Arthur Rothstein/FSA photo from the collections of the Library of Congress

A Prologue to the Protest Movement

Duke Historical Series

A PROLOGUE TO THE PROTEST MOVEMENT

The Missouri Sharecropper Roadside Demonstration of 1939

Louis Cantor

Duke University Press, Durham, North Carolina, 1969

L.C.C. card no. 70–86480
S.B.N. 8223–0215–2
Printed in the United States of
America by Heritage Printers, Inc.

To two great teachers
who inspired me
to become a teacher:
William D. Miller and Mary F. Gyles

Preface

Among the many factors affecting the process of historical change within the United States today, one, more than any other, seems to stand out. This is the increasing use of the protest demonstration, both as a means of calling public attention to social ills, and as a way of prodding local and federal government to take the necessary action to correct those ills. The effectiveness of the demonstrations of the 1950's and 1960's cannot yet, of course, be accurately measured. At least one earlier group protest, however—a sharecropper roadside demonstration in Southeast Missouri in 1939—does provide an excellent case study of how this device was used successfully during the depression as a peaceful weapon for social change. The 1939 sharecropper demonstration bears remarkable similarity to the contemporary protest movement. It was outdoors in the public view; it attracted national attention; it exposed conditions that shocked the public conscience; it was composed mostly of Negroes; it drew charges that it was inspired by outside agitators and Communists; it fomented cries of police terrorism; it brought about an investigation by the FBI; and it aroused considerable activity on the part of local citizens and state government. Finally, although it caused a stir in the upper echelons of the federal government, it apparently failed to bring about any fundamental change in the attitude of the later New Deal toward the sharecropper and the tenant.[1]

It is not the intent of this book to suggest that the 1939 sharecropper demonstration in Southeast Missouri was the beginning of the modern protest movement in the United States. The origin of that phenomenon is far too complex to be summed up in so simple an explanation. Rather, this study is concerned with how the protest demonstration was used in one instance by one group during the economic depression of the 1930's. By analyzing the demonstration

1. For an excellent discussion of the attitude of the Roosevelt administration toward the sharecropper and the tenant in the early years of the New Deal, see David Eugene Conrad, *The Forgotten Farmers: The Story of Sharecroppers in the New Deal* (Urbana, 1965).

closely, the author has attempted to determine just how effective a weapon it was at calling attention to the plight of the cropper and at stimulating both private and public action on his behalf.

The sharecropper, whose condition was ordinarily bad, sank to new depths during the depression. The cropper felt neglected by the New Deal; the administration's major farm program—the AAA—virtually ignored him. The leader of the 1939 demonstration, Owen Whitfield,[2] was convinced that the only way to awaken the conscience of the nation to the cropper's plight was to dramatize it by having an open protest demonstration. By resorting to this method, Whitfield broke sharply with previous tactics employed by farm leaders in their efforts to improve the cropper's conditions during the thirties.

The author feels it is necessary to caution the reader against reading into the past modern-day values. It must be kept in mind that while the Southeast Missouri demonstration was a peaceful, non-violent protest, in 1939 the tactic was still considered to be a radical tool by those who objected to its use. Because it was a more radical approach toward solving the sharecropper problem in 1939, and because it attracted national attention, this study also attempts to evaluate the New Deal's response to it. Although I have made no exhaustive study of farm tenancy during the depression, by focusing on this single dramatic incident, it is hoped that some light might be shed on the later New Deal's farm tenancy program, and perhaps a better understanding might be gleaned of the Roosevelt administration's political philosophy in general.

It is a pleasant duty to express gratitude to a number of colleagues and friends whose judicious comments and suggestions on the manuscript provided invaluable assistance. To Professor Eugene Nutter of Southeast Missouri State College, I owe a double debt; not only did he originally suggest the subject for study, but he offered essential criticisms as well. I also want to express my appreciation to John Bierk, David Eugene Conrad, and Clifford Scott, who read the entire manuscript and made indispensable recommendations. Many others read parts of the manuscript in the various stages of its development; Fancher Coe, Harold Dugger, Larry Grisvard, Nolan Porterfield, Joseph Preston, and George Suggs offered advice and criticisms that were uncommonly helpful,

2. For an alphabetical listing of the individuals involved in the demonstration, see Appendix, Table 1.

and to them I am also deeply grateful. Any remaining errors are, of course, my own.

Several librarians provided exceptional assistance, but I owe a special debt to Janice Nunnelee of the Southeast Missouri State College Library and Helen Finneran of the National Archives in Washington; their patience and careful guidance during my many hours of research made my task much easier. Finally, I wish to thank Mrs. Carole Elenbaas, who typed the entire manuscript, which was no mean task, since she performed this chore at the same time that she was typing her husband's dissertation, keeping house, and raising a lovely daughter.

Louis Cantor

Fort Wayne, Indiana
January 20, 1969

Contents

1

A Prologue to the Protest Movement

2

1 The Problem: Rich Land, Poor People

Today a traveler driving along the new interstate highway between Memphis and St. Louis finds very little when he passes through Southeast Missouri to remind him of the sharecropper roadside demonstration which occurred there in January of 1939. The new superhighway—Interstate 55—completely removes the motorist from any memory of the event by bypassing most of old Highways 60 and 61, the sight of the earlier roadside strike. At Sikeston, if the traveler bothers to drive over from the Interstate, he will find that a shiny new Holiday Inn now stands where Highways 60 and 61 intersect. This very spot in 1939 was the gathering place for many of the demonstrators and later served as the unofficial headquarters for the multitude of newspaper reporters who flocked to the scene at the time. It is hard to imagine that this luxurious Holiday Inn stands on ground once covered with hundreds of indigent, ragged sharecroppers who startled the nation in the winter of 1939 by marching to the side of the highway in what was then an unprecedented protest demonstration.

Very few visible remnants of the demonstration remain. Indeed, it is now quite possible to grow up in Southeast Missouri and never hear of the event that put the region on the front pages of newspapers around the country. Generally, very little is said about it. Occasionally, a child might hear about the story at school, and upon request, the parent will give a personal recollection of it as best he remembers. Or someone might recall that, in a day when protest demonstrations have become commonplace, Southeast Missouri has the dubious distinction of being a region where one of the first occurred. It is therefore unlikely that the event will fade completely from the public mind. But many have tried to forget it, and there are still people living in Southeast Missouri who are reluctant to discuss the incident. In talking with them, the independent observer gets the distinct impression that they would like to forget completely that the nasty business ever happened.[1]

The 1939 demonstration occurred in the region of Missouri popularly referred to as the "Bootheel," a sobriquet resulting logically from the peculiar geographical shape of the area.[2] In the extreme southeastern corner of the state, the Missouri border drops about fifty miles below the 36″30′ parallel, and its shape on the map gives the distinct appearance of a heel jammed down in between Arkansas and Tennessee. Physiographically, the Bootheel is significant, however, not because of its geographical resemblance to the heel of a boot, but because it is the northernmost extremity of the Mississippi Delta cotton area, which begins in the north at Sikeston, Missouri, and extends along the lowlands of the Mississippi River through Arkansas and Louisiana to the Gulf of Mexico.[3]

While the region's boundaries are not precisely fixed, the seven

1. The author, for example, attempting to interview a local newspaper editor who had closely covered the demonstration at the time, asked him his recollection of it, and was told: "Why don't you fellows stop beating a dead horse. There was enough written about it when it happened. As far as I'm concerned, the less that is said about it, the better."

2. For earlier accounts of the demonstration, see Carey McWilliams's chapter, "A Kick from the Boot Heel," in *Ill Fares the Land* (Boston, 1942); Ben M. Ridpath, "The Case of the Missouri Sharecroppers," *Christian Century*, LVI (Feb., 1939), 146–148; Charles S. Hoffman and Virgil L. Bankson, "Crisis in Missouri's Boot Heel," *Land Policy Review*, III (Jan.–Feb., 1940), 1–14; Cedric Belfrage, "Cotton-Patch Moses," *Harper's Magazine*, CXCVII (Nov., 1948), 94–103; Fannie Cook's novel, *Boot-Heel Doctor* (New York, 1941), is a fictional version of the 1939 demonstration and the 1937 flood in Southeast Missouri. Pictures of the demonstration might be conveniently seen in Harvey Wish, *Contemporary America: The National Scene Since 1900* (3rd ed.; New York, 1955), following p. 522, and Harvey Swados, *The American Writer and the Great Depression,* American Heritage Series (Indianapolis, 1966), following p. 246.

3. Max R. White *et al., Rich Land, Poor People,* Farm Security Administration Research Report No. 1 (Indianapolis, Jan. 1938), p. 12. Cited hereafter as *FSA Report.*

lowland counties—Butler, Dunklin, Mississippi, New Madrid, Pemiscot, Scott, and Stoddard—make up the area usually defined as the Bootheel, although most of these counties are located north of 36″30′ and thus are not actually in the heel of the boot. Even though the seven Delta counties are not located geographically in the South, from an economic standpoint they are much like that section of the country primarily because they are the cotton producing counties. During the thirties cotton was the Bootheel's prime cash crop, the seven Delta counties alone producing 98.5 per cent of all the cotton grown in the state.[4]

Such, however, was not always the case. As a farming area, the Bootheel is relatively young. Indeed, until the latter part of the nineteenth century, Southeast Missouri was largely a swampy area, thinly populated and rich only in virgin timber. Then, several things happened that brought about a sudden transformation of the territory. The economic history of the Bootheel is a story of a rapid evolution of agriculture in the short span of one generation.[5]

The starting point for Southeast Missouri's sudden change from swampland to high-yield cotton country was 1890. It was then that lumber companies came into the area and thoroughly stripped the timber resources. After the timber barons had denuded the forests, levees were built and drainage districts organized. The chief impetus for draining the swampland was to increase the value of the property. Landowners were instrumental in organizing the Little River Drainage District in 1905, which helped drain over half a million acres of swampland extending from Cape Girardeau, Missouri, to the Arkansas line. As hundreds of miles of levees and dikes were

4. Farm Security Administration, *Southeast Missouri: A Laboratory for the Cotton South* (U.S. Department of Agriculture, Dec. 30, 1940).

5. One government official, later studying the farming problem in the Bootheel, wrote that the sudden evolution of agriculture in the region could be compared rightfully to the biological law of Ernest Haeckel, i.e., the history of the embryo recapitulates the history of the species. "The evolution of agriculture in Southeast Missouri," he wrote, "recapitulates in a small area in a very short span of time the history of the development of commercialized farming in general." Another government farm expert suggested that the region could accurately be described as a "laboratory for the cotton South," pointing out that "the history of Southern agriculture for the last 150 years has been repeated in Southeastern Missouri within the span of a single generation" (*ibid.*; N. G. Silvermaster, Memo to C. B. Baldwin, "Subject: Southeast Missouri," Oct. 12, 1940, National Archives, Washington, D.C., Record Group 96, Records of the Farmers Home Administration. Cited hereafter as NA, RG 96).

constructed within the drainage district, thousands of acres of land were reclaimed for agricultural use.[6] Prior to drainage, government officials estimated that over 70 per cent of the land in the Bootheel was unfit to raise any crop; by 1930, less than 3 per cent was incapable of being farmed.[7]

As soon as the land was drained, it was cleared for the plow and crops were planted. The reclaimed earth—made especially rich by centuries of deposits left by the floods of the Mississippi River—was excellent farmland. After a brief experience with corn and wheat—the latter grown to meet the demands of World War I—cotton became the chief crop in the Bootheel during the twenties when the boll weevil in Arkansas and Mississippi pushed planters north into Missouri. Between 1920 and 1925, acreage in cotton increased more than 330 per cent, and cotton production jumped more than 200 per cent.[8]

The rapid expansion of cotton farming in the Delta counties during this period was accompanied by a corresponding increase in population. The attraction of farming the reclaimed fertile soil caused settlers to swarm into the region from the South. Between 1900 and 1930, the total population of the seven Delta counties in the Bootheel increased 75 per cent. Although it tapered off some soon thereafter, in the decade between 1930 and 1940, the increase in all of the seven counties was still nearly 30 per cent, while several of the counties gained as much as 50 per cent. By contrast, the total population of Missouri during the same ten years increased only 4.0 per cent, and that of the entire country only 7.2 per cent.[9]

Because large-scale migration to the area took place so late, the Southeast Missouri Delta country has been characterized by some as one of the last great American agricultural frontiers. Unlike

6. *FSA Report*, p. 14. For a more elaborate discussion of this entire operation, see Gary L. McDowell, "Local Agencies and Land Development by Drainage: The Case of 'Swampeast' Missouri" (unpublished Ph.D. dissertation, Columbia University, 1965); and Leon P. Ogilvie, "The Development of the Southeast Missouri Lowlands" (unpublished Ph.D. dissertation, University of Missouri, 1967).

7. *FSA Report*, p. 15. See Appendix, Table 2.

8. E. J. Holcomb *et al., Report to the Tolan Committee on the Cooperative Study of Farm Labor and Tenancy in Southeast Missouri* (U.S. Department of Agriculture, Nov. 1941), Pt. I, p. 1. Cited hereafter as *Report to the Tolan Committee.*

9. *Ibid.*, Pt. II, p. 5; *FSA Report*, p. 4; *Southeast Missouri: A Laboratory for the Cotton South.*

earlier frontiers, however, the Bootheel held few fortunes for the great majority of the people who came into the area at this time. Although the vast land resources available in the region beckoned to the landless farmer, few farmers who arrived became landowners.[10]

High development costs discouraged small landholding. Large land speculators, interested primarily in quick profits, invested vast sums in clearing the cut-over land. Moreover, the drainage system was financed by bonds that were retired through the payment of taxes by landowners. During the farm depression of the twenties and thirties, drainage taxes, which ran as high as three dollars an acre, contributed to mortgage foreclosures. Since 70 per cent of the land area in the Bootheel was within the drainage districts by the thirties, many small farmers lost their farms because of the drainage tax.[11] After the 1939 demonstration, the FBI conducted an investigation of the incident, and its report, which had examined the history of Southeast Missouri, concluded that the drainage tax was undoubtedly "a prime factor in the downfall of the small farmer."[12]

Large land speculators increased their holdings when small landowners were forced to sell. The trend toward large-scale consolidation at the expense of the small farmer continued in the late thirties. The 1940 census indicated that the number of farms in the seven Delta counties decreased by 10.9 per cent from 24,117 in 1935 to 21,486 in 1940, while the total acreage under cotton, despite the government's AAA program, actually increased. A dramatic illustration of this tendency can be shown in the counties of Pemiscot, New Madrid, and Mississippi, which jumped altogether from a total of 186,767 acres in cotton in 1934 to 230,213 acres in 1939, an increase of over 20 per cent.[13]

Because of the intensive speculation in land there was little room for the small landowner. The usual procedure was to sell in tracts of five hundred or a thousand acres, which meant that the small

10. See McWilliams, *Ill Fares the Land*, p. 282.

11. *FSA Report*, pp. 14–15.

12. The FBI report itself is still unavailable to the public. The findings or conclusions of the investigations, however, were released to the papers at the time. See St. Louis *Post-Dispatch*, *Southeast Missourian*, Memphis *Commercial-Appeal*, New York *Daily Worker*, all March 13, 1939.

13. N. G. Silvermaster, memo to C. B. Baldwin, Oct. 12, 1940, NA, RG 96.

operator was unable to buy. In addition, large land speculators would frequently eliminate the small farmer only after the farmer had spent his time and money in clearing the land. The scheme was simple and highly successful. A speculator would buy a large tract of uncleared land for five to fifteen dollars an acre and sell this land to small farmers for a much higher price. Unable to clear the land and make his crop at the same time, the farmer would get behind in his payments. After his mortgage was foreclosed, another farmer would buy the partially cleared land, and again the mortgage would be foreclosed when he got into trouble. By the time the land was actually cleared, several farmers had had their mortgages foreclosed, while the speculator continued to make a profit by then selling the cleared land for a high price.[14]

In this way huge tracts of land were bought up by insurance companies, banks, land development corporations, and large individual landholders. By the time of the demonstration in 1939, over half of the nearly two million acres in farms in Southeast Missouri were owned by landowners who held two hundred acres or more each; one third of the total was owned by landholders who held five hundred acres or more each; at least one quarter was held by owners of a thousand acres or more each; two hundred thousand acres were owned by insurance companies; and two companies alone held more than forty thousand acres each. Individual holdings of two thousand, three thousand, and four thousand acres were not unusual, and holdings of from five hundred to two thousand acres were quite common.[15]

The speculators who actually owned the land seldom farmed it. Occasionally, in the case of small farms, the landowner might be an owner-operator, but more often than not, on the large farms—the prevalent type in the Bootheel—the owner was a landlord only, or the title was held by an insurance company. Some insurance companies simply hired agents to manage the farms, while other companies followed the practice of many large individual landholders in selling or in leasing land for rent to persons who could

14. *Southeast Missouri: A Laboratory for the Cotton South.*

15. *FSA Report*, p. 33. Large-scale land consolidation was not a phenomenon peculiar to Southeast Missouri. Although no accurate figures are available, one author has estimated that by the time of the depression, one-third of the South's cotton land was owned by banks and insurance companies. See Very Rony, "Sorrow Song in Black and White," *New South* (Summer, 1967), Southern Regional Council publication.

afford it. Frequently those who bought or rented leased land were the cotton ginners who became prevalent in the area during the twenties, when gins mushroomed to meet the increased amount of cotton being grown. The number of active gins in the Bootheel leaped from 53 in 1921 to 165 in 1925.[16]

Many of the ginners rented several hundred acres as a speculative commercial venture. Most already owned some land and grew cotton themselves, all of which went to their own gin. They could easily purchase foreclosed farms cheaply, or rent them from the insurance company or bank. Renting more land, they would then either grow the cotton themselves by hiring tenants, or rerent it to hard-pressed farmers for as much as or more than they paid to the owner, always with the stipulation that the farmer gin his cotton at the landlord's gin. In either case, the ginner could control production and the ginning of the cotton produced. Usually they preferred to rent since this relieved them of the task of producing the crop while at the same time it insured them a supply of cotton for their gins. In 1939, for example, while ginners owned about one quarter of the total farmland in New Madrid County, they actually operated only 87 out of the 632 farms they possessed, and in 1940, only 44 out of 640.[17]

These middlemen—the salaried agents of the insurance companies or the ginners who rented land—became a kind of "over-tenant."[18] Although technically a tenant himself—because he did not actually own the land—the over-tenant nonetheless was virtually a landlord in his own right. Ginners who rented land frequently acted as agents or managers for the nonresident owner. Perhaps most importantly, the over-tenant had the responsibility of hiring and firing the tenants and farm workers who actually farmed the soil and performed the necessary labor to make the crop. In the eyes of the tenant, the over-tenant was the rent collector, cotton buyer, cotton ginner, bookkeeper, and banker.[19]

Ginners frequently served in the capacity of money lenders in addition to their other functions. In 1940, in New Madrid County, for example, ginners made loans on over six hundred farms which contained more than seventy thousand acres of cropland. These loans, which varied from 6 to 12 per cent, were almost always made

16. *Ibid.*, p. 9; *Report to the Tolan Committee*, Pt. II, p. 1.
17. *Ibid.*, pp. 2–3.
18. See *Ibid.*, Pt. I, p. 2.
19. *Ibid.*, Pt. II, p. 4.

from funds which the ginner had borrowed at a lower rate. By one means or another, ginners in New Madrid County were able to control the planting, processing, and disposition of the cotton crop on over one thousand farms containing over a hundred thousand acres of cropland—nearly 50 per cent of the total cropland in the entire county.[20]

Thus, a kind of unofficial class system grew up in the Bootheel, with nonresident landowners at the top, over-tenants below them, and at the bottom of the economic hierarchy, the landless tenant, who supplied the labor. The maldistribution of land ownership in the Bootheel led to a quasi-feudal system of cotton production very much like that of the old South, with most of the land being worked by sharecroppers and small tenants. Because of one-crop farming, with its demand for seasonal work, the type of labor utilized on farms in Southeast Missouri was like that commonly found throughout the Cotton Belt. Farm workers fell into three general categories: sharecroppers, day laborers, and tenants who paid a fixed amount of cash or crop for the use of the land. In Southeast Missouri, those in the last category were usually classified simply as "renters."[21] Completely dependent upon and subservient to the landowners, these croppers, laborers, and tenants spent a lifetime working land that belonged to someone else.[22]

20. *Ibid.*, pp. 4, 7.

21. Although there was a great deal of variation in the types of renter, in Southeast Missouri, more often than not he paid in crop rather than cash. Most of the time, he paid one-third in cotton and one-fourth in corn. See *FSA Report*, p. 34. For a general classification of the Southern tenancy system, see Conrad, *The Forgotten Farmers*, pp. 6–8; T. J. Woofter, Jr., *et al.*, *Landlord and Tenant on the Cotton Plantation*, Research Monograph V, Works Progress Administration (Washington, 1936), pp. 9–14; and Fred C. Frey and T. Lynn Smith, "The Influence of the AAA Cotton Program Upon the Tenant, Cropper, and Laborer," *Rural Sociology*, I (1936), 483–505.

22. The farm tenancy system was born in the South after the Civil War, largely because the newly freed Negroes owned no land and had no cash with which to buy any. The landlord supplied a "furnish" of food, seed, mules, fertilizer, farm implements, and a shack to live in in return for a set share of the crop. Later, when many small white farmers lost their land, they dropped into the ranks of the farm tenants. See A. F. Raper, *Preface to Peasantry* (Chapel Hill, 1936); A. F. Raper and Ira De A. Reid, *Sharecroppers All* (Chapel Hill, 1941); Norman Thomas, *The Plight of the Sharecropper* (New York, 1934); Howard Kester, *Revolt Among the Sharecroppers* (New York, 1936); J. D. Black and R. H. Allen, "Growth of Farm Tenancy," *Quarterly Journal of Economics*, LI (1937); Paul V. Maris, "Farm Tenancy," *Yearbook of Agriculture, 1940*, U.S. Department of Agriculture, 76th Cong., 3rd Sess., House Doc. 695 (Washington, 1940).

In 1935, 74 per cent of all the farms operated in the Bootheel were operated by tenants. While this figure was no higher than elsewhere in the South—in 1930, for example, 75 per cent of all cotton farms in the South were operated with tenant labor—in New Madrid and Mississippi counties, farms operated by tenants reached 90 per cent, and in Pemiscot County the figure was more than 80 per cent.[23]

Most of the tenants located in Southeast Missouri in the thirties were not born in the state. Out of nearly four hundred heads of tenant families interviewed by government officials in New Madrid County in 1940, only seventy-seven—less than one in five—had been born in one of the seven Delta counties. In 1939, the Social Security office of Scott County reported that nine out of ten social security recipients in that county were born out of the state.[24]

Some tenants were brought into the area by the landlord when he moved up from the South. Others were imported by landlords who went down to the Southern states after them. Many who were brought in at this time came from Arkansas, Mississippi, and Tennessee. In New Madrid County, for example, one-third of the renters interviewed in 1940 listed one of these three states as their birthplace, as did more than half the sharecroppers, and almost two-thirds of the regular wage laborers.[25]

A large number of these farm workers were Negroes. In the decade before 1930, while white rural population increased in the Bootheel by 3,183, the Negro rural population increased to 15,267, and by 1935, two-thirds of the Negro farm population in Missouri was located in the seven Delta counties.[26]

Although there was considerable variation in the distribution of the Negroes in the different farm tenure groups, generally speaking, Negroes were more heavily concentrated among the sharecroppers and day laborers than among the renters, since the latter usually had to furnish their own workstock, food, and capital, while the cropper and day worker owned nothing but their labor. The

23. *FSA Report,* p. 33; W. A. Turner, *A Graphic Summary of Farm Tenure,* U. S. Department of Agriculture, Misc. Pub. No. 261 (Washington, 1936), pp. 1–3.

24. *Report to the Tolan Committee,* Pt. V, p. 25; *Post-Dispatch,* Jan. 22, 1939.

25. *FSA Report,* p. 19; E. P. Coleman, a large planter in Sikeston, recalls bringing several hundred cropper families with him when he moved up from Mississippi. Mr. E. P. Coleman, interview with author, Dec. 31, 1966; *Report to the Tolan Committee,* Pt. V, p. 25. See Appendix, Table 3.

26. *FSA Report,* p. 18. See Appendix, Table 4.

cropper lived from harvest to harvest because the landlord supplied him with a subsistence "furnish" in advance of the crop. The day laborer occupied the lowest rung of the economic ladder. He received only wages in return for labor, worked usually about 120 days, and had nothing at other times.[27]

In a survey of the types of tenancy by color in Dunklin, New Madrid, and Pemiscot counties, Negroes made up only 8 per cent of the total in the renter class as opposed to over 30 per cent of the whites in the same class, while Negroes contributed only 70 per cent of the total in croppers and laborers as against 50 per cent of the whites in the same two classes.[28]

By the time of the depression, the general living conditions of the sharecroppers and farm workers in the Bootheel were deplorable for both blacks and whites. The regional office of the Farm Security Administration (FSA) conducted a survey of the area in 1938, and its findings give an excellent picture of how most of the people lived. The report concluded that the living conditions "refute the American myth that a region of rich agricultural lands will always be populated by healthy, happy, farm people living in security and enjoying the benefits of a rich community life," and decided that the area could best be described as a "paradox of rich land and poor people."[29]

Since low income groups tend to be at a marked disadvantage in such areas as housing, education, and rights before the law, perhaps the plight of Missouri's tenants can best be understood by first examining their annual income. The government surveyors found that in 1936 white renters had an average gross income of $845,

27. *Ibid.*, pp. 34–35. For a more elaborate discussion of the Negro's role in the whole Southern plantation economy, see Gunnar Myrdal, *An American Dilemma: The Negro Problem and Modern Democracy* (New York, 1944), pp. 230–250; Allison Davis, Burleigh B. Gardner, and Mary R. Gardner, *Deep South: A Social Anthropological Study of Caste and Class* (Chicago, 1941), pp. 379–391; Hortense Powdermaker, *After Freedom: A Cultural Study in the Deep South* (New York, 1939), pp. 75–110; and Raper, *Preface to Peasantry.*

28. *FSA Report,* p. 20. See Appendix, Table 5.

29. *Ibid.*, p. 2. Most of the information in the following pages was drawn from one chapter of this FSA report, which was based mostly on interviews with approximately 1,500 families in Dunklin, Pemiscot, and New Madrid counties. "Because careful methods of sampling were used," the report stated, "it is believed the conditions among the families interviewed are fairly representative of the conditions which prevail among all farm families in these counties" (*ibid.*, p. 37).

white sharecroppers $415, white laborers $264, and Negroes of all tenure classes only $251.[30]

Incredible as it may seem, the real income for the sharecropper was far less than the figure given here because from this amount he had to repay the landlord for the "furnish" supplied him between March and January, plus interest. While no official evidence existed on the actual rate of interest charged in the Bootheel, the FSA reported that it had reason to believe that the interest was not less than the 10 per cent or more traditionally charged in many areas of the Deep South. Very seldom were questions raised about the interest charged, not only because the landlord kept the books, but also because the tenants were frequently too uneducated, or in the case of the Negro, too afraid to question their bosses. One landlord perhaps best expressed it when he said rather candidly: "No matter how much the cropper grew or how hard he worked, when settling up time came, he always seemed to break about even."[31]

Most of the houses occupied by tenants in the Bootheel were little more than crude shacks. A large number of them were unpainted, wooden constructions, without plastering or insulation. While many of the white owners and renters lived in "weatherboard" houses, consisting of a simple frame with drop siding, most of the white croppers, laborers, and Negroes were in even worse condition, living either in "strip" or "box" houses. Both were made of nothing more than rough timber placed together vertically, the first with

30. *Ibid.* See Appendix, Table 6. A general rule throughout the entire South was for the Negro agricultural worker to have a lower income than white farm workers. One survey of 646 Southern cotton plantations in 1934 indicated that Negro sharecroppers had a mean net income of $295, while the figure for white sharecroppers was $417. See Woofter *et al.*, *Landlord and Tenant on the Cotton Plantation*; and Richard Sterner, *The Negro's Share: A Study of Income, Consumption, Housing and Public Assistance* (New York, 1943), p. 67.

31. Mr. Robert Delaney, a Charleston, Missouri, planter, interview with author, Nov. 23, 1966. A popular story that circulated in the South told of a clever old Negro cropper who, although unable to "cipher," figured out how to outwit the planter. The cropper turned in three bales of cotton at the gin, the story goes, then stood by, seemingly unconcerned, as the planter weighed his goods and went through the ritual of making complicated calculations concerning the amount owed him for the "furnish," interest, items purchased at the planter's store, etc. After this formal procedure, the planter announced, to no one's surprise, that the cropper had broken even again. At this point, the Negro produced a previously concealed fourth bale and asked that he be paid for it. The planter calmly remarked: "Well, I guess I'll just have to figure the whole thing again."

stripping over the cracks to keep out the weather, the latter with no stripping. When not left bare, the inside walls of these shacks were covered with old newspapers, pieces of cardboard or building paper.[32]

For protection in times of flood, most of the houses were built on concrete blocks, or, if near the levee, on cypress blocks, several feet high. None of the houses had cellars, and most of the roofs were in such poor condition that they afforded little protection from rain and snow. One FSA surveyor told of a housewife he visited who said: "I'm sorry the house is so upset, but since it rained I had to move the furniture out in the middle of the floor to keep it from getting wet."[33]

The interior of the homes, FSA investigators described as "a picture of squalor, filth, and poverty." Floors were usually single layers of rough lumber with cracks that exposed the earth; furniture consisted of homemade tables and box-crate cabinets, and since beds were always in demand, it was not unusual to find children sleeping on blankets or pallets spread out on the cracked board floors.[34]

Because the majority of the houses were made of old unpainted lumber with large gaps caused by warped wood, insects created health problems in the summer and the heating difficulties created health problems in the winter. The problem during the summer was compounded by inadequate screening. While nearly all houses had screening of some sort, most were in such disrepair that they offered little resistance to flies and mosquitoes. Landlords were reluctant to fix screens because they felt it was a waste of time and money. Perhaps indicative of the prevalent attitude of the planter class toward the tenants was the remark made by a landlord when asked to provide screens on the door: "There is no use to buy screens," he reportedly said, "they leave them open anyway. Perhaps they want to let the flies out."[35]

Sanitation conditions were undoubtedly the most pathetic problem. Ninety-eight per cent of the households had no indoor toilet facilities; most of the outdoor toilets were open, unscreened, and often close to the source of water, testament to the large number of cases of typhoid fever, dysentery, hookworm, and other intestinal

32. *FSA Report*, pp. 5, 41.
33. *Ibid.*, p. 43.
34. *Ibid.*
35. *Ibid.*, pp. 41, 44–45.

diseases which plagued the area. Unless drainage ditches were dredged every two or three years, the water became stagnant. Undrained swamps and improperly drained ditches were natural breeding places for the mosquito, and because most houses were not adequately screened, malaria was a chronic problem. In fact two-thirds of all the deaths from that disease in the state of Missouri were counted in the Bootheel. Cases of typhoid, tuberculosis, and pneumonia also ran far beyond the state average. These diseases—all preventable—were attributed to poor living standards, lack of medical and hospital service, and inadequate nutrition.[36]

The customary diet of the Bootheel tenant farmer was salt pork, corn pone, and dried beans. Eggs, butter, milk, fresh vegetables, and fruit were a rarity, as evidenced by the prevalence of pellegra, colitis, and malnutrition. Although some households had cows and chickens, they were usually too small in number to produce sufficiently for regular consumption. A few had gardens of some sort, but these too were small and inadequate.[37]

Preservation of food presented another major problem, which was insurmountable in the summertime. Some dug pits in the ground or used caves, but these were generally unsatisfactory because of the possibility of seepage. Many others tried using a tub of water placed under the house. But none of these methods was adequate for more than several hours at a time. Thus, during the hot summer months, the average family was forced to plan food for immediate consumption. The FSA report pointed out that largely because of improper preservation of food and poor diet, the infant mortality rate in some counties was twice as high as the state average.[38]

Despite the high infant death rate in the Bootheel, the farm population continued to rise rapidly among the tenant farmers because of a high birth rate. The population increase was greater among whites, since most of the infant deaths occurred in the Negro families. Since landlords tended to select tenants with large families to help out during the peak seasons, a family with many children was considered an economic asset. Yet, because large numbers contributed to the constant availability of a large labor force, the landlord could continue to work tenants at a minimum cost. Thus

36. *Ibid.*, pp. 47–50.
37. *Ibid.*, p. 45.
38. *Ibid.*, pp. 46, 51.

the high birth rate in Southeast Missouri tended to perpetuate the prevailing economic system.[39]

Children born to tenant families in the Bootheel had very little hope of ever changing their status. Because of the pressing need to work, most had to drop out of school at an early age. The average number of grades completed among all families in Dunklin, New Madrid, and Pemiscot counties was only 5.5, while among the Negroes in the same counties, it was only 2.6. In addition, because of the extremely poor condition of the school system, the children who spent the few years there profited very little from it. "Inefficient grade schools, inadequate high schools, and still poorer opportunities for Negroes," the FSA survey reported, "are the chief characteristics of public education in the Lowlands counties."[40] The report went on to give a vivid description of the public educational system in the Bootheel. For most of the children living in the rural areas, it said, "the system of elementary education is one of multiplicity of school districts, of one-teacher schools, of unapproved schools, or poorly trained and low-paid teachers, and of irregular attendance. . . ."[41] Only twenty-four schools out of a total of over four hundred located in the rural districts of the Bootheel were approved by the State Department of Education as having met the standard for elementary schools. The majority of the county population attended schools whose buildings and grounds were in deteriorated condition, equipment was frequently inadequate, library facilities were very poor, and the teaching was far below standard.[42]

Most of the teachers were not properly trained for their profession. Only one-seventh of them had completed college; a great many had attended only a year or two, while 20 per cent had no college training at all.[43]

It was not unusual for students to be kept out of school to work in the fields. The rural pupil, the FSA reported, attended school on the average a little more than half the time it was in session. Moreover, most rural schools dismissed in the fall and spring for cotton picking and chopping. In an effort to compensate, school was held during a part of the summer when there was no work in the fields. Weather in the Bootheel during the summer, however, was not very conducive to efficient study. Nearly one-half of the children of high

39. *Ibid.*, p. 23. See Appendix, Tables 7 and 8.
40. *Ibid.*, pp. 25, 59.
41. *Ibid.*, p. 59.
42. *Ibid.*
43. *Ibid.*

school age in the seven Delta counties lived in districts which had no high schools, and in the rural areas poor transportation facilities discouraged those who otherwise might have attended.[44]

As with so many other factors in Southeast Missouri, while educational opportunities were poor for white farm families, they were even poorer for Negroes. "The system of public education for Negroes," to quote from the FSA survey, "is distinctly inferior to that for whites."[45] Negro schools were fewer in number—only six Negro high schools, for example existed in the entire area, while Dunklin and Stoddard counties had none—teachers were not as well trained, buildings and facilities were frequently less adequate, and the average salary for Negro teachers in the rural districts was about $370 a year, while white rural teachers averaged about $500. Given all the handicaps, it is not surprising that the illiteracy rate for both white and Negro tenants in the Bootheel was far beyond the state average—in some counties running as high as 10 per cent.[46]

In summary, the low income, wretched housing, poor diet, and constant disease all combined to make a miserable existence for the overwhelming majority of the people, with little hope of changing the conditions under which they lived. "A journey through the area," the FSA investigators asserted, "presents a picture of poverty, deprivation, and hopelessness, with but few avenues of escape even for those who keep alive a flickering desire for something better."[47]

It was largely the effort to keep alive the sharecropper's desire for something better that the Southern Tenant Farmers Union (STFU) was organized in the South in 1934. By the time of the depression, the landless tenant farmers of the Bootheel, like their counterparts in the South, had reached the nadir of their fortune. To these disinherited souls—the "forgotten farmers," one historian has labeled them—the union held out hope for what must have seemed at the time to be a near hopeless situation.[48]

44. *Ibid.*, pp. 59–60.
45. *Ibid.*, p. 60.
46. *Ibid.*, pp. 24, 59–60.
47. *Ibid.*, p. 40.
48. Conrad, *The Forgotten Farmers.*

2 The Farmer Takes a Union

The STFU was born in Tyronza, Arkansas, in July of 1934, fathered by two Socialists, H. L. Mitchell and Clay East.[1] Mitchell had once been a sharecropper, but by the time of the depression both he and East were making their living in the city, Mitchell in a small dry cleaning business in Tyronza, and East as an operator of a gas station there. After an unsuccessful attempt to organize Socialist locals in Arkansas, Mitchell and East turned their efforts to organizing a union. They drew inspiration from Norman Thomas, who was already vitally interested in the problems of Arkansas sharecroppers during the early thirties. Fearing Communists would find America's farming proletariat a fertile field for exploitation, Thomas hoped to give the Arkansas sharecroppers a Socialist alternative. With Thomas's blessing, Mitchell and East decided to organize a sharecroppers' union, which would be, according to the

1. The papers of the STFU have been deposited in the Southern Historical Collection at the University of North Carolina, Chapel Hill, N.C. For the history of the union in the early thirties, see Jerold S. Auerbach, "Southern Tenant Farmers: Socialist Critics of the New Deal," *Labor History*, VII (Winter, 1966), 3–18; Conrad, *The Forgotten Farmers*; Kester, *Revolt Among the Sharecroppers*; and Donald H. Grubbs, "Gardner Jackson, That 'Socialist' Tenant Farmers' Union, and the New Deal," *Agricultural History*, XLIII, No. 2 (April 1968), 125–137.

STFU preamble, "dedicated to the complete abolition of tenantry and wage slavery in all its forms. . . ."[2]

Fearing the favorite planter practice of playing whites against blacks, and vice versa, Mitchell and East decided to have one union for both races. Even though a Negro minister was named as vice-chairman, however, and although membership was biracial, the real union leadership—at least in the early days—tended to be concentrated in the white men who shared its birth pangs: East, its first president; Mitchell, the executive secretary and also the key figure in guiding union policy; J. R. Butler, who later served as president; and Howard Kester, who was sent to the union as Norman Thomas's personal representative.[3]

The union concentrated its efforts on what it considered to be the gross inequities of the New Deal's farm program. Specifically, the union charged that the AAA program adversely affected the cropper in two ways: In the first place, the acreage reduction cut down on the number of croppers needed to work the land; and in the second place, the parity program frequently resulted in the cropper's eviction from the farm. The union attacked the failure of the AAA parity payment to reach the cropper, because, it charged, many unscrupulous landlords were switching the status of tenants in order to retain the entire parity check for themselves.[4]

According to the AAA program, the parity check was always made payable to the owner of the land. The landlord was then supposed to share it with the tenants according to the amount each tenant held in the crop. Many landlords found it easy to evict their croppers, keep the entire check, and work their land with day laborers, who had no stake in the crop. The economic rule was simple. When the price of cotton was low or the crop risk great, the planter favored the sharecropper method, and thus had his tenant share with him half of the risk of a possible loss on the crop.

2. See M. S. Venkataramani, "Norman Thomas, Arkansas Sharecroppers, and the Roosevelt Agricultural Policies, 1933–1937," *Mississippi Valley Historical Review*, XLVII (Sept. 1960), 225–246; Auerbach, "Southern Tenant Farmers"; H. L. Mitchell, "Biographical Sketch"; J. R. Butler and Howard Kester, "The STFU, 1940," p. 2, STFU Papers.

3. Mitchell, "Workers in Our Fields: The Story of a Union That Would Not Die," p. 3, STFU Papers; Auerbach, "Southern Tenant Farmers"; Howard Kester, interview with author, Aug. 6, 1966.

4. Mitchell, "Workers in Our Fields," p. 3, STFU Papers.

Conversely, when the price of cotton was high and its return assured—in this case the guaranteed government parity payment—he switched to the cheaper form of day labor, and thus did not have to split the higher income with the cropper.[5]

AAA planners had anticipated the problem of landlords switching sharecroppers to day laborers in order to keep the entire parity payment, but had done very little to guard against it. The government argued that, because of the large number and various types of farm tenants, separate checks to each one would be an insurmountable administrative problem. The sheer paper work involved would have been enormous, since there were already over a million cotton contracts dealing with landowners alone. Had an effort been made to pay tenants separately, the number of checks would have been infinitely larger. Moreover, there were so many different types of farm tenants—sharecroppers, cash renters, share renters, etc.—that AAA planners concluded it would be hopeless to determine accurately just how much each tenant should be paid. Thus they decided to make out the checks directly to the landowner, who they thought could be the best judge of determining the tenants' share of the crop.[6]

Perhaps an equally important reason for making the parity payment to the landlord was political expediency. The New Dealers had placed high hope in the farm program's economics of scarcity—raising prices by limiting production—and they thus sought landlord cooperation in their effort to make it work. Taking land out of production was a radical concept, and AAA planners feared landlords might rebel, especially in the early years when standing crops had to be destroyed. Thus, concessions were made wherever possible to the landholders. Although AAA regulations established after 1933 provided for withholding parity checks from landlords who sought to divert payments from tenants by switching from croppers to day laborers, and although the final arbiter in all matters of dispute between the landlord and the tenant was the secretary of agriculture, the local AAA county committees were given broad power. This was especially unfortunate for the tenant because these

5. Harold Hoffsommer, "The AAA and the Sharecropper," *Social Forces*, XIII (May 1935), 494–502.

6. See Conrad, *The Forgotten Farmers*, pp. 52–54; and Frey and Smith, "The Influence of the AAA Cotton Program Upon the Tenant, Cropper, and Laborer," pp. 488–489.

committees were notoriously weighted in favor of large planters.[7]

The actual wording of the law made possible a broad general interpretation by the local county committees. Section 8 (f) of the Agricultural Adjustment Act of 1938 provided that "any change between the landlord and the tenants or sharecroppers . . . shall not operate to increase the landlord's payments." While the section went on to say that the Agriculture Department might "withhold or reduce" the parity payment of those landlords found guilty of changing the status of tenants in order to "receive a greater share" of the benefit payment, it was the final sentence in the paragraph that was the most significant one: "Such limitation shall apply only if a county committee finds that the change or reduction is not justified and disapproves such change or reduction."[8]

In other words, the county committee was to judge the landlord's intent, i.e., whether the landlord, in evicting the croppers, intended to chisel them of their parity payment, or if his intent was honest because he legitimately no longer needed their help. "Most county committees," one observer sarcastically noted, "have found it difficult to be sure as to the true nature of the planters intent," since "the committeemen were planters themselves."[9]

The secretary of agriculture's position was that the county committee, freely elected, was the fairest judge of these matters. "Since the county committee is elected by the community committeemen," Henry Wallace wrote, "and the community committeemen are

7. *Ibid.*, pp. 120–135. Conrad, who studied carefully the writing of the law in the Cotton Section of the AAA, concluded that "the men of the Cotton Section . . . knew it would be disturbing to the normal workings of the system if the government made payments directly to tenants." Thus, the main reason for giving priority to landlords over tenants in the writing of the law "was that unless AAA got the voluntary cooperation of the landlords the cotton program would fail" (*ibid.*, pp. 52–53). See also William E. Leuchtenburg, *Franklin D. Roosevelt and the New Deal, 1932–1940*, New American Nation Series (New York, 1963), pp. 137–138; Myrdal, *An American Dilemma*, pp. 258–259; Davis, Gardner, and Gardner, *Deep South*, pp. 283–284; and Carl T. Schmidt, *American Farmers in the World Crisis* (New York, 1941), p. 264.

8. AAA Division of Information, *Tenant-Protection Provisions under AAA* (U.S. Department of Agriculture, March, 1940), p. 1; S. B. Bledsoe, memo to Henry Wallace, March 9, 1939, p. 1, NA, RG 96.

9. Thad Snow, unsent letter to St. Louis *Post-Dispatch*, Thad Snow Papers. These papers are presently in the possession of Mrs. Robert Delaney, of Charleston, Missouri, Thad Snow's daughter. I am indebted to Mrs. Delaney for permission to examine them.

elected by cooperating cotton producers who may be tenants and sharecroppers, it seems that an appropriate safeguard to tenants has been provided for in the Act."[10]

STFU disagreed totally with Wallace's view. The union charged that although all farmers were theoretically eligible to vote in county committee elections, those elections were frequently not publicized, seldom held on a uniform date in any state, and perhaps most important, that those tenants and croppers who attempted to exercise their right by voting, usually evoked the wrath of the large planters.

Undoubtedly, the union's charges were not without foundation. Since the burden of proof was clearly upon the tenant to demonstrate that the change from cropping to day labor was not justified, its enforcement was doomed from the beginning. It was common practice for county committees to inform landlords immediately if a cropper registered a complaint. A lowly cropper would hardly think of fighting a landlord and owner after his eviction and thus jeopardize the only chance he had to continue working on that farm as a day laborer.[11] Indeed, even the high-ranking members of the Agriculture Department were aware of the fact that the planter-controlled county committees afforded little protection for the tenants and croppers. "When one takes into account the fact that most of the members of the county committees are [hard pressed] landlords," one official wrote to Henry Wallace, coupled with the "increasing tendency to mechanization of cotton farms . . . it is apparent that this protection is inadequate."[12]

It is then no wonder that the union charged in the early days of the New Deal that the parity payment "stopped at the landlord, and operated to drive the sharecroppers off the land."[13] In 1934, STFU got its initial organizational impetus when it fought Arkansas absentee landlord Hiram Norcross, who had evicted fifty of his

10. Henry Wallace to Senator Hattie W. Caraway, March 18, 1939, National Archives, Washington, Record Group 16 (Records of the Office of the Secretary of Agriculture). Cited hereafter as NA, RG 16.

11. Mitchell, "Report of the Secretary, 1939," p. 13; Butler and Kester, "The STFU in 1940," p. 6, STFU Papers; See Senator William B. Bankhead, U.S. Congress, Senate, Subcommittee of the Committee on Appropriations, *Hearings, Agriculture Department Appropriations Bill, 1943*, 77th Cong., 2nd Sess., 1943, p. 1090.

12. S. B. Bledsoe, memo to Henry Wallace, March 9, 1939, NA, RG 96, p. 2.

13. Mitchell, "Workers in Our Fields," p. 3, STFU Papers.

sharecroppers in part, the croppers alleged, because he wanted to obtain their parity checks.[14]

STFU continued to argue that the New Deal's AAA program helped those farmers who needed it least—the large landowner—and hurt those who needed it most—the sharecroppers and tenants. Already, by 1930, about 90 per cent of the total cash income from agriculture came from 50 per cent of the total farm population, while the other 50 per cent of the farmers in the United States struggled for the remaining one-tenth of the income. By insisting that the AAA parity payment continued pouring money into the hands of the large planters, STFU became a major New Deal critic. It is not surprising, therefore, that a union which sought to be a voice for the southern tenant farmer should quickly acquire an enthusiastic following during the early days of the New Deal's farm program.[15]

By the time of the demonstration in 1939, the union claimed a five-state membership of over 35,000 in Arkansas, Tennessee, Mississippi, Missouri, and Oklahoma. Union activity in Southeast Missouri was slow in getting started, however, primarily because STFU's major efforts in the early thirties focused on eastern Arkansas, where, like the Bootheel of Missouri, cotton planting was relatively new and problems seemed worse than elsewhere in the South.[16]

The union encountered a virtual "reign of terror" in eastern Arkansas during the early thirties, when planters violently resisted union organization. With headquarters a relatively safe distance away at Memphis, union organizers frequently had to flee for their lives over the Harahan bridge at Memphis to escape angry Arkansas planters. STFU was doubly devious in the Southern planters' eyes, since it not only attempted to organize workers in the field, it attempted to do so biracially. Nevertheless, the union gradually succeeded in making itself heard; it played a large role in helping to

14. *Ibid.* STFU also charged in *West v. Norcross* that Norcross had evicted his croppers because they were union members. See Conrad, *The Forgotten Farmers*, pp. 87–88.

15. Farm Security Administration, *Security for Farm Tenants* (Washington, 1940), p. 5; see Auerbach, "Southern Tenant Farmers."

16. Mitchell, "The STFU in 1938," p. 9, STFU Papers; see Conrad, *The Forgotten Farmers*, pp. 83–104; Auerbach, "Southern Tenant Farmers"; Venkataramani, "Norman Thomas," pp. 225–246.

publicize the growing problems of farm tenants. So great had these problems become by 1935 that President Roosevelt appointed a special committee to study farm tenancy in the United States.[17]

The opening paragraphs of the committee's report to the president, released in February, 1937, vividly revealed the problem of farm tenancy in the country at the time. "Half a century ago," it began, "one of every four farmers was a tenant. Today two of every five are tenants." The committee pointed out that new tenants had been increasing at the rate of forty thousand a year for the past ten years. Indicative of the instability in farm tenancy was the high rate of mobility. "Many change farms every 2 or 3 years," the report stated, "apparently one out of three remains no longer than 1 year." Many farm owners, the committee found, were little better off than tenants in terms of farm security. "In some areas the farmers' equity in their property is as little as one-fifth," the report said. It then concluded that "fully half the total farm population of the United States has no adequate farm security."[18]

It was largely because of this report that the Farm Security Administration was established. Although STFU agreed in the main with the committee's recommendations, W. L. Blackstone, representing the union, wrote a minority report, taking strong exception to several committee proposals. Blackstone's report recommended that the FSA be established as an independent federal agency, separate from the Department of Agriculture. In Blackstone's view, the Department of Agriculture was dominated by planter interests and represented "the top third of the farmers in the country." Blackstone pointed out that the union had been quite disillusioned over the AAA program thus far. "Our experience has been such," his report stated, "that we cannot believe the Department of Agriculture will be able in any near future to remove itself from domination by the rich and large landowning class of farmers and their political-pressure lobbies." Blackstone charged that "the county agricultural agent" was "often paid in part by chambers of commerce or the Farm Bureau Federation," and argued that the county agent had become a symbol of domination by the wealthy class.[19]

17. J. R. Butler, letter to author, Jan. 7, 1966; Conrad, *The Forgotten Farmers*, pp. 83–104.

18. U.S. Congress, House, *Farm Tenancy: A Message from the President Transmitting the Report of the Special Committee on Farm Tenancy*, 75th Cong., 1st Sess., 1937, House Doc. 149, p. 1.

19. *Ibid.*, pp. 24–25.

STFU endorsed the committee's recommendation that tenants be represented on local farm committees, but suggested that the representation be in proportion to the number of tenants involved "as compared with the number of landlords or landowners. That clearly would be in keeping with true democratic processes."[20] The union also enthusiastically concurred in the committee's recommendations to continue the Resettlement Administration's rehabilitation-loan program.

On July 22, 1937, just months after the report appeared, the Bankhead-Jones Farm Tenant Act was approved by the Congress. The act called for the establishment of the Farm Security Administration—created in September, 1937—to administer the aid-to-tenant provisions of the law. FSA was authorized to make long-term, low-interest loans to landless farmers. It also absorbed the functions of the Resettlement Administration, continuing the rehabilitation-loan program, as well as administering the subsistence homestead and resettlement communities, which had been established earlier to help relocate destitute farm families.[21]

STFU was undoubtedly pleased with the establishment of the FSA in 1937. Although it was not entirely what the union wanted, STFU felt that the government had made a step in the right direction. The union did not relinquish, however, its efforts to continue to publicize the plight of the cropper and to organize new locals in the fields.

In 1937, STFU took a rather bold step; it decided to become affiliated with the newly formed CIO. STFU wanted direct affiliation as a national union, but the CIO decided to organize it instead as a part of the United Cannery Agricultural Packing and Allied Workers of America (UCAPAWA). H. L. Mitchell, whose name by this time had become synonymous with STFU policy, was skeptical of UCAPAWA from the beginning, primarily because of what he considered to be the high-handed tactics of its president, Donald

20. *Ibid.*, p. 26.

21. *Ibid.*; U.S. *Statutes at Large*, L, 522; Murray R. Benedict, *Can We Solve the Farm Problem* (New York, 1955), p. 362; FSA, *Security for Farm Tenants*, p. 4; Venkataramani, "Norman Thomas," pp. 241–244. For an excellent analysis of how FSA tried to help the croppers, see Paul V. Maris, "How May the Conditions of Tenant Farmers and Share Croppers Be Improved," (address delivered before the American Country Life Association, Lexington, Ky., Nov. 4, 1938), Fannie Cook Collection, Missouri Historical Society, St. Louis; and Sidney Baldwin, *Poverty and Politics: The Rise and Decline of the Farm Security Administration* (Chapel Hill, 1968).

Henderson, a known Communist. But Mitchell decided to join anyway because he endorsed the CIO's "program of industrial unionism." After receiving assurance that its autonomy would be respected by the International UCAPAWA, STFU crossed the Rubicon and voted to join at a meeting in Denver in 1937. STFU was chartered as District IV of UCAPAWA, with a federated membership.[22]

STFU's troubles with UCAPAWA, however, started almost immediately. Essentially it was a fight between local autonomy and central control; from the beginning, Mitchell wanted organization and administrative autonomy for STFU, and he strenuously resisted the efforts of Henderson to exert control over STFU locals. Despite its large membership, STFU had little say in determining policy. Mitchell charged the UCAPAWA executive council was composed of members from "paper districts," who were all "hand-picked men"—nothing more than "personal friends of Henderson."[23] During 1938, bitter fighting occurred between STFU and UCAPAWA over the collection of per capita dues, the chartering of STFU locals, and charges by STFU that UCAPAWA wanted to convert the sharecroppers' union into a political body, "responsible to an outside group," since UCAPAWA was dominated by members of the Communist Party.[24]

In 1938, when E. B. McKinney, a Negro who had been vice-president of STFU for four years, tried to obtain separate recognition by UCAPAWA for thirteen Negro locals in Arkansas, Mitchell and Butler charged that Henderson had "hired" McKinney "to try to split the STFU along race lines in order to weaken it."[25] In August of the same year, J. R. Butler claimed that Claude Williams, a union leader, had sent a letter to Communist party headquarters, asking support for a campaign to win control over STFU.[26] Williams at the time was president of Commonwealth

22. Press release, STFU, June 23, 1937; Mitchell, "Oral History," copy of material collected for Oral History Project, Columbia University, New York, p. 86; An Open Letter to Friends of STFU, Oct. 1, 1939, p. 2, STFU Papers; see also Very Rony, "Sorrow Song in Black and White," *New South* (Summer, 1967), Southern Regional Council publication.

23. An Open Letter to Friends of STFU, Oct. 1, 1939, p. 2, STFU Papers.

24. Butler and Mitchell to Members Executive Board CIO, Feb. 14, 1939; undated memo, "Activities of Donald Henderson, Communist specialist of Cannery and Agriculture Workers Union," *ibid.*

25. An Open Letter to Friends of STFU, Oct. 1, 1939, p. 5; J. R. Butler to National Executive Council, June 18, 1938, *ibid.*

26. J. R. Butler to Claude Williams, August 22, 1938, *ibid.*

College, in Mena, Arkansas, an institution long suspected of harboring Communist activities. Both incidents confirmed Mitchell's suspicions that Henderson and the Communists were out to take over the union. A special session of the STFU executive council voted to expel McKinney and Williams, and the action was sustained by the members at the Fifth Annual Convention of STFU at Cotton Plant, Arkansas, on December 28, 1938.[27]

When Henderson proposed that STFU locals be chartered directly by UCAPAWA and all dues payments and reports go directly to the International, rather than through the STFU office in Memphis, Mitchell resisted openly, and at the Cotton Plant meeting, STFU passed a resolution asking UCAPAWA for the right to collect dues through the Memphis office and for complete autonomy in all its affairs.[28] By the end of 1938, STFU and UCAPAWA were heading for a showdown. The showdown came over the roadside demonstration in Southeast Missouri early in 1939.

27. Mitchell, "Oral History," p. 109, STFU Papers. For the record of Williams's trial, see "Complete Proceedings, Trial of Claude C. Williams by the Executive Council," STFU, Sept. 16 and 17, 1938, *ibid.*

28. An Open Letter to Friends of STFU, Oct. 1, 1939, p. 6; Mitchell to All Locals, STFU, Jan. 1, 1939, *ibid.*

3 The Bootheel Gets a Leader

Because STFU's chief concern in its early years was eastern Arkansas, it was not until 1936 that it sent an organizer into Southeast Missouri to try to build a union there. STFU got started in the Bootheel largely at the invitation of Thad Snow of Charleston, Missouri.[1] Snow was a relatively large plantation owner and a man of unusual skill and talent. To many people in the area he was known variously as the "Cottonfield Confucius," the Bootheel philosopher, or the "Sage of Swampeast Missouri." The latter name was acquired because Snow liked to refer jokingly to the Bootheel as "Swampeast Missouri," and he made the label well known to readers of the St. Louis *Post-Dispatch* by constantly writing witty letters to its editors about the region and the activities of its inhabitants.

Thad Snow was something of an anomaly for his time. Although he was a fairly prosperous man and had about twenty sharecropper families on his thousand-acre farm in Charleston, he spent a great deal of his time lecturing his planter colleagues on their failure to provide a better life for their tenants, and in constantly laboring to help his own sharecroppers pull themselves out of their miser-

1. Mitchell, undated memo to Rev. David S. Burgess, "Re: Early Organization in Southeast Missouri," General Histories Folder, STFU Papers.

able existence. While he had the respect and admiration of his planter associates, Snow was frequently eyed with a great deal of suspicion by many because there was no doubt about whose side he would be on in the planter-tenant confrontation that was about to take place in the Bootheel. "In so far as we have a class struggle in the cotton country," he once wrote, "my sympathies are definitely with the poor devils who bend their backs to do our work."[2]

Snow had come into Missouri as a migrant from the North, born in Indiana and educated at the University of Michigan. Thus he did not share the traditional Southern attitude toward the sharecropper in general and the Negro in particular. Snow believed that his being born and bred in the North was a distinct advantage for him in the Bootheel, for it enabled him "to observe the southern-planter psychology with a degree of objectivity. . . ."[3]

An avid reader of Thorstein Veblen, he understood the problems of Southeast Missouri in broad economic terms, and he saw himself surrounded in the thirties with absentee landlordism and the maldistribution of land and wealth. Like Veblen, Snow had a perceptive eye for detecting the causes of problems, especially those of an economic nature.

Thad Snow was undoubtedly happiest when writing of the problems in the Bootheel, which meant that he rarely had a sad moment. During his lifetime his facile pen covered a broad range of topics. At one time or another, he was concerned with the difficulty of the cotton farmer, the need for good roads in Southeast Missouri, the failure of the engineers in preventing periodic floods of the Mississippi, and of course, most importantly, the great roadside demonstration of 1939.[4]

His witty, often sarcastic, method of writing, however, was frequently misinterpreted by Southeast Missourians, and as a result, his general reputation was more myth than fact. To those who had never met him, he was labeled a Communist, while to his intimate

2. Undated letter to *Post-Dispatch*, Thad Snow Papers.

3. Snow, U.S. Congress, Senate, Subcommittee of the Committee on Agriculture and Forestry, *Hearings on S. Res. 158*, 7th Cong., 2nd Sess., 1937, p. 4548.

4. Snow left his memoirs in his book, *From Missouri* (Boston, 1954), which is still the best popular account of the 1939 strike. Although it is autobiographical, over half of the book is devoted to the demonstration. While Snow was mostly critical of the Bootheel, one cannot read *From Missouri* without being immediately impressed by the fact that Thad Snow loved the land and the people he wrote about.

planter associates, who always regarded him as a close friend, he was, at best, an eccentric and a "radical" with foreign ideas. The most popular myth that circulated about him in the Bootheel was that he kept a shortwave radio in the basement of his home, on which he would make periodic calls to Russia, presumably to chat with Joseph Stalin or other high officials in the Soviet government.[5]

Snow actually requested STFU to come organize on his plantation, and the union responded by sending John Hancox, a young Negro poet and songwriter, who set up the first STFU local in the state.[6] Hancox was not destined to play a dominant role in STFU's history in Southeast Missouri though, for the man who quickly emerged as the unquestioned leader of the union in this area, the man who was to mastermind the highway demonstration of 1939, was Owen H. Whitfield, a Negro sharecropper and a part-time peripatetic preacher, who joined STFU a few months after it started in the Bootheel.

Whitfield was born in 1892 in Jamestown, Mississippi, and as a youth traveled around in Tennessee and Arkansas before returning to Mississippi to attend Okolona College there for two years while earning money by working with his uncle on a farm. Later he spent time working at various jobs—as a fireman on a train, as a tap dancer traveling in a minstrel show—before finally settling down in 1923 to sharecropping with his family on the plantation of Al Drinkwater, about nine miles from Charlestown, where he helped raise some of the first cotton ever grown in Missouri.[7]

Whitfield was a tireless worker, frequently rising long before it was time to be in the fields in an effort to make a better life for his rapidly growing family. He toiled diligently throughout a day that stretched from "can to can't," which was the way the cropper liked to describe his work day; i.e., he worked from the time you can see in the morning when the sun comes up until you can't see any longer after it goes down. Yet, Whitfield later recalled, it seemed that no matter how early he rose or how assiduously he labored, he was never able to get very far ahead. Then one day,

5. This story is still commonly accepted in the Bootheel today. During interviews with supposedly well-informed people, the author encountered it, with numerous variations, on at least a half-dozen occasions.

6. Mitchell, undated memo to Rev. David S. Burgess, General Histories Folder, STFU Papers.

7. *Ibid.*; Mrs. Zella Whitfield, interview with author, Dec. 19, 1965; Mitchell, "Oral History," p. 112, STFU Papers.

out in the field, Whitfield had what he liked to refer to as his "argument with God."

It was the end of a long hot summer day in 1936, and as usual, he had been plowing since long before dawn. The sun had already gone down, his wife and children had returned to the house, and he was now all alone in the field. Just as he was about to leave the field, one of the children came running out and informed him that they were completely out of food, and that there would be no supper. A religious man and a minister of God, Whitfield fell on his knees in supplication. He was angry, and he cried out to God to explain to him the reason for his fate. All his life he had tried to live by the Good Book, which taught that the Lord always rewarded those who served Him. He had been an obedient servant and kept the faith. He had worked hard to provide for his wife and children, and yet he was constantly threatened with hunger. Suddenly a voice came to him, he recalled, and said: "I give you enough to fill your barns, as I promised. But you let someone take it away." That ended Owen Whitfield's dilemma and began a new life for him. He now understood that it was not the Lord's fault that he was hungry, but his own. God had always given him plenty; it was now up to him to get it.[8]

It was shortly after this experience that Whitfield joined STFU in an effort to obtain what he considered to be his fair share of the Lord's bounty. The Negro was apprehensive about joining STFU at first, primarily because he felt it was dominated by whites, and it could therefore do little to help his people in the Bootheel, the majority of whom were Negroes. He changed his mind, however, after talking to STFU officials, and soon became very enthusiastic about the potential the union held for improving the lot of the tenant farmer, both black and white.[9]

Whitfield had first started preaching in 1923, and by the time he joined the union in 1937, he had become pastor of a number of rural churches in the Bootheel. It was the church that proved to be the indispensable aid in Whitfield's unionizing efforts. It assisted him in a number of ways. First of all, it was through the churches that he made most of his personal contacts. Rural churches had mostly farm worker members, and it was not long before many of Whitfield's church members became union members. Secondly, the

8. Mrs. Zella Whitfield, interview with author, Dec. 19, 1965.
9. *Ibid.*

church could be used as a surreptitious meeting place for many of the early union gatherings. They were often held there at night, away from the watchful eye of the planters. Lastly, and most importantly, the pulpit served as the vehicle by which Whitfield was able to communicate his ideas to his parishioners and potential union members.[10]

His speech was eloquent and his sermons powerful. Although Whitfield probably had never heard of Walter Rauschenbusch, the message which came from the pulpit was the social gospel. "Take your eyes out of the sky," he was fond of telling his sharecropper congregation, "because someone is stealing your bread."[11] Whitfield liked to refer to his ministry as "applied religion." By this he meant that there should be less emphasis on the rewards of the afterlife—the "pie in the sky"—and more on the effort to apply God's teachings to life on this earth. "I'm not preachin' 'bout heaven," he once remarked during an interview. "No sir! I'm preachin' the brotherhood of man . . . the applied religion!"[12]

Whitfield had charisma, and it did not take long before he attracted a large following. He did not confine his message to the Negroes in his churches, however; he worked equally hard communicating to the whites in the fields, and soon became one of STFU's best organizers. He liked to carry a hand drawn cartoon into the fields with him, which he believed helped to sell the idea of the union to both races. In the first caption, the cartoon showed two roped mules—one black and one white—tugging in opposite directions toward two piles of hay. By pulling in different directions, they cancelled each other's efforts and therefore neither was able to reach his objective. In the second caption, the two mules decided to pull together, first toward one bale, then toward the other. The message required little explanation; only by pulling together, he would point out, could whites and Negroes hope to improve their lot.

Surprisingly enough, Whitfield found that the white sharecroppers

10. *Ibid.*

11. Quoted in Mitchell to James Myers, Feb. 10, 1939, STFU Papers. See also Cedric Belfrage, "Cotton-Patch Moses," *Harper's Magazine*, CXCVII (Nov. 1948), 94–103.

12. Quoted in Ben M. Ridpath, "The Case of the Missouri Sharecroppers," *Christian Century*, LVI (Feb. 1939), 148. Later in his life, Whitfield joined an organization called the People's Applied Religion. Mrs. Zella Whitfield, interview with author, Dec. 19, 1965.

were far more hostile toward the planters than were the Negro sharecroppers. After indicating to the whites the many injustices of the tenancy system, Whitfield claimed they were quite obstreperous, often wanting to burn barns or kill the offending planters, unlike the Negro workers, who tended to accept their unjust treatment as only another phase of their normally difficult life.[13]

It is not surprising that two men as remarkable as Thad Snow and Owen Whitfield, located less than ten miles from one another, should sooner or later come together and get to be friends. Snow, steeped in Thorstein Veblen, and Whitfield, a socially conscious minister, had a great deal to say to one another. Snow was the theoretician, understanding the often subtle and complicated forces which gave rise to the plight of the tenant workers; Whitfield was the practical union organizer, grappling with the real day-to-day problems in the fields.

Whitfield openly discussed the problems of the Bootheel sharecropper with Thad Snow, who was one of the few plantation owners the croppers trusted. Whitfield was not always completely candid with all white people he met. Whenever he encountered a white he thought might be hostile, his favorite practice was to cast himself in the role of the "poor dumb nigger from Mississippi," and let his otherwise hostile acquaintance assume that he was in the presence of just another happy, carefree darkie who knew his place. By letting whites continue to live in this fictional world, Whitfield found that many would-be antagonists soon assumed a more friendly attitude. The Negro minister greatly admired and respected Thad Snow, however, always spoke freely with him, and listened attentively when Snow spoke.[14]

Snow soon became a kind of unofficial economic and political mentor, as well as a very close personal friend. Apparently, it was largely due to Snow's efforts, working with STFU, that Whitfield and his family got the opportunity to move into the LaForge Project in New Madrid County, an FSA housing cooperative built in 1937 to help rehabilitate displaced sharecroppers.[15]

LaForge was an FSA "experiment" to try to determine the

13. Mitchell, undated memo to Burgess, General Histories Folder, STFU Papers; Mrs. Zella Whitfield, interview with author, Dec. 19, 1965; Mr. John Stewart, interview with author, May 1, 1966.

14. *Ibid.*

15. *Ibid.*; Mitchell, undated memo to Burgess, General Histories Folder, STFU Papers.

efficacy of the "family-type" cooperative farm and its value in helping to solve sharecropper and tenant problems. The FSA purchased a 6,700 acre tract in New Madrid County and attempted to rehabilitate 100 sharecropper families by providing them with a four- or five-room house for each family and a loan averaging about $1,300 for the purchase of livestock, feed, machinery, and other equipment. In addition, FSA provided trained farm experts and home supervisors to assist in learning farming practices, such as soil conservation and crop diversification, as well as canning, consumption of food, and other vocational training. The LaForge "Cooperative Association" was also established on the project, which provided the community with a gin, a warehouse, and other facilities and services.[16]

Since the Whitfields were not living in New Madrid County at the time LaForge was built, they were not eligible for entrance, but STFU persuaded Thad Snow to pull strings, and the Charleston planter got them in. At LaForge, Whitfield came into contact with Hans Baasch, its director. Baasch was a Norwegian who was sold on the advantages of cooperative farming. He also became Whitfield's close friend and adviser.[17]

Owen Whitfield was elected vice president of STFU in 1937. Under Snow's careful guidance, and Hans Baasch's sympathetic support, he began to spread the union's gospel throughout the Bootheel. By the end of 1938, there were over twenty locals in Southeast Missouri with an estimated membership of nearly five thousand. The union was the indispensable tool Whitfield needed to improve his people's conditions. For the first time, the lowest field hand in the Bootheel was provided a vehicle for expressing his discontent.[18]

16. LaForge was one of ninety-nine New Deal farm communities. See Paul K. Conkin, *Tomorrow a New World: The New Deal Community Program* (Ithaca, 1959), pp. 332–337; "LaForge Project Review," Farm Security Administration, Oct. 5, 1940, NA, RG 96; *One Hundred Families* (Second Anniversary, LaForge Farms Resettlement Project, USDA, Dec. 20, 1939, New Madrid, Missouri); John M. Collins, "100 Missouri Sharecroppers Move Into a Land of Promise: An FSA Experiment Gets Underway in the Cotton Country," Fannie Cook Collection; and *Southeast Missouri: A Laboratory for the Cotton South.*

17. Mrs. Zella Whitfield, interview with author, Dec. 19, 1965.

18. Mitchell, "The STFU in 1938," unnumbered page following p. 10, STFU Papers.

Apart from its constant campaign to publicize the croppers' condition, STFU's most effective job was calling strikes in the fields to help raise workers' wages. The union organized strikes in 1935, 1936, and 1938 in an effort to raise wages for farm workers. In some areas of eastern Arkansas, wages were as low as thirty cents a hundred pounds for cotton pickers. Although STFU claimed a victory in its 1938 strike, its efforts in the Bootheel were largely unsuccessful, owing mostly to efforts of planters who brought in strikebreakers from across the river in southern Illinois.[19]

At the time of the 1938 strike, Whitfield went to STFU headquarters at Memphis and tried to persuade the union against it. "Personally," he later argued, "I am against strikes."[20] When the decision was made to carry out the strike at the executive meeting in the fall of 1938, Whitfield voted against it. "The union must fight through the government," he said at the time; "nothing [can] be gained by fighting in the field."[21] This did not mean that Whitfield was convinced that strikes were without any kind of beneficial effect. He later wrote that he hoped that his position would not be mistakenly interpreted by some as an "apology" for the strikers action, "for everyone knows that if these poor people dont do something for themselves there will be nothing done."[22] Indeed, at the time that he opposed the 1938 strike, Whitfield vehemently defended the workers' right to strike as well as the efficacy of organizing farm unions. "I wonder whats all the howling about?" he wrote to those who criticized the farmers' efforts to organize in the fields. "Arnt all the big folks organized. what about kiwanis club and all the other clubs? what about chamber of commerce? what [about] the ginners association and all the other associations?" Whitfield felt that it was about time for the sharecroppers—the "poor devils both white and black—[to] get together for protection of ourselves

19. See Auerbach, "Southern Tenant Farmers"; Mitchell, "The STFU in 1938," pp. 3–4, STFU Papers; Mitchell, "Oral History," p. 55; Snow, undated letter to *Post-Dispatch*, Thad Snow Papers; and National Advisory Committee on Farm Labor, *Farm Labor Organizing, 1905–1967* (July 1967), pp. 24–25.

20. Whitfield, unsent letter to the Charleston *Democrat*, Oct. 16, 1938, Thad Snow Papers.

21. Whitfield, "Summary Minutes of the National Executive Council meeting of the STFU," Sept. 16–17, 1938, Memphis, STFU Papers.

22. Whitfield, unsent letter to the Charleston *Democrat*, Oct. 16, 1938, Thad Snow Papers.

and our families as well as the big folks for after all we are human beings."[23]

Whitfield opposed the union's 1938 strike, therefore, not because he opposed using the strike as a means of helping the sharecropper. Rather, his opposition rested largely on the fact that the Negro leader had much larger aspirations for the lowly Bootheel farm workers. His goal envisaged gains greater than those usually obtained by calling strikes in the field to help raise wages. Whitfield's opportunity to help fulfill that goal came early in 1939.

23. *Ibid.*

4 The Demise of the Sharecropper System

The abysmal living conditions of the tenant farmer described in the first chapter no doubt helped to make the Bootheel ripe for social protest. Moreover, the union's "proletarianization" of the farm workers made all union members aware of the injustices of the farm system that caused their miserable existence. But poor living conditions for tenant farmers did not make the Bootheel unique because they were not unlike conditions elsewhere in the cotton South at this time. Nor was the union's effort at organizing peculiar to Southeast Missouri; as indicated, STFU had much greater strength in other southern states. Thus, while it is true that the sharecropper's conditions and the activity of the union in the area no doubt helped set the stage for action, they alone do not account for the highway demonstration of 1939. Even with the charismatic leadership of Whitfield, something more was needed to galvanize the feelings of discontent prevalent in the Bootheel in order to trigger a massive uprising. That decisive event occurred at the end of 1938, when hundreds of croppers were evicted from their homes because many planters were converting from sharecropping to day labor in order that they might receive the entire AAA parity payment themselves.

The problem of landlords' diverting parity payments by switching the status of a tenant, as already indicated, was a major impetus for the STFU's coming into being. It was to be one of the union's major concerns in the Bootheel, because there the problem had already existed prior to the New Deal's farm program. Indeed, the temptation of obtaining the full parity check by converting from sharecropping to day labor caused Bootheel landlords to accelerate a process that had already been taking place in Southeast Missouri in the thirties largely as a result of mechanization and the bountiful supply of cheap labor.

The fierce competition of large-scale mechanized farming was already destroying the traditional sharecropper system in the Bootheel by the mid-1930's. As indicated in the first chapter, the trend in Southeast Missouri in the 1930's was for the size of the farm to increase, while the number of farms decreased, a trend which converted many plantations into large highly mechanized "farm factories." The sharecropper system simply was not conducive to mechanization and the farm factory.[1]

Under the old system, cotton had been grown in the Bootheel either by small owner-operators performing the manual labor, or, more often than not, by large owners or renters, who used a great many sharecroppers to perform the bodily work. With mechanization, however, the trend was toward agricultural industrialism; machines and a few day hands took the place of a great many croppers. Day laborers could operate machines and were quite cheap because they could be paid by the hour and, unlike croppers, the planter did not have to care for them year round. An FSA report in 1940 indicated that farming meant at best "day laborers during peak season and harvesting time only, rather than for small owner-operators or tenants permanently rooted on the land."[2]

The shift in Southeast Missouri toward large-scale farm factories with fewer farm workers was also taking place during the thirties—albeit on a more gradual scale—throughout the entire nation. For example, there were about 900,000 tractors on farms in the United States in 1930, but by 1938 the figure had jumped to over 1,500,000. By 1939, because of mechanization, government officials estimated that 1,500,000 fewer farm workers were needed to supply both foreign and domestic markets than the country had in 1929. Yet during the same period, the government reported, the entire farm population actually increased by 1,830,000.[3]

1. *Report to the Tolan Committee*, Pt. III, p. 7.

2. FSA, *Security for Farm Tenants* (Washington, 1940), p. 6.

3. *Ibid.*, p. 8. W. C. Holley, Ellen Winston, and T. J. Woofter, Jr., *The Plantation South, 1934–1937*, Research Monograph XXII, Works Progress

Of greater importance than mechanization in eliminating the sharecropper in Southeast Missouri, however, was the prevalence of an abundant labor supply in the region. This excessive labor supply was due to a number of factors. As was indicated earlier, a high birth rate in the Bootheel was already producing a large labor surplus. This problem was periodically aggravated by the influx into the region of unemployed laborers during the peak periods of picking and chopping. Many of these workers were recruited by planters from out of the state, some from as far away as Texas.[4]

Moreover, since Southeast Missouri was the northern end of the cotton belt, additional migrant seasonal workers passed through on their way to Berrien County, Michigan, which was the next stop on their migratory journey. Government officials, later investigating the Bootheel's problems, found that 60 per cent of the migratory workers in Berrien County, a cherry-picking region, originated in Southeast Missouri and northern Arkansas. To complicate the Bootheel's problems further, because of the huge labor surplus, many migrants were unable to find work in Southeast Missouri once they arrived; thus many were forced by lack of funds to remain through the winter before moving on to the next area requiring seasonal labor.[5]

Indicative of the landlords' frequent use of migrant seasonal labor was the high rate of mobility of tenant farmers in the Bootheel. According to the 1935 Census of Agriculture, 43 per cent of the tenants living in Southeast Missouri had been on their present farms less than one year. While mobility among tenants was not unusual, the rate in the Bootheel was far above both the state and the national average of 34 per cent.[6] Among farm families interviewed in Dunklin, New Madrid, and Pemiscot counties, 34 per cent of white croppers and 44 per cent of white laborers moved on the average at least twice—some more frequently—during a

---

Administration (Washington, 1940), pp. 17–22. Although denied by Department of Agriculture officials, there is some evidence to indicate that the AAA program actually speeded up mechanization because it gave cotton planters cash needed to buy the machinery. See Paul Taylor, "Power Farming and Labor Displacement," *Monthly Labor Review*, XLVI (March 1938), 595–607, 852–867; Schmidt, *American Farmers in the World Crisis*, pp. 263–264; and Raper and Reid, *Sharecroppers All*, pp. 43–46.

4. N. G. Silvermaster, memo to C. B. Baldwin, "Subject: Southeast Missouri," Oct. 12, 1940, p. 4, NA, RG 96.

5. *Ibid.*; *Southeast Missouri: A Laboratory for the Cotton South*, p. 2; Henry Wallace to F. D. Roosevelt, Jan. 21, 1939, NA, RG 16.

6. *FSA Report*, p. 53. The president's committee on farm tenancy found

period of five years, and the number of Negroes was slightly higher in both categories.[7]

Finally, it was not unusual for members of sharecropper families who had small tracts of land to travel short distances to work on other farms to supplement their meager incomes. This was especially true during the chopping and picking season.[8]

The shift to mechanization, the high birth rate, and the increase of migrants into the region were the principal factors that contributed to a huge labor surplus. Thus, the Bootheel problem was simple: there were always more farm workers than there was farm work. In 1935, for example, according to one study, in the four major counties in the Delta, the labor available greatly exceeded the required labor for every month except June, October, and November. From January to May, 35,737 workers were available, which meant a surplus for these months ranging from 17,000 to 30,000 laborers in the four counties.[9] Although not as large, surpluses also existed from June to September. Not until October, when cotton picking started, was the surplus eliminated, and even then, it was not completely wiped out.[10]

Several experts, studying the problem in 1940, computed that if it were possible to provide an equal distribution of the work load, the average per farm worker in Southeast Missouri would vary from a low of 3.3 days in January and 3.5 in February to a peak of 22.2 days in November and 23.9 in October. Moreover, there was little opportunity for those farm workers to find jobs in nearby

---

that "in the spring of 1935, there were more than a third (34.2 per cent) of the 2,865,000 tenant farmers of the Nation who had occupied their present farms only 1 year" (U.S. Congress, House, *Farm Tenancy* . . . 1st Sess., 1937, House Doc. 149, p. 7). See Appendix, Table 9.

7. *FSA Report*, p. 55. See Appendix, Table 10.

8. *Report to the Tolan Committee*, Pt. III, p. 27.

9. Philip Brown, "Farm Labor in Southeast Missouri," *Agricultural Situation*, XXIV, No. 4 (April 1940), 11. See also Charles S. Hoffman and Virgil L. Bankson, "Crisis in Missouri's Boot Heel," *Land Policy Review*, III, No. 1 (Jan.–Feb. 1940), 2–3, 6–8.

10. In October, there were still 214 extra workers. Moreover, "these estimates," the author stated, "are conservative. They are based on census figures as of the first week in January 1935, which showed 29,687 family laborers and 6,050 day laborers in the area. January is a slack season of the year and the labor supply was at a minimum when the census was taken. The number of agricultural laborers has increased since 1935. Furthermore, family labor on a farm is utilized to its utmost and performs a share of the work that is not in proportion to its size" (Brown, "Farm Labor in Southeast Missouri," p. 11).

cities during the off season. The 1930 United States Census indicated that only 10 per cent of the population in the Delta lived in areas described as urban residences, while three-fourths of the remaining rural population resided on farms.[11]

All the statistical evidence available strongly suggests that the switch from sharecropping to the less expensive form of day labor was already occurring in the Bootheel—at least on a small scale—in the thirties. Between 1929 and 1936, for example, some 36 per cent of farm tenants in the seven Delta counties who were sharecroppers became day laborers, while only 20 per cent who were day laborers in 1929 became sharecroppers by 1936.[12] While there was no data available for the entire area, a survey of the types of tenure among a sampling of farm families in Dunklin, New Madrid, and Pemiscot counties indicated that by 1936 there was already a greater percentage of day laborers in those counties than croppers or renters.[13] In New Madrid County, during the decade of the thirties, the number of tenants who had been sharecroppers increased slightly, share renters remained almost the same, while wage laborers practically doubled, increasing slowly year by year.[14]

Thus, by the thirties, not only was the trend to fall back from ownership into tenancy in Southeast Missouri, but because of the shift from muscles to machines and the availability of cheap labor, the trend for many farm families was from sharecropping back further into the ranks of day laborers.

If mechanization and cheap labor only whetted the Bootheel planter's appetite to switch from sharecropping to day labor, when the New Deal's farm program came along, the planter practically feasted. The temptation of receiving the entire portion of the parity payment proved to be too tantilizing to resist.

Since both the cropper and day laborer were without workstock, equipment, or capital, the only major distinction between the two, so far as the landlord was concerned, was the method of paying for the labor, and so the shift from sharecropper to day laborer could be made easily. It was subject only to the arbitrary whim of

11. Hoffman and Bankson, "Crisis in Missouri's Boot Heel," p. 8.

12. *Ibid.*, pp. 9–10. Information from which these figures were compiled was taken from "unpublished data in the files of the Farm Security Administration, Region III, Indianapolis, covering sample areas" in the seven Bootheel counties.

13. *FSA Report*, p. 35. See Appendix, Table 11.

14. *Report to the Tolan Committee*, Pt. V, p. 16.

the individual landlord, and more particularly, to how strongly the landlord was tempted to switch.

In 1938, the temptation to switch to day labor was doubled. After a bumper cotton crop in 1937, New Dealers sought to eliminate the surplus by cutting cotton production 40 per cent. In part because the AAA program had already eliminated jobs for farm workers, and no doubt in part because of STFU's criticism, the Department of Agriculture decided to change the cotton regulation in 1938. Anticipating the additional loss of income to sharecroppers by its proposed reduction, AAA planners tried to mitigate the shock by doubling the amount to be given to the cropper, increasing his share from 25 per cent, according to the 1937 regulation, to 50 per cent in 1938.[15]

In other words, in 1937, the landlord received 50 per cent of the parity check, the renter 25 per cent, and the cropper 25 per cent, or if there was no renter, it was 75–25. In 1938, according to the new law, the landlord would receive 25 per cent, the renter 25 per cent, and the cropper 50 per cent, or again if there was no renter, 50–50. In either case, the landlord theoretically was to turn over an additional one-fourth of the crop payment to the cropper.[16]

One common arrangement in the Bootheel, as already noted, was the absentee owner and sharecropper setup—with the salaried overseer in between. In this case, a 75–25 arrangement was converted into 50–50 in 1938. Perhaps more significantly, in the case of the renter, where the setup was 50–25–25, the landlord would go to 25–25–50 in 1938. In this instance, it was tempting for the landowner to evict both renter and cropper and keep the entire payment for himself.[17]

Finally, there was still another variation in the outcome of the new law. At least a few large renters and salaried agents apparently evicted croppers at the end of 1938, switched to day labor, and failed to inform their landowners, keeping the difference in pay themselves. Whitfield, who observed the peculiar but unfortunate experiences of croppers dealing with salaried agents, maintained that many agents and overseers frequently cheated both croppers and companies.

15. See *Post-Dispatch*, Jan. 22, 1939.

16. See Snow, *From Missouri*, p. 231; Mitchell, "The STFU in 1938," p. 1; press release, STFU, Jan. 14, 1939, STFU Papers.

17. There were at least a few instances of this occurring at the end of 1938. One renter with sixty acres who had been evicted participated in the demonstration. See *Daily Worker*, Jan. 15, 1939.

In all instances, it was easy for the overseer to keep the check from the cropper if he so desired. "In 80 per cent of the cases we don't see the check," Whitfield later argued. "In 50 per cent of the cases, we don't even know there is a check."[18] It was this temptation on the part of the landowner, the large renter, and the salaried agent to double, or at least increase their share of, the parity payment by simply removing the cropper that precipitated the mass evictions at the end of 1938.

Actually, evictions had already been taking place in Southeast Missouri prior to this, but not on a large scale. Because of charges of evictions in the Bootheel in 1934 and 1935, for example, the AAA sent an investigator to the area. The investigator concluded, however, that the reports had been grossly exaggerated.[19] At the end of 1937, moreover, twenty-one families were evicted from Sikeston and twenty-five from Wyatt, Missouri.[20] Whitfield wrote to Roosevelt at the beginning of 1938, complaining of evictions, and requesting protection for croppers in the farm law. The government's only response was a letter informing Whitfield that he should urge those tenants needing help to see the FSA supervisor.[21]

Not until 1939 did wholesale evictions occur, apparently because of the new law. The prospect of not having to double the croppers share of the parity payment for 1939 by eliminating him completely caused about seventy planters to evict croppers in wholesale numbers at the end of 1938.[22]

Ironically, in attempting to help the cropper by providing for a larger share of the parity payment, the result of the AAA's program was the very antithesis, because it only encouraged planters to switch from sharecropping to day labor. "The law and rulings which have sought to 'freeze' the ancient sharecrop system," Thad

18. Whitfield, quoted in *ibid.*, Jan. 16, 1940.

19. See "Report of the Adjustment Committee on Investigation of Landlord-Tenant Complaints under the Cotton and Tobacco Contracts," Sept. 1, 1934, pp. 44–46; "A Report on a Survey to Determine What Relationship, If Any, Existed between the Cotton Acreage Reduction Program and the Number of Tenants Enrolled as Emergency Relief Clients in the Period January 1, 1934 to March 15, 1935," Sept. 1, 1935, pp. 45–48, National Archives, Record Group 145 (Records of the Agricultural Adjustment Administration). Cited hereafter as NA, RG 145. See also Conrad, *The Forgotten Farmer*, pp. 77–78.

20. See "Preliminary Report on Labor Displacement on Cotton Plantations," Jan. 15, 1938, STFU Papers.

21. Whitfield to FDR, Jan. 5, 1938; H. G. Reynolds to Whitfield, Feb. 4, 1938, NA, RG 96.

22. *Southeast Missouri: A Laboratory for the Cotton South*, p. 3.

Snow acutely noted, "have had exactly the opposite effect of breaking it rapidly down."[23]

By eliminating the cropper in making the switch, absentee landlords, remaining personally anonymous, had no serious pangs of conscience. The planter-operator, however—the resident owner who lived and worked on the farm in the Bootheel—had to salve his conscience by arguing that since he was the actual landowner, it was he who had to pay taxes on the "idle-land" taken out of production in the AAA program. As indicated, in the Bootheel these taxes could run as high as three dollars an acre. Certainly, there was at least some justification for this argument, especially in the case of the planter who was technically not a landowner, but a "titleholder," if—as was frequently the case in the Bootheel—he was himself mortgaged to an insurance company.

One resident owner expressed his discontent with the croppers' accusation that the planters' mass evictions were heartless and without justification. Insisting that the planter was "carrying all of the load," by "trying to pay for a farm, pay his interest, upkeep and taxes," this middle-sized Bootheel "titleholder" gave an example of his problem under the AAA program. Let us say the owner of 160 acres of land has cooperated in this program and made the reduction of one-half of the acreage of this farm, he postulated. This means that he actually farms only 80 acres, with the remaining 80 acres "going into soil conservation crops on which he gets nothing and pays out money for seed, for preparing the ground and for upkeep." He might then rent the 80 acres he is farming "for one-fourth of the cotton and one-third of other crops, or cash rent, as the case might be."

According to the 1938 law, to continue his example, when the parity payment comes in on the 80 idle acres, "one-fourth [goes] to the owner of the land and three-fourths to the tenant and his sharecroppers." Thus, the landowner, or titleholder—to use his phrase—has to pay taxes, upkeep, and interest on his farm loan and 160 acres out of "the rent revenues from 80 acres" of farmed land, "plus one-fourth of the government subsidy" on the idle land. Given this arrangement, he concluded, it was almost impossible for the middle-sized planter to make a living under the provisions of the 1938 law. "You can readily see," he said, "that the man

23. Thad Snow, unsent letter to the *Post-Dispatch*, Thad Snow Papers. An abbreviated version of this letter appears in the *Post-Dispatch*, March 1, 1940. See also Myrdal, *An American Dilemma*, p. 257.

who owns this land must either make arrangements to farm it himself" without tenants and croppers as one way out of the dilemma, "or he must sell it to the only prospective purchaser, the man who operates large tracts of land with day labor and owns his own gin."[24]

Since most Bootheel planters felt Southeast Missouri was not given sufficient acreage allotments anyway,[25] the thought of sharing the parity check, when not compelled to do so, was absurd. Thad Snow, who probably understood planter attitudes better than anyone else in the Bootheel, noted that "most planters believe deeply, and with entire sincerity, that the croppers are neither entitled to, nor benefited by, a money return for their labor in excess of the minimum required to keep the bodies in going condition during work seasons." Snow pointed out that it was not unusual for a landlord with a hundred acres of cotton to get as much as $25 an acre. Thus, if he kept his sharecropper, he got one-half of what could be $2,500. If he was clever, he kept the $2,500 and worked the land with day labor.[26] One planter with two hundred acres estimated in 1939 that he might save $1,500 to $2,000 a year by a simple conversion.[27] "Planters, of course," Snow said on another occasion, "react like anybody else to a stimulus of that nature."[28] The "original sin of the cotton program," Snow frequently observed, "was the failure to make the 'labor' payment accrue only for labor performance." The government had made it entirely too convenient for him. "It is not a matter of bad men," Snow noted, displaying his usual ability for pithy summations, "but of a bad system."[29]

Actually, the landlord-tenant relationship was largely a pater-

24. Quoted in *Southeast Missourian* (Cape Girardeau), Jan. 19, 1939.

25. See Henry C. Dethloff, "Missouri Farmers and the New Deal: A Case Study of Farm Policy Formulation on the Local Level," *Agricultural History*, XXXIX, No. 3 (July 1965), 141–146.

26. Thad Snow to Victor E. Anderson, Special Attorney, AAA, Oct. 20, 1934, Thad Snow Papers; Snow, *Post-Dispatch*, Jan. 22, 1939; Snow, *From Missouri*, p. 231.

27. *Post-Dispatch*, Jan. 15, 1939. See also S. B. Bledsoe, memo to Henry Wallace, March 9, 1939, p. 1, NA, RG 96.

28. Snow, testimony before a Congressional Committee on Defense Migration in St. Louis, undated, 1940, Thad Snow Papers.

29. Snow, *Post-Dispatch*, March 1, 1940; Snow, *Southeast Missourian*, Feb. 21, 1939. The attitudes of the landowners are best represented in the Charleston *Enterprise Courier*, April 21, 1938; *Southeast Missourian*, Jan. 11, 1940; Memphis *Commercial-Appeal*, Jan. 15, 1939; Memphis *Press-Scimitar*, Jan. 17, 1939; and Sikeston *Standard*, Jan. 24, 1939.

nalistic one anyway. Many croppers were largely illiterate in economic matters, and almost entirely at the mercy of the landlord from the start. Unfortunately, however, since the cotton economy was imported late into Southeast Missouri, and since many of the actual landowners were nonresident insurance companies, land banks, and real estate corporations hundreds of miles away, the landlord-tenant relationship in the Bootheel tended to be less paternalistic than that in the Old South. Absentee ownership usually meant speculators who were more interested in profits than people. The local representative of the absentee owner, more often than not, had little personal feeling for his employees.

For example, when the shift was made from sharecropping to day labor, the tenant was moved to the lowest stratum in the economic hierarchy. "Way down underneath" the class structure, Thad Snow said, was the semistarved day laborer, "with no stake in the crop, no status in law, no hope on earth, and so far as I know, no prospects in heaven."[30] He usually got seventy-five cents a day for no more than 120 days a year; the rest of the time he was either cared for by a benevolent landlord or went on relief. In the older South, it was not uncommon for the planter to assume the responsibility of caring for the cropper during the off-season. In Southeast Missouri, however, the tendency was to work seasonal day labor and to shift the burden to the relief agencies during the off-season. That the planters assumed that the relief agency would take up the burden for the laborers during the off-season is indicated by the fact that the percentage of day laborers receiving relief in Dunklin, New Madrid, and Pemiscot counties at some time during the year was as high as 30 per cent by 1935. The FSA found in its survey a direct correlation between seasonal work and relief. "In the winter months after cotton is picked the relief rises," the report said; "in the spring after cotton chopping begins the load declines."[31]

The problem of lack of work during the winter months was especially acute for the Negro in the Bootheel, because although his need was frequently greater than the whites, it was harder for him to get relief. "Before a Negro can receive relief," the FSA report stated, "he must be in much more desperate straits than a white man. Among many members of the Negro group [inter-

30. Snow, undated and unpublished article, Thad Snow Papers.
31. *FSA Report*, pp. 6, 55. See Appendix, Table 12.

viewed] there was a general attitude that relief was not for them."[32]

Since federal relief was always administered locally, many Negroes met resistance upon application. Attitudes of the white citizens toward the Negro in the Bootheel were frequently hostile, as evidenced by the long history of Negro lynchings and racial violence in Southeast Missouri. Much of the violence was caused by the large influx of Negroes into the Bootheel between 1890 and 1920. These Negroes apparently threatened the poor whites in the area who feared that they would depress the wage scale. "The Bootheel's sordid record of violence," one author has pointed out, "cannot be understood apart from this simple conflict of economic interests."[33]

Many Negroes who later participated in the demonstration spoke during interviews afterward about the problems they had had in receiving relief. These interviews were conducted by Herbert Little, a former newspaper man, and a member of the staff of the National Youth Administration. After the Bootheel demonstration had started, President Roosevelt asked Aubrey Williams of the NYA to obtain as much information about the croppers as he could. Williams, who had earlier been interested in STFU's problems in Arkansas, sent Herbert Little to Southeast Missouri to investigate.[34] Little interviewed 102 people who had participated in the demonstration, and these histories provide an excellent source of information concerning the problems of the Bootheel croppers.[35]

During these interviews, many Negroes said that they had applied for WPA or FSA aid in 1937 and 1938 and had been refused. One

32. *Ibid.*, p. 56. See Appendix, Table 12. Negroes in all tenure groups received a considerably smaller amount of relief than the whites in the same classes. As in the case of overall income, this rule was general throughout the entire rural South. See Sterner, *The Negro's Share*, pp. 219–230.

33. Irvin G. Wyllie, "Race and Class Conflict on Missouri's Cotton Frontier," *Journal of Southern History*, XX (May 1954), 186.

34. Mr. Howard Kester, interview with author, Aug. 6, 1966; Aubrey Williams to Roosevelt, Jan. 16, 1939, *Selected Documents from the Papers of Franklin D. Roosevelt Concerning Sharecropper Demonstration in Southern Missouri* (Microfilm, Sept. 1966), Franklin D. Roosevelt Library, Hyde Park, N.Y. Cited hereafter as *Selected Documents*, Roosevelt Library.

35. Little submitted the 102 case histories, along with his report, to Aubrey Williams. Williams sent the report to Roosevelt, who in turn sent it to Henry Wallace, who sent it to Attorney-General Frank Murphy. See Report of Herbert Little to Aubrey Williams, Jan. 16, 1939; Williams to Roosevelt, Jan. 19, 1939; Roosevelt to Wallace, Jan. 21, 1939; Wallace to Murphy, Jan. 24, 1939, *Selected Documents*, Roosevelt Library.

succinctly remarked: The WPA "kept putting me off."[36] Another Negro man who said he had applied for WPA aid, expressed his frustration: "They told me to go to Sikeston. That man told me to get out and not to come back until he notify us and he don't notify us yet." Another told of applying for help at Cooter, Missouri, and was told "they wasn't helping no niggers over there," while still another applied for work on a WPA project at Charleston, Missouri, and reported: "Every time I went up there they tell me to come back. Never did get no papers or nothing."[37]

To make matters worse, Negroes were frequently the first to be evicted on the farm. One Negro man told Little that a farm on which he was working in 1938 was rented in 1939 to "a white operator, who uses white labor," and thus he was told to leave.[38]

At least a few of the Negro sharecroppers longed for an opportunity to return to the earlier days, where there was at least some paternalistic reward. One cropper summed up this feeling when he told a *Post-Dispatch* reporter:

> "Gran'pap told me the slaves weren't so bad off," he said folding his eviction notice. "He used to say that there always was a warm cabin and somethin' for the pot and griddle. The worst drawback was the constriction—couln't go an' come like they pleased. Now it looks like its just turned 'round. I'd be pleased to trade some non-constriction for a side of meat."[39]

Paternalism, however, STFU felt, was foreign to the Bootheel planters' way of thinking. The mass evictions were perhaps an obvious indication of that. Although evictions had been taking place throughout the South in the thirties, they were more prevalent in Southeast Missouri than elsewhere.[40] "The Bootheel planters," J. R.

36. "Interviews with campers, Case No. 91." The names of the 102 individuals interviewed were deleted to insure privacy. *Selected Documents*, Roosevelt Library.

37. Even the FSA, perhaps the most liberal of all the New Deal agencies, was administered locally and thus subject to pressure to discriminate against the Negro. See Myrdal, *An American Dilemma*, pp. 274–275.

38. Case Nos. 98, 66, 56, 15, *Selected Documents*, Roosevelt Library. Also, Negroes were usually the first to be replaced by mechanization—another practice prevalent throughout the entire South. See Myrdal, *An American Dilemma*, pp. 259–261.

39. *Post-Dispatch*, Jan. 29, 1939.

40. Conrad, *The Forgotten Farmers*, pp. 77–78.

Butler, STFU president, later wrote, "were the worst offenders."[41]

Thus, as we have seen, by the 1930's, the old sharecropper system was already dying in Southeast Missouri before the AAA's method of paying parity helped kill it completely, simply because it was cheaper for landlords to substitute machines and day laborers during the peak periods than to employ croppers who had to be cared for year round. The temptation of lowering the status of a tenant in order to obtain the parity check only dealt the system the final death blow.

When demotion to seasonal day labor status forced the former sharecropper to turn to relief agencies during the off season, Negroes especially complained that it was difficult to obtain help because local relief officials tended to be unsympathetic. Whitfield, who had closest contact with the Negro farmer in the Bootheel, saw the demotion to day laborer stir the black sharecropper's wrath as never before. The Negro minister now realized that he at last had a cause that would serve to convert the cropper's discontent—born out of years of oppression and suffering—into action. Whitfield sensed that his people were finally ready to resist demotion into this lowest tenure class. The Negro sharecropper, long quiet suffering in his already deplorable status, refused to accept the final degradation without a fight.

41. Butler, letter to author, Jan. 7, 1966.

5 Gettin' Ready to Move

It was toward the end of 1938, when Whitfield learned that wholesale evictions of Southeast Missouri sharecroppers were to take place in January 1939. Later, in a radio interview, Whitfield said he had learned in August of 1938 that croppers would be evicted at the end of the year.[1] It was customary practice on cotton plantations to serve croppers with two eviction notices; one on the first of November, and the second, which served as the final notification, sixty days later, on January 1 of the new year. Upon receipt of the first notice, the cropper immediately began looking around for work elsewhere, and hopefully, found it before the sixty days expired. It was also customary to permit a ten-day "grace period" in case the cropper had received late notification, or was still without work on "moving day," January 1. Thus, although agreements technically expired on January 1, the final day for eviction for those croppers who were to leave in the Bootheel was January 10, 1939.[2]

Whitfield estimated that there were about nine hundred families who were to be evicted on January 10. There is no way of knowing the exact number, because very few croppers received actual written notices. The overwhelming majority of them received oral no-

1. Whitfield, radio interview over KMOX, St. Louis, reported in the Charleston *Enterprise Courier*, Jan. 19, 1939.

2. See Harriet Young to New York *Times*, Feb. 23, 1939, STFU Papers.

tices, according to the prevailing custom, telling them simply that their services were no longer needed.[3]

After the croppers had moved to the highway, many people in the area who were hostile to the demonstration, especially the local newspapers, charged that because there were no written notices the croppers had not legally been evicted.[4] Although technically the allegation was correct, the entire question was only a semantic one. In order to be legally evicted, the tenant who received the eviction order had to register it officially with the proper legal authorities. The few who received written notices failed to do this, and those who were told to leave, of course, had no tangible evidence that they had been legally evicted.

In most instances, planters apparently felt it unnecessary to have written notices for tenants. One cropper reported later to a government investigator: "Man I was working for said he would not have any work to do until cotton picking time. He never told me to get off the place." At least one man was "evicted indirectly" when his employer "sent him word by [his] neighbor last December 29, saying he would not need him further."[5] There is some evidence to indicate that a few tenants requested written evictions and were refused.[6] The *Post-Dispatch* talked to one evicted Negro cropper at the time of the demonstration who reported he had paid a visit to the courthouse at Charleston to inquire if written orders were necessary to move, and was told: "You niggers don't need written notices. Bet you couldn't read it anyway. When your boss tells you to get off, get off."[7]

Very few croppers were evicted at gunpoint, since in most instances they were too docile to resist forcefully. Thus, in most cases, a verbal notification was sufficient to remove the cropper from the farm. STFU had long worked for written contracts, the lack of which was something that had plagued southern farm tenancy for years. The 1935 census, for example, indicated that more than

3. Whitfield to Mitchell, Dec. 1, 1938, STFU Papers; Ridpath, "The Case of the Missouri Sharecroppers," p. 147.

4. See especially the Sikeston *Standard*, the Charleston *Enterprise Courier*, and the *Southeast Missourian*.

5. Case Nos. 4, 43, Aubrey Williams to Roosevelt, Jan. 19, 1939, *Selected Documents*, Roosevelt Library.

6. See "Letters Written on Backs of Survey Blanks," undated, 1939, STFU Papers.

7. *Post-Dispatch*, Jan. 24, 1939.

80 per cent of all farm leases were oral agreements, "recorded only," one government report said, "in the memory of the tenant and his landlord."[8] The situation had improved little by 1940, despite STFU's efforts. One writer, summarizing the problems of farm tenancy in the country in 1940, pointed out that most tenants operated "under nothing more than a vague verbal understanding."[9] Others estimated in 1940 that "three-fourths of all tenant farmers in the United States operate farms under inadequate oral agreements."[10]

The usual procedure under the landlord-tenant agreement was that the tenant assumed that he was hired for the following year unless he heard to the contrary usually sixty days prior to the termination of the tenancy. There was little doubt that the majority of the croppers in Southeast Missouri were notified verbally that their services were no longer needed in 1939. Of the 102 participants interviewed by Herbert Little, the NYA investigator found only three written notices, "couched in legal language," but he was completely convinced that all had been evicted.

The 102 personal histories, his report stated, "are full of statements obviously truthful because of the circumstantial details given to the interviewer. . . ." In most instances, the planter orally informed the croppers "that (1) he was switching from sharecropping to day labor basis, (2) that he wanted the house for a larger family, (3) that he would not be wanted next year." Little reported that while there were many variations in the story the landlord used, in nearly all cases, the landlord "gave the worker to believe that there was nothing for him to do at that place."[11] The FBI investigation concluded essentially the same thing. "The great majority of the participants interviewed," the report stated, "had received . . . oral . . . instructions to vacate their premises on the first of the year."[12]

8. FSA, *Security for Farm Tenants*, p. 8. See also press release, STFU, Jan. 14, 1939, STFU Papers; and T. J. Woofter *et al.*, *Landlord and Tenant on the Cotton Plantation*, p. 11.

9. Paul V. Maris, "Farm Tenancy," *Yearbook of Agriculture, 1940*, U.S. Department of Agriculture, 76th Cong., 3rd Sess., House Doc. 695 (Washington, 1940).

10. H. W. Hannah and Joseph Ackerman, "Legal Aspects of Farm Tenancy in Illinois," Bulletin 465, *University of Illinois Agricultural Experiment Station* (April 1940), p. 250.

11. *Ibid.*; Wallace to Murphy, Jan. 24, 1939, p. 2., *Selected Documents*, Roosevelt Library.

12. FBI Report, *Southeast Missourian*, March 13, 1939.

When word about evictions reached Owen Whitfield at the end of 1938, he immediately attempted to solicit help for his people who were to be dismissed at the first of the year. He had contacts in St. Louis, and since the distance there was not too great, he began to travel to that city to speak to groups he thought might be sympathetic with the plight of the sharecropper in adjacent Southeast Missouri. In December of 1938, he spoke before the St. Louis chapter of the Urban League and also to the St. Louis Industrial Union Council, the central CIO body in the city.[13]

While appealing for aid in St. Louis, the Negro leader quickly became embroiled in the rapidly growing power conflict that was then taking place between STFU and UCAPAWA. From the beginning, Owen Whitfield had been more enthusiastic about UCAPAWA than Mitchell and the other STFU members because he felt its affiliation with the CIO would give the union more power. Affiliation with the CIO, Whitfield said early in 1938, "gives us not 40,000 but 40,000,000 voting power."[14] To demonstrate his faith in the efficacy of the CIO, he used the example of a man shipwrecked at sea in a storm. At first, Whitfield said, the man reached for a piece of sail, then a piece of wood, but they sank before him. "Then suddenly," he went on, "he felt something solid and held onto it for it was a rock and he was saved." To Owen Whitfield, the CIO was STFU's rock in a stormy sea. The tenant farmer's union had "been tossed about by many storms and often our support has disappeared from us," he said, "but we have reached out and found a rock to cling to and I say to you brothers . . . that rock is the CIO."[15]

Whitfield's enthusiasm for UCAPAWA and the CIO was vividly demonstrated by the fact that he had hitchhiked to attend the Denver meeting in 1937, at which time STFU decided to become a part of the CIO. Because of his obvious zeal, the Negro minister became one of four STFU members elected by that convention to the UCAPAWA executive council of twenty-one members.[16]

While in St. Louis appealing for help at the end of 1938, Whitfield made contact with Al Murphy, a former Communist party

13. Whitfield to Mitchell, Dec. 1, 1938; Josephine Johnson to Mitchell, Dec. 21, 1938, STFU Papers; Whitfield to John T. Clark, the executive secretary of the St. Louis Urban League, Aug. 3, 1938, Fannie Cook Collection.

14. Whitfield, "Proceedings of the Fourth Annual Convention of STFU," Feb. 25–27, 1938, Little Rock, Ark., STFU Papers.

15. *Ibid.*

16. An Open Letter to Friends of STFU, Oct. 1, 1939, p. 2, *ibid.*

organizer in Alabama and once head of the defunct Sharecroppers Union in that state. Murphy promised support for the Bootheel croppers about to be evicted, and Whitfield openly welcomed it. Mitchell, however, who had had difficulty earlier with the Communist-dominated Alabama Sharecroppers Union, was convinced that this was another effort by the Henderson faction to destroy STFU.[17]

As 1938 drew to a close, relations between Whitfield and the STFU Memphis office began to weaken. Mitchell and STFU did push Whitfield for executive office at the Second International Convention of UCAPAWA in San Francisco in early December 1938, but at that meeting, the split between STFU and UCAPAWA became irreconcilable. Because of the great distance to California, and because union funds were short, STFU had very few representatives. Thus, Henderson's faction dominated the convention, defeated a STFU proposal for local autonomy, and kicked Whitfield and three other STFU officers off the UCAPAWA executive board. Whitfield, however, was elected vice-president of UCAPAWA at this convention. Apparently, the Negro's strong support of the International won him this high post, although Mitchell later claimed that UCAPAWA gave the job to Whitfield as a sop to STFU in an effort to heal the rift between the two organizations.[18]

The first indication Mitchell had that Whitfield was not with STFU completely was when the Negro minister failed to show up at the Cotton Plant Convention at the end of December 1938. Whitfield sent a telegram to Mitchell saying that upon his return from the UCAPAWA convention in San Francisco earlier in the month he found a team of mules missing and was trying to locate them.[19]

STFU, still smarting from the recent fight at San Francisco, had anticipated trouble from the Henderson faction at Cotton Plant, but at this time they apparently still thought they had Whitfield's support. This was evidenced by the fact that less than a week earlier,

17. Mitchell to Clarence Senior, Aug. 21, 1935; Mitchell to Gardner Jackson, Sept. 3, 1936; Executive Committee, STFU to John L. Lewis, undated Jan., 1939; Al Murphy to Whitfield, Jan. 9, 1939; Butler to Henderson undated 1939, *ibid.*; Al Murphy, interview with author, Dec. 29, 1966.

18. Mitchell to Whitfield, Dec. 4, 1938; Mitchell to A. G. Poole, Dec. 4, 1938; Mitchell to Evelyn Smith, Dec. 13, 1938; Mitchell, "Oral History," p. 97, STFU Papers.

19. Telegram, Whitfield to Mitchell, Dec. 30, 1938, STFU Papers.

on December 24, 1938, Butler had sent Whitfield a telegram saying that the Memphis office had heard that some locals were being advised against sending delegates to Cotton Plant. Butler and Mitchell suspected that E. B. McKinney and Claude Williams were behind it, and asked Whitfield to "get this situation in hand."[20] Indeed, despite Whitfield's absence at Cotton Plant, he was re-elected vice-president of STFU. He now had the unique distinction of being vice-president of STFU and UCAPAWA simultaneously.[21]

Henderson flew to the Cotton Plant convention to try to work out a compromise on the sticky question of STFU's dues payments, but it was to no avail. STFU insisted on collecting its own dues, while Henderson was equally insistent that dues payments be sent to UCAPAWA, and he in turn would return the funds to the Memphis office for STFU's use.[22] The convention ended with both sides hopelessly split.

After the Cotton Plant meeting, STFU was entirely too occupied with its rapidly growing struggle with UCAPAWA to be especially concerned about immediate problems in Southeast Missouri. It could only assume that Whitfield was still on its side in the struggle, and that he would do nothing in the Bootheel without first notifying the Memphis office. By the end of 1938, however, the Negro minister was indeed already making plans on his own.

Apparently as soon as Whitfield learned that the Bootheel planters were in fact going to carry out the planned evictions, he decided to use the occasion to call national attention to the plight of the cropper in Southeast Missouri. Although he spent much of his lifetime working to assist the sharecropper in any way he could, Whitfield, surprisingly enough, rarely spelled out exactly what his ultimate goal for the landless tenant was, beyond "improving his condition." He once wrote that the objective of the southern tenant farmer was "to obtain (1) land for the landless. (2) clothes for the naked. (3) food for the hungry. (4) and freedom for the wage slaves."[23] Most of the time when he discussed his objectives, he spoke in generalities such as these. Only occasionally did he get down to specifics.

20. Telegram, Butler to Whitfield, Dec. 24, 1938, *ibid.*

21. Butler to Whitfield, Jan. 7, 1939; Mitchell, "Report of the Secretary, 1939," p. 2, *ibid.*

22. Henderson to Mitchell, Jan. 28, 1939, *ibid.*

23. Whitfield to editor, Charleston *Enterprise Courier*, Oct. 16, 1938, Thad Snow Papers.

One of the things that was apparently foremost in his mind at all times was a fervent hope one day to obtain for all croppers some kind of government housing.[24] In early 1938, Whitfield had written a letter to Roosevelt, asking for help for those croppers evicted in that year. In it he argued that a "colonization plan is our only hope."[25] After learning of the evictions set for 1939, Whitfield wrote to John T. Clark, the executive secretary of the St. Louis Urban League, that he was organizing a campaign to get his people "in readiness for a drive on the federal government" in order to get "the FSA to continue its homesteading projects" similar to the one already established at LaForge.[26]

Whitfield was undoubtedly very fond of the living accommodations he had at the LaForge colony, and he longed for the day when the government would provide additional colonies for all sharecroppers in Southeast Missouri. Although he and his family enjoyed security at LaForge, Whitfield's soul was restless with the constant awareness that there were thousands of his church parishioners still living in cabins without floors or windows. He would not rest until they also had a decent place to live.[27]

If better housing for the Bootheel croppers was Whitfield's immediate goal in January 1939, however, he never emphasized it, because by the time of the demonstration, he seemed to be less concerned about specific goals and more interested in publicizing the evictions. He constantly announced, both during and after the strike, that the primary purpose of the demonstration of 1939 was to awaken the nation to the croppers' sorrowful conditions. Although he undoubtedly hoped to receive tangible gains in the long run, his immediate purpose was to gain publicity. At first, Whitfield entertained the idea of organizing a group march on the county courthouse in order to publicize the dismissals.[28] However, after

24. Later in her life, Whitfield's daughter recalled that she could remember as a child her father frequently talking about how nice it would be to provide a permanent home for sharecroppers—especially a place for old folks to live after their working days were over. Mrs. Cora (Whitfield) Terry, interview with author, Dec. 9, 1965.

25. Whitfield to FDR, Jan. 5, 1938, NA, RG 96.

26. Whitfield to John T. Clark, Aug. 3, 1938, Fannie Cook Collection.

27. Mrs. Zella Whitfield, interview with author, Dec. 19, 1965; see also Fannie Cook, "Speech made in accepting Tuttle Memorial at St. Louis Urban Banquet in behalf of Owen Whitfield," Jan. 18, 1940, *ibid.*

28. Mitchell, undated memo to Burgess, General Histories Folder, STFU Papers.

he held several special meetings with his followers in Bootheel churches in November and December of 1938, he changed his strategy and decided to carry out a massive roadside sitdown demonstration.

It is difficult to determine precisely when Whitfield decided upon the idea of a roadside sitdown strike. Later in life, the Negro leader liked to recall how the notion of the strike came to him in a vision, but it is by no means certain that he even originated the idea. Thad Snow, later recounting the events leading to the demonstration, said the whole thing started as a joke. At one of the special meetings called at the churches, Snow reported, one of the sharecroppers was asked where he was going when he was evicted, and he replied: "Out on the road, I guess." The story was repeated at subsequent church meetings and soon began to gain support among the croppers.[29] "If we are going to starve," Whitfield said at a church meeting in December, "let's starve out there where people can see us!"[30]

Certainly, Whitfield had plenty of examples of group protests from which he could draw lessons. Precedents had been established in the United States as early as the nineteenth century. There were instances of sitdown protests during the great railway strike of 1877, but perhaps the idea gained its greatest momentum when the method was adopted by Bill Haywood and the "Wobblies" in the early years of the twentieth century. Of course, 1930 was the year of Gandhi's famous salt march, but certainly the immediate progenitor in the United States were the numerous CIO sitdown strikes in 1937 at General Motors and Chrysler auto plants in Flint, Michigan, but even these were supposedly inspired by the French "folded arms" strikes of 1936.[31]

There had even been instances of small sharecropper roadside encampments in Arkansas prior to 1939 involving STFU members, although the union itself apparently never officially endorsed the idea. After a small roadside demonstration in Arkansas, Sherwood Eddy, former secretary of the YMCA, helped establish the Delta cooperative farm near Rochdale, Mississippi. Because of the size

29. Josephine (Johnson) Cannon, letter to author, Oct. 29, 1967; Mrs. Zella Whitfield, interview with author, Dec. 19, 1965; *Southeast Missourian*, Feb. 21, 1939.

30. Quoted in Ridpath, "The Case of the Missouri Sharecroppers," pp. 147–148.

31. See the St. Louis *Post-Dispatch*, March 5, 1939, for a brief pictorial history of the sitdown strike.

of the demonstration in the Bootheel, however, and because the scene was the main highway between Memphis and St. Louis, the publicity given to the event in Southeast Missouri was without precedent.[32]

Undoubtedly, Whitfield decided that a large-scale demonstration could take place safely in the Bootheel of Missouri because he felt that the political climate there was better than it was in the Deep South, where STFU had already encountered bloody resistance to union organization. "We staged the protest in Missouri," a union handbill stated in 1940, the year after the demonstration, "not because cotton labor is treated more unfairly in Missouri than elsewhere. We know that is not true. We staged it in Missouri because we had less fear of bloody violence in Missouri."[33]

Once the decision was made to move to the highways, Whitfield instructed the croppers to remain absolutely silent, and to tell no one about the proposed plan. If word got out beforehand, he feared the "law" might attempt to head it off. Moreover, the element of surprise, he thought, might increase its dramatic effect. Thad Snow said that even he was not given very early information of the fateful event. To the best of his knowledge, he later stated, Whitfield, at the very start, had informed only one outsider, Hans Baasch, the director of LaForge, of what was going to take place.[34]

At the last moment, however, Whitfield changed his mind, and decided to bring several other people into his confidence. Fearing disastrous consequences should bad weather hit the unprotected croppers on the roadside, Whitfield appealed at the eleventh hour to Orville Zimmerman, the congressional representative from the area, about the possibility of obtaining protection from the elements. He hoped to acquire army tents from either the state or federal government, should the need arise.[35]

About December 10, Whitfield went to see Zimmerman to ask about the chance of getting tents. Zimmerman suggested that Whit-

32. Auerbach, "Southern Tenant Farmers"; J. R. Butler, letter to author, Jan. 7, 1966; Mitchell, "Oral History," pp. 66–68; Mitchell to J. E. Cameroon, Jan. 13, 1936, STFU Papers. Nine STFU members picketed the Department of Agriculture in 1935 and received some publicity, but nothing comparable to that given the Bootheel strike. Mitchell, letter to author, Oct. 17, 1967; see also Very Rony, "Sorrow Song in Black and White," *New South* (Summer, 1967), Southern Regional Council publication.

33. Handbill distributed by the Missouri Agricultural Workers Council, undated, Thad Snow Papers.

34. Snow, *From Missouri*, p. 246. 35. *Ibid.*, p. 247.

field tell Thad Snow about the proposed strike, since Snow and the congressmen were supposed to take a trip together sometime in the next few days. Zimmerman told Whitfield: "We may stop and see if the Governor has any tents."[36]

Next day the Negro farm leader told Snow of his plans, and the following week when Snow and Zimmerman drove to Columbia, Missouri, together on other business, the two men discussed what Whitfield had told them, and decided to pass along the information to the governor and the adjutant-general of the state. At this point, the account of what happened is somewhat conflicting, but it seems highly probable that the two men made state officials aware of what they had been told. According to an account attributed to Zimmerman which appeared in the Charleston *Enterprise Courier* on January 26, 1939, the two men were incredulous at first, and "decided it would be foolish to spread the rumor further." However, on the "off chance" that a demonstration might come off, they thought it would be wise to pass along what little information they had to Governor Lloyd C. Stark and Lewis M. Means, the adjutant-general of the state and the head of the National Guard. Just in case some of the rumors proved to be true, state officials would be prepared to act "if they chose to do so. . . ." According to Zimmerman's account, if Stark and Means were "caught unprepared for the event, the blame properly rests on Mr. Snow and me," he said, because both Snow and Zimmerman had emphasized to the state officials that they "regarded an organized demonstration as only a remote possibility."[37]

On February 9, the *Enterprise Courier* carried a telegram received from Zimmerman, saying the statement which appeared on January 26 was not his statement, and that he had authorized "no one to make a statement for me." The newspaper went on to say that the January 26 account was obtained from information received from Thad Snow, who had considered it to be a verbatim account of a telephone conversation he had had earlier with Mr. Zimmerman.[38] After denying the account, Zimmerman did not give his version of the story, and Snow does not discuss the trip with Zimmerman at all, either in his book or in his private papers.

In any event, state officials were made aware of the proposed

36. *Ibid.*
37. Charleston *Enterprise Courier,* Jan. 26, 1939.
38. *Ibid.,* Feb. 9, 1939.

demonstration, along with the general public, two days before it started. An account of the strike that was to take place on January 10 appeared in the St. Louis *Post-Dispatch* on January 8. This was the result of the meeting which had taken place earlier between Whitfield and Snow.

When the Negro minister first came to Thad Snow with the story, Snow insisted that a newspaper reporter should be on hand so that the strike might be given the publicity Whitfield so fervently sought. This was against Whitfield's better judgment, and it was only after Snow convinced him that the *Post-Dispatch* would not let the word out early if he so desired, that Whitfield agreed to it. The Negro then drove to St. Louis and asked Sam Armstrong, a *Post-Dispatch* reporter and friend of Thad Snow's, to come down and attend the proposed final church meeting which was to be held on Saturday, January 7, 1939. Whitfield emphasized that Armstrong was to attend the meeting only to obtain " background" on the demonstration, and he made it clear that he was not to put the story in the papers until the croppers had moved to the roadside.[39]

Once again, however, Whitfield had a change of mind at the very last moment. Armstrong attended the meeting on January 7 with Thad Snow, and after it was over, Whitfield saw the reporter and decided to give him permission to print it. Whitfield was now convinced that no one would believe the story anyway. Armstrong thus related his account of the final meeting, foretelling of the strike set for January 10 to the readers of the *Post-Dispatch* on the front page of the Sunday paper, January 8.[40]

At this final meeting, which was held at the First Negro Baptist Church in Sikeston, Whitfield spoke with customary eloquence, making frequent references to the Bible, and reminding his people how Moses led the children of Israel from Egypt to the land of Canaan. Whitfield was careful to put his words into the vernacular of his audience, pointing out how Moses escaped at the Red Sea from "old Boss Pharoh's ridin' bosses in their chariots." The crowd shouted "Amen" as Whitfield said: "We also must make an exodus. Its history repeatin' itself in 1939."[41]

39. Snow, *From Missouri,* p. 248.

40. *Ibid.*, pp. 250–251. Both the Sikeston *Standard* and the *Southeast Missourian* also carried stories of the church meeting on Jan. 9, 1939.

41. *Post-Dispatch,* Jan. 8, 1939.

Armstrong estimated the crowd to be about 350, composed predominantly of Negroes, "but with a scattering of white sharecroppers." The *Post-Dispatch* reporter said the gathering "partook of the character of a church service, as well as a mass meeting called to meet a crisis."[42]

Marshals were elected for each camp to direct activities and keep order. Whitfield emphatically stated that the demonstration was to be orderly and nonviolent. "We must obey the law," he said, and "don't let anyone say we're tryin' to make trouble. It seems to be almost a criminal offense to wake people up so they take peaceful group action."[43]

The Negro minister was confident that his people had very little to lose in the experiment they were about to undertake, since they were already at rock bottom. Most of the croppers later told government investigators that they would "just as well starve and freeze on the highways" as in their shacks. After January 10, there was no work for them until chopping started in April, and no credit was immediately available.[44] "These courageous evicted sharecroppers," Whitfield later said, "decided to just walk along the highway until 'I starve out and die.' "[45]

Whitfield was careful to emphasize to the crowd that the demonstration was to be strictly voluntary. He said that he in no way wanted to jeopardize the jobs of those croppers who had them. "We don't want to break up any deal any cropper has made with his boss," he said. "If he's got a share-croppin' deal for next year, let him sit right tight."[46]

The stage was now set for the mass exodus. Although Whitfield had mentioned the problem of evictions of the Missouri croppers to Mitchell as early as December 1, 1938, no one in STFU anticipated that a massive demonstration would take place. Whitfield had written to Mitchell on December 1 that the evicted croppers were "planning to pile their household goods on [the] sides of the highway and see what happens. And you know if such thing [*sic*] happens we must be ready to do what we can."[47] After this terse

42. *Ibid.* 43. *Ibid.*

44. Henry Wallace to Frank Murphy, Jan. 24, 1939, *Selected Documents,* Roosevelt Library.

45. Quoted in *Southeast Missouri: A Laboratory for the Cotton South,* p. 3.

46. *Post-Dispatch,* Jan. 8, 1939.

47. Whitfield to Mitchell, Dec. 1, 1938, STFU Papers.

comment, however, Whitfield said no more. He never gave any indication to the Memphis office that a huge protest demonstration was actually being planned or was imminent. When the Bootheel sharecroppers moved to the highways in January of 1939, it came as a complete surprise to Mitchell and the union, for it was secretly organized, planned, and directed entirely by Mr. Whitfield.

6 The Bootheel Backfires

Sam Armstrong's story in the *Post-Dispatch* on Sunday, January 8, told in detail the plans for the proposed demonstration set for the following Tuesday, January 10. Despite the *Post-Dispatch*'s front-page warning, the demonstration caught the Bootheel completely unaware. Many Southeast Missourians read the *Post-Dispatch* regularly, but apparently Whitfield had accurately gauged the sentiment of the Bootheel at the time he gave Armstrong permission to print the story, since most residents seemed unwilling to believe that the croppers would actually carry out their threatened move.

Although the majority of the croppers did not move out until the morning of the tenth, several hundred started out after sundown January 9, and spent the night on the highway. Early on the morning of January 10, therefore, motorists passing along U.S. Highways 60 and 61 were shocked to see the roadsides strewn with broken-down autos, old wagons, trucks piled with bedding, pots and pans, wire chicken coops, and of course, poorly clad croppers.[1]

Thad Snow, writing of the event later, took an obvious delight in describing how Whitfield had pulled it off. "It was entirely spontaneous, even if beautifully organized," he said. "There was a sweet simplicity about it that almost passed belief." Even though the

1. *Post-Dispatch*, Jan. 10, 1939; New York *Times*, Jan. 11, 1939.

demonstration had been "brewing for months," Snow went on, displaying his usual light sarcasm, "no rumor of it had escaped up to a social level above that of the lowly conspirators themselves. Not a single planter or other respectable citizen . . . had an inkling of what was planned until shortly before the event." The entire business defied all the rules of the book, Snow said. "It all came off like a batter stealing first, ahead of the first pitched ball. . . ."[2]

By noon of the tenth, the highway patrol estimated there were over 1,000 persons camped along the roadsides. The precise number of families and individuals who participated in the demonstration is difficult to determine, as was the exact location of all the various camps, primarily because there was so much shifting around. The size of the crowd and the number of camps increased and decreased slightly on a day-to-day basis.

The Highway Patrol later said that there were 330 families—a total of 1,307 persons.[3] The FBI report is probably closest to being accurate. It stated there were 251 families, comprising 1,161 individuals. These families, the report stated, formed thirteen camps located intermittently along seventy miles of Highway 61, north and south, between Sikeston and Hayti, Missouri, and thirty-eight miles between Sikeston and Charleston, east and west, on Highway 60. Sikeston was the center of the activity, since it was the point where Highways 60 and 61 joined. The size of each camp varied a great deal. Several were small, while the largest of them, reported to be in Mississippi and New Madrid counties, numbered several hundred each.[4]

No effort was made to interfere with the traffic on the highways or to obstruct activity of any kind. The majority of the croppers simply moved immediately to the side of the road, out of the way of passing traffic, and began to make camp. Most camps had a stove, a few pieces of ragged furniture, pots and pans, some bedding, occasionally a dog, but all were without permament shelter of any kind. A few signs appeared the first day, but most were gone after that. One said: "Roosevelt or Bust—We are Busted." Another said:

2. *Post-Dispatch,* March 5, 1939. 3. *Ibid.,* Jan. 14, 1939.

4. FBI Report, *ibid.,* March 13, 1939. See also Report of Herbert Little (dictated over the telephone), to Aubrey Williams, Jan. 16, 1939, *Selected Documents,* Roosevelt Library. Little reported that there were 291 persons in a camp in Lilbourn in New Madrid County on January 16.

"We Voted for Roosevelt. Now Look Where We Are At."[5]

Mitchell later claimed that 90 per cent of the demonstrators were STFU members, but government investigators later reported that while STFU may have helped organize the protest, many campers "were apparently unaquainted with the organization."[6] Undoubtedly many were members of Whitfield's churches, who had never joined the union. Government officials on the scene estimated that 90 to 95 per cent of the demonstrators were Negro.[7] There were sprinklings of whites in many of the camps, and the newspapers made quite an effort to emphasize this fact, but this was probably to drive home the point that the demonstration was a protest of croppers and farm workers, and not a racial upheaval.[8]

Whether union members or not, the majority of those who participated in the demonstration had been evicted and were without a place to live. Some others had spontaneously joined the movement to the roadside because they were generally unhappy and hoped to improve their lot. Government officials later reported to Roosevelt that while many had been forced to leave their homes, there were some demonstrators who had joined the strike "voluntarily out of profound dissatisfaction with the arrangements under which they were living and working." This led to a great deal of confusion in the beginning about the purpose of the demonstration, since there were at least some participants who were not actually homeless.[9]

Much of the confusion was compounded by the fact that the landlords led the press to believe that the croppers would be taken back to work if they so desired. It sounded like an invitation to return to cropping, when in fact it was nothing more than an effort to have the former cropper return to the farm either to be hired as a day laborer, or to remain in the shack until some kind of menial work was found for him to do. For example, one farm owner—

5. Charleston *Enterprise Courier,* Jan. 12, 1939; *Southeast Missourian,* Jan. 16, 1939.

6. Mitchell to Rev. Ben Morris Ridpath, Jan. 30, 1939, STFU Papers; Wallace to Murphy, Jan. 24, 1939, *Selected Documents,* Roosevelt Library.

7. Report of Herbert Little (dictated over the telephone), to Aubrey Williams, Jan. 16, 1939; Roosevelt, memo for Secretary of Agriculture, Jan. 19, 1939, *Selected Documents,* Roosevelt Library.

8. See *Southeast Missourian,* Jan. 10, 1939; *Post-Dispatch,* Jan. 8 and 11, 1939.

9. Aubrey Williams to Roosevelt, Jan. 16, 1939, *Selected Documents,* Roosevelt Library.

according to a captain of the Highway Patrol—offered to "take back" 121 Negroes who left his farm to march to the highway, but all refused to return to the farm, presumably because of the anticipated working conditions there.[10]

Referring to the landlords' statement that the croppers could "go back to their shacks any time they wanted to," one author acutely observed that "little if any emphasis has been given to the conditions implicit in such invitation or the question as to how the sharecroppers and their families will live after they are back on the land."[11]

To further add to the confusion, there were at least some families who had been evicted as croppers the year before, and were then working as day laborers, who decided to join the demonstration. Of the 102 heads of families interviewed by Herbert Little, he estimated that "about two-thirds were sharecroppers at some stage, although some had been kicked down to day laborers. Maybe one-fourth [had been] day laborers and two or three of them tenant [renter] farmers."[12]

Most evicted sharecroppers who had been offered jobs as day laborers refused. The majority of them felt simply that they would be unable to make a decent living as a day laborer. Perhaps this feeling was best expressed by a former cropper, who was not ordered to vacate the premises, but instead asked to stay on as a day laborer: "Left [the] last place," he said, and participated in the demonstration, "because I could not make a living. There was seven in the family and I could not support them on a dollar a day."[13]

Among the 102 participants interviewed by Herbert Little, there were numerous instances of farm workers who left to join the demonstration because of general dissatisfaction. One Negro worker who received no eviction notice apparently decided to join the movement to the highway when his boss refused to fix his house. "I was stayin' in a log house with no floor and asked the boss to fix it and he wouldn't do it," so he decided to leave. Another person who

10. Report of Herbert Little (dictated over the telephone), to Aubrey Williams, Jan. 16, 1939, *Selected Documents,* Roosevelt Library.

11. Ridpath, "The Case of the Missouri Sharecroppers," p. 147. See also Josephine Johnson, "What Became of the Sharecroppers," *Post-Dispatch,* April 3, 1939.

12. Report to Herbert Little, *Selected Documents,* Roosevelt Library.

13. "Interviews with campers," Case No. 48, Aubrey Williams to Roosevelt, Jan. 19, 1939, *Selected Documents,* Roosevelt Library.

was not ordered to leave, but who participated in the demonstration, said he left his job "because he did not have a house in which to live." He reported that he "lived in a 'cotton pen' . . . since last October and wanted to live elsewhere, so moved to the highway."[14]

General dissatisfaction, though, according to the planter way of thinking, was hardly justification for a demonstration. One writer toured the Bootheel and talked with planters after the croppers had moved to the highway. One large planter was "greatly perturbed because the croppers wanted better conditions," the writer noted. "He called it something nearly as bad as sedition."[15]

Although many demonstration participants interviewed said that they had been offered work as day laborers for 75¢ a day, apparently not all of them were even that lucky. After the demonstration, STFU conducted a survey among 286 farm families in the Bootheel, many of whom had undoubtedly been participants in the roadside strike. Its survey found that out of 229 heads of families who categorized themselves as day laborers, 190 had no promise of work, while 39 had been offered jobs varying from 50¢ to $1.25 a day. Of the total number, many were then receiving relief, but over half were not, although they already had applied. Some of these were turned down, while others' cases were still pending.[16]

Apparently a large number, both of those who had been evicted and those who had not, decided to join the movement to the highway with the hope of receiving a permanent home similar to the FSA project at LaForge, where Whitfield lived. One government report said the mere presence of LaForge in the vicinity was "a large factor in leading the workers to make their demonstration." Other government officials were more explicit. They pointed out most of the demonstrators had been "led to believe" that by indicating their need to the FSA they would induce the federal agency "to establish a project for them similar to one operating at LaForge, Missouri. . . ." Apparently they had hoped to express this need simply by marching to the highways, the officials said, because "they had neither formed a cohesive organization nor presented definite demands to any public agency" prior to the demonstration.[17]

14. Case Nos. 63, 35, *Ibid.*

15. Josephine Johnson, *Post-Dispatch,* Jan. 23, 1939.

16. "STFU Report of Relief and Farming Survey Made January 1939," STFU Papers.

17. Wallace to Murphy, Jan. 24, 1939; Aubrey Williams to Roosevelt, Jan. 16, 1939, *Selected Documents,* Roosevelt Library.

The manager of the LaForge Project, Hans Baasch, reported in February of 1939 that more than 10,000 applications had been received for entrance to the project, and STFU's survey found that out of 286 individuals interviewed, 250 listed a job on a farm project under FSA control, similar to the LaForge experiment, as the type of work they would like to have.[18]

Among the 102 heads of families interviewed by Herbert Little, there was almost unanimous agreement that those sharecroppers whose tenure had been terminated had been evicted in order that the landlord could keep the entire parity payment.[19] Practically all the croppers were convinced of this, and most of those who spoke to the croppers after the strike were convinced also. One out-of-town newspaper farm editor, after conducting his own investigation, found that "in at least some cases the sharecroppers have been required to sign over to the farm owner their share of the benefit payment or else get off the farm."[20]

The immediate reaction to the demonstration at the local level was quite hostile. Most newspapers in the area charged it was the work of outside agitators and, as already indicated, accused those who claimed to have been evicted, but had no written eviction notices, of deception. Capitalizing on the fact that only a handful of tenants had received written evictions, many papers tried to suggest that those who had participated in the demonstration had not actually been forced to leave their farms. "NOT MORE THAN 10 PER CENT ACTUALLY EVICTED FROM HOMES," was the headline in the Charleston *Enterprise Courier*.[21] The St. Louis *Globe-Democrat* called the charge of mass evictions "a cruel hoax on the public" and countered with the accusation that the strike was unquestionably instigated by "ambitious union promotors who mustered their following by promises of extravagent largess from the government." Most of the participants, the *Globe-Democrat* alleged, expected "a white house with a poarch [*sic*], a dug well, a team of mules, garden patch, chickens and hogs, a roof that never leaks, an automobile that always runs, and money for now and then to buy some

18. New York *Times,* Feb. 19, 1939; "STFU Report of Relief and Farming Survey Made January 1939," STFU Papers.

19. Report of Herbert Little to Aubrey Williams, Jan. 16, 1939, *Selected Documents,* Roosevelt Library.

20. Des Moines *Register,* Jan. 19, 1939.

21. Jan. 12, 1939.

clothes."[22] Another local paper, charging outsiders had exaggerated the severity of the croppers' conditions, showed a picture of one group of homeless campers with the caption: "The group above seems to be having a picnic or an outing. . . ."[23]

Robert K. Ryland, the director of the National Emergency Council of Missouri, perhaps best expressed local feeling, when he said he was certain that the demonstration was "fostered by subversive elements." Most of the Negroes he talked to, he reported—echoing the *Globe-Democrat*'s charge—were "waiting for Uncle Sam" to give them forty acres of land, "a white house with a porch, a barn, a dug well, and a span of mules."[24]

Most press accounts emphasized that the demonstration was the work of ne'er do wells. As one paper put it, the strike was carried out by a "rapidly growing contingent of hangers-on who expect to get something for nothing. . . ."[25] Another familiar newspaper theme was that the otherwise well-meaning Negroes had been duped. These accounts tried to claim that it was not the Negro who was at fault, but the union officials who had misled them. "The white people of Sikeston have been good to the Negro people," the *Herald* said. "The colored people are not altogether to blame for they are being influenced by outside agitators who are believed to be 'fifth columnists.' "[26]

The planters in the area charged that 90 per cent of the croppers were not residents of Missouri, but transients from other states. Bootheel landowners called special meetings and passed resolutions denying they were evicting croppers in order to receive the full parity check.[27] Twenty-four landowners from New Madrid, Dunklin, Pemiscot, and Scott counties met at New Madrid on January 12. The meeting was presided over by J. V. Conran, the prosecuting attorney of New Madrid County. The landlords passed a resolution asking for a public hearing and a federal inquiry into the strike.

The resolution specifically asked for an FBI investigation into

22. Cited in the Charleston *Enterprise Courier,* Jan. 19, 1939.

23. *Southeast Missourian,* Jan. 12, 1939.

24. *Ibid.,* Jan. 16, 1939.

25. Charleston *Enterprise Courier,* Jan. 12, 1939.

26. Undated Sikeston *Herald* clipping, Owen Whitfield Papers. These papers are presently in the possession of Whitfield's wife, Mrs. Zella Whitfield. I am indebted to Mrs. Whitfield for permission to examine them.

27. Telegram, Glen W. Kirkbridge to Secretary Wallace, Jan. 12, 1939, K. W. Marshall *et al.*, to Orville Zimmerman, Feb. 11, 1939, NA, RG 16.

the affairs of Owen Whitfield and Hans Baasch. Whitfield, it said, "has been going about southeast Missouri collecting dollars from the poor people of these communities and telling them that if they would move out on the highways the Government would give them 40 acres of ground and the tools to cultivate it." Baasch, the resolution pointed out, "is reliably reported to have made various communistic remarks leading to this trouble," one of which suggested that it would " 'not be long before all the ground in New Madrid County will be owned by the Government and given to the poor people when divided into 40-acre tracts.' " Most of those who had gone to the highways had not done so because of evictions, the resolution continued, but as "a result of their own voluntary act," and only after "the instigation of certain agitators who claimed to be representatives of the United States Government. . . ."[28]

On January 13, some fifty Mississippi County landowners met in Charleston Courthouse and passed a resolution which also requested a full government investigation to determine the extent of outside influence. Arguing that the total number of participants in the demonstration was "less than 3 per cent of the total tenants and sharecroppers of the county," the resolution said that the evictions in 1939 were actually "less than the normal moving from farm to farm each year. . . ." The resolution stated that the demonstration was the result of "unscrupulous and scheming agitators" who deceived the tenants "by making them believe that they were going to be given property and money by the Government and that they will not have to work." Furthermore, the statement asked all public and private relief agencies to "refrain from encouraging the movement by giving aid and assistance. . . ."[29]

Both resolutions were sent to the governor of Missouri, the two United States senators, congressmen representing the district, the Dies Committee on un-American activities, Vice-President Garner, and Secretary of Agriculture Henry Wallace. Both resolutions were subsequently published in the Congressional Record, Senator Harry Truman printing the documents on the Senate side, and Orville Zimmerman placing them in the House Record. Truman made no comment, but Zimmerman pointed out that "the landowners are not responsible for this much publicized demonstration," and sug-

28. *Cong. Record,* 76 Cong., 1st Sess. (Appendix), 143–144, 187 (Jan. 17 and 18, 1939).

29. *Ibid.*

gested that the resolution should be published officially in the Record "in order that Congress and the country may further know the facts about the highly colored and distorted stories which have been published" about Southeast Missouri's croppers. Zimmerman blamed the publicity of the "so-called uprising" on "overzealous reporters who are looking for good stories for their papers," and insisted that the landlords were correct in pointing out that "there was less moving this year . . . than usual." A great many changes "are always made with the beginning of each year," Zimmerman said, and "as a rule only undesirable tenants are ever asked to move."[30]

Government officials of the state were equally unsympathetic with the demonstrators. State Senator James C. McDowell drove from the state capital to attend the landlord's meeting in Mississippi County at the Charleston Courthouse and announced: "This is the culmination of a damnable scheme. There is someone behind this," he insisted, "and it is our duty to find out who put them up to it. I guess the CIO is back of it, but someone in these counties gave them a hand." The Senator was not being entirely objective, since he was one of the biggest planters in the area. Significantly, he had prefaced his remarks with the statement that "agitators" had induced eight of his Negroes to leave his own farm to participate in the demonstration.[31]

Most local officials echoed the sentiment of the Mississippi County planters' resolution that government aid to the campers would be foolish because it would only serve as a further enticement. One paper quoted a local county prosecutor as saying that governmental assistance would "only encourage [the croppers] and we'll have the same condition next year and the year after. . . . Just leave 'em alone."[32]

The hostility of the state officials was further evidenced by the uncomfortable atmosphere which representatives of the federal government encountered when they arrived on the scene. Federal officials were very sensitive about their presence in the area, as is suggested by this recorded telephone conversation between Aubrey Williams and Herbert Little, the man Williams sent to Southeast Missouri to investigate the situation for the NYA:

30. *Ibid.*, 144, 187. See Appendix, pp. 178–182.

31. *Post-Dispatch*, Jan. 13, 1939.

32. *Daily Worker*, Jan. 14, 1939.

Williams: I would like for you to stay on . . . and get the whole view of the thing. Be careful, though, that nobody finds out you are there.

Little: The State Police tried to arrest one of the NYA boys that came along with me and I told them who I was—that I was making a study.

Williams: I mean the papers.

Little: I am avoiding any newspaper people and I don't think the State Police will do anything about it.[33]

Governor Lloyd C. Stark was convinced the demonstration was organized by transients from outside of the state, "and a considerable number of town negroes," most of whom "had been promised federal aid and an individual farm of their own." The Governor wrote Henry Wallace that an investigation would reveal "un-American and communist practices, which I am reliably informed can be traced directly to certain employees of the Farm Security Administration."[34] The Governor expressed a point of view generally shared by a large number of Bootheel planters. Most landowners in the area were certain that the FSA project at LaForge was "communistic" and that its director, Hans Baasch, was a Communist. At the time that LaForge was constructed in the Bootheel in 1937, there was a general outspoken criticism of it. Orville Zimmerman, the Bootheel representative, wrote to Thad Snow, at the time, that he had received editorials, "letters, petitions, resolutions and what not" protesting the establishment of the LaForge project, "but 'nary' a word from anybody" supporting it.[35]

Although Governor Stark asked state officials to cooperate with the Red Cross, that organization announced it did not recognize the situation as being in their field. "Our position is that it is a matter for State and Federal agencies," William Baxter, director of the midwestern branch of the American Red Cross, said. "It is primarily their responsibility and we don't want to take any step that would muddy the water."[36] Baxter later told the FBI that the Red Cross

33. Report of Herbert Little, *Selected Documents,* Roosevelt Library.

34. Stark estimated that 60 per cent of the demonstrators were from other states. Stark to Henry Wallace, Jan. 16, NA, RG 16. The papers of Governor Lloyd Stark have been deposited in the Western Historical Manuscript Collection of the University of Missouri, Columbia, Mo., but are not open to all scholars. The author was denied permission to examine them.

35. Zimmerman to Thad Snow, May 8, 1937, Thad Snow Papers.

36. Quoted in *Post-Dispatch,* Jan. 11, 1939.

did not provide assistance during the demonstration because his investigation indicated that the croppers had "ample foodstuffs and sufficient available housing." He was therefore convinced "that the participants were suffering a self-imposed hardship."[37] Baxter further recommended to the War Department that the army not send tents to assist the campers. "Adequate shelter can and will be provided by the local communities or farm owners, to any of these people who are willing to accept this," he said. "I do not feel that any useful purpose would be served by providing tentage to enable these people to remain on the highway."[38]

After receiving Aubrey Williams's report, President Roosevelt recommended that the Federal Surplus Commodities Corporation make available the supplies they had on hand—"especially milk, eggs, butter, citrus fruits, meats and cereals."[39] The Commodities Corporation responded and made supplies of food available, but the distribution was in the hands of state officials, who declared that commodities would not be delivered as long as the croppers remained on the highway. To receive help, application had to be made in person and forms filled out properly. But most croppers had no transportation, and many could not write.[40]

Carl Ross, the district supervisor for the Farm Security Administration, located at New Madrid, began receiving applications for emergency subsistence grants right away, but they required about ten days for approval. If approved, the applicants would receive two dollars a month per head of family. The grants were for one month only, he said, "although they might be extended to three months."[41]

When Thad Snow and C. L. Blanton, a Sikeston publisher, requested Lewis Means, the state's adjutant-general, to provide National Guard tents for the campers, Means said he did not have the authority to do this and could not do it without the approval of the Secretary of War. When officials sent telegrams directly to Washington, however, pointing out that the adjutant-general had indicated that aid was "possible upon authorization of the War Department,"

37. FBI Report, *Post-Dispatch,* March 13, 1939.

38. Marlin Craig, Chief of Staff, "Confidential Memo," Jan. 12, 1939, *Selected Documents,* Roosevelt Library.

39. Roosevelt, memo to Secretary of Agriculture, Jan. 19, 1939, *Selected Documents,* Roosevelt Library.

40. Henry Wallace to Roosevelt, Jan. 21, 1939, NA, RG 16; Aubrey Williams, memo to Roosevelt, Jan. 16, 1939; Roosevelt, memo for Secretary of Agriculture, Jan. 19, 1939, *Selected Documents,* Roosevelt Library.

41. *Post-Dispatch,* Jan. 12, 1939.

Means himself then wrote to the War Department, and asked that the army send no tentage until he personally requested it.[42]

The Chief of Staff of the Army, Malin Craig, apparently accepted the word of Means and Red Cross director Baxter, both of whom had assured him that the matter could be handled locally. At the bottom of his confidential memorandum for the Secretary of War was a section labeled "Off the Record," which said: "The Adjutant General of Missouri is particularly anxious that this [off-the-record part of the message] not be released," because he is "afraid of the repercussions which might occur if some of this stuff got in the paper." General Means had sent word to him, Craig said in this confidential memo, assuring him that the state of Missouri was "actively in touch" with the whole situation in the Bootheel and therefore would not require his services. "This is an organized protest against working conditions in which the CIO IS INVOLVED," Craig wrote. The adjutant-general "would prefer that the War Department adopt a 'hands off policy' at this time."[43]

Craig complied with the wishes of the adjutant-general, and the War Department kept "hands off." The War Department further complied with the wishes of General Means when Craig wrote to the White House that the demonstration "appears to be a local political proposition," and recommended that no federal action be taken.[44]

Since STFU had not been informed of the demonstration, no plans had been made for emergency relief. On the morning of the tenth, Whitfield sent a telegram to Mitchell, which succinctly told the story of the differences he was having with STFU. It said simply: "Evicted Sharecroppers Moving to Highway. You and Butler Keep Out."[45] Both Mitchell and Butler first learned of the demonstration indirectly. Butler saw Sam Armstrong's story in the *Post-Dispatch* on the ninth, and sent a telegram to Mitchell in New York City.[46] Mitchell was in New York just for the weekend to make plans for

42. Telegram, Stark to Butler, Jan. 11, 1939; Butler to Secretary of War Harry A. Woodring, Jan. 12, 1939; Secretary of War Woodring to Butler, Feb. 24, 1939, STFU Papers; Telegram, Luther Slinkard to Roosevelt, *Selected Documents,* Roosevelt Library.

43. Malin Craig, Chief of Staff, "Confidential Memo," Jan. 12, 1939, *Selected Documents,* Roosevelt Library.

44. Malin Craig to Marion H. McIntyre, Secretary to the President, Jan. 13, 1939, *ibid.*

45. Telegram, Whitfield to Mitchell, Jan. 10, 1939, STFU Papers.

46. Telegram, Butler to Mitchell, Jan. 9, 1939; Mitchell, "Oral History," p. 110, *ibid.*

National Sharecroppers Week, an annual money-raising event sponsored by STFU, which was to be held in March. During most of January, Mitchell had been in Washington, making arrangements to take a job with the National Youth Administration, in an effort to increase STFU's sagging funds. This idea was dropped as soon as he learned of the demonstration.[47]

Both Butler and Mitchell took immediate action when they got the news of the Bootheel exodus. Butler sent a night letter on the tenth to President Roosevelt, asking him to urge Governor Stark of Missouri to provide shelter for those on the highways, and to advise Secretary Wallace to withhold all parity checks on crops worked by day labor. Mitchell quickly sent Whitfield a telegram in care of Hans Baasch, at LaForge, telling him to keep the people on the highway, and informing him that he was going to Washington right away to get help. He then called Butler in Memphis, who told him of Whitfield's telegram advising STFU to keep out of Southeast Missouri. Mitchell advised Butler to go to Missouri despite Whitfield's warning, and also to appeal to other locals for relief.[48]

Mitchell then went back to Washington, where he contacted NYA head Aubrey Williams, who was a personal friend of Mitchell's and a supporter of STFU.[49] Williams in turn suggested that Mitchell consult the Red Cross and also see Will Alexander of the FSA. The Red Cross told Mitchell what Red Cross agents in the Bootheel were telling the officials there, i.e., that the problem on Missouri's highways was a man-made disaster, not a natural one, and they therefore refused to act.[50]

Either Aubrey Williams or Will Alexander got Mitchell an appointment with Mrs. Roosevelt. The First Lady promised that she would request the President to order the National Guard to send

47. *Daily Worker,* Jan. 11, 1939; Mitchell, "Oral History," p. 110, STFU Papers; Mitchell, letter to author, Jan. 21, 1966.

48. Butler to Roosevelt, Jan. 10, 1939; Mitchell, undated Memo to Burgess; Mitchell to All Locals, STFU, Jan. 17, 1939, STFU Papers.

49. Williams also frequently handled problems relating to Negroes for Roosevelt and later came to be regarded as a kind of New Deal troubleshooter on racial matters. In terms of general attitude toward the Negro's plight, Williams was doubtless one of the most sympathetic members of Roosevelt's administration. See Leslie H. Fishel, Jr., "The Negro in the New Deal Era," *Wisconsin Magazine of History,* XLVIII (Winter, 1964–65), 111–126.

50. Mitchell, "Oral History," p. 111, STFU Papers; Mitchell, letter to author, Jan. 21, 1966.

tents and field kitchens to the shelterless campers. She also wrote an appeal for aid in her column the next day.[51] Will Alexander gave authority to his agency to make emergency grants for subsistence purposes to families in need of aid and, upon recommendation of FDR, "to assist through the rehabilitation loan program any eligible families for whom tenant farms can be found."[52] Although Alexander instructed FSA representatives in the Bootheel "to obtain land for as many of these families as possible, and to give them rehabilitation loans to make a crop," he noted at the time that "the amount of available land is limited and in all probability, only a limited number can be taken care of in this way."[53]

Alexander also sent Virgil Bankston to Sikeston to begin an immediate FSA investigation of STFU charges that tenants had been evicted in order that planters could receive the entire parity check. Claude Wickard, AAA North Central Division director at the time, also began an investigation into the charges. At the same time, Wickard announced that all benefit payments would be withheld from those planters "shown to have evicted tenants or reduced their status to day laborers for the purpose of obtaining a larger share of AAA benefits." When AAA officials arrived on the scene in Southeast Missouri, they stated emphatically that those landlords who were converting to day labor in order to keep the benefit payment might be deprived of their payments.[54]

Mitchell next wired Howard Kester to go to Sikeston to set up a relief center. The political climate in Missouri was considered unsafe, however, and the union shifted its location to Blytheville, Arkansas.[55] Kester was "advised by local people," Mitchell later wrote, that an office in Sikeston "would be dynamited by the planters and he might expect to be lynched."[56]

51. *Ibid.*; Mitchell to Mrs. Roosevelt, Feb. 2, 1939; Mitchell, "Oral History," p. 111, STFU Papers; Wilma Dykeman and James Stokeley, *Seeds of Southern Change: The Life of Will Alexander* (Chicago, 1962), p. 241.

52. Telegram, Alexander to Mitchell, Jan. 11, 1939, STFU Papers; Paul H. Appleby to J. R. Butler, NA, RG 16; Roosevelt, memo for Secretary of Agriculture, Jan. 19, 1939, *Selected Documents,* Roosevelt Library.

53. Will Alexander to Henry Wallace, with attached memo for Mr. Henry Kennee, Jan. 19, 1939, NA, RG 16.

54. *Daily Worker,* Jan. 12, 1939; *Post-Dispatch,* Jan. 11, 1939.

55. Mitchell to Officers, All Locals in Missouri, Jan. 15, 1939; press release, STFU, Jan. 23, 1939; Butler to Alfred Love, Jan. 24, 1939; Butler to Paul Eisen, Eden Seminary, Feb. 10, 1939; Butler to Oliver Hotz, Dec. 2, 1939, STFU Papers.

56. Mitchell, undated memo for Burgess, *ibid.*

Having started the machinery to grapple with the immediate problem in the Bootheel, Mitchell now began the long-range, and perhaps more difficult, task of trying to raise funds. STFU had never been a wealthy organization. Members paid a twenty-five cent entrance fee and one dollar per year for membership dues. Most of its financial support came from outside sympathizers who made large contributions. One of its big problems in 1939 was that many of its outside supporters had mistakenly assumed that it would no longer need their help after the union joined UCAPAWA in 1937 because the CIO would offer it financial support.[57]

Direct CIO support never materialized, however, and by early 1939, STFU was in an economic crisis. The day before the Southeast Missouri roadside demonstration, Mitchell and Butler had sent out a request to "Friends" of the STFU, pleading for financial support. Mitchell sadly related in this appeal that STFU's biggest contributor, the American Fund for Public Service, headed by Roger Baldwin, had informed the union early in 1939 that their customary two-hundred-dollar monthly contribution would no longer be sent.[58]

Mitchell first tried immediately after the demonstration to obtain a thousand-dollar loan from the CIO, but that failed.[59] The national labor organization gave no financial assistance, but did enthusiastically support the Bootheel strike. John Brophy, national director for the CIO, sent numerous telegrams to government officials urging that aid be sent to the Southeast Missouri croppers. In the name of the CIO, Brophy requested Wallace, Alexander, WPA head F. C. Harrington, and Jesse W. Tapp, head of the Federal Surplus Commodities Corporation, to take immediate steps to provide relief. Brophy also echoed STFU's proposal that benefit checks to landlords be withheld from planters "until they change their unhuman policies toward these American families."[60]

Although Mitchell undoubtedly welcomed the CIO's verbal support, this did not help STFU's economic problems. Failing to obtain financial aid from the CIO, the union secretary borrowed three hundred dollars from David Clendenin of the Socialist party's

57. See Mitchell, "Annual Report of STFU, Memphis, Tennessee, for the Year Ended December 30, 1939"; David Clendenin to J. R. Butler, Oct. 22, 1937, *ibid.*

58. Mitchell and Butler, to Friends of the STFU, Jan. 9, 1939, *ibid.*

59. Mitchell, "Report of the Sec. for 1939," pp. 2–3, *ibid.*

60. Cited in *Daily Worker*, Jan. 13, 1939.

Workers Defense League.[61] Mitchell was also able to contact Baldwin later and, with some assistance from Norman Thomas, who spoke to Baldwin personally, wrest the regular two-hundred-dollar monthly appropriation from the American Fund.[62]

These undertakings helped to solve the immediate financial crisis. Yet, to provide supplies for over a thousand homeless sharecroppers required far greater resources, and STFU would indeed have had extreme difficulty meeting the need had aid not begun pouring into union headquarters almost immediately after the demonstration started from sympathizers all over the country. The contributions were large and small, the great majority of them from individuals who had seen the campers' picture and read of their plight on the front pages of their paper. Many sent money; others sent old clothing or medical supplies.[63]

Two private committees helped raise a great deal of the funds used to support the croppers. Jim Meyers, the industrial secretary for the Federal Council of Churches, organized the Church Emergency Relief Committee, and Harriet Young, the eastern representative for STFU, helped set up the Emergency Committee for Strikers' Relief, under the auspices of the League for Industrial Democracy, headed by Norman Thomas, Reinhold Niebuhr, and John Herling.[64]

All together, the union collected $3,293.56 for relief. Virtually all of the money was spent directly on the campers in the form of cash, food and clothing, and other supplies. An incidental amount was applied to union expenses, mostly traveling fees, organization needs, and office administration.[65]

Because union headquarters were located at Blytheville, Arkansas, a considerable distance from Sikeston, the center of the strike activity, the supplies were slow in getting to the croppers. By the

61. Mitchell, Report of the Secretary for 1939, pp. 2–3; Butler to David Clendenin, April 24, 1939; Harriet Young to Mitchell, March 17, 1939, STFU Papers.

62. Baldwin to Butler and Mitchell, Feb. 8, 1939; Harriet Young to Butler and Mitchell, Jan. 19, 1939, *ibid.*

63. There are two complete folders in the STFU files labeled Missouri Relief Contributions, I and II, 1939, containing correspondence with individuals who contributed something in the way of relief. See *ibid.*

64. John Herling to Mitchell, Jan. 25, 1939; Paul Eisen to Howard Kester, Jan. 26, 1939, *ibid.*

65. "Statement of Receipts and Disbursements, Southeast Missouri Relief Fund, from Jan. 1, 1939 to Feb. 18, 1939"; F. R. Betton, "Report on Relief Distribution in Southeast Missouri, STFU, Jan. through Feb. 18, 1939," *ibid.*

end of the second day, the meager resources which the croppers had brought with them were almost depleted. Most had carried all their possessions to the roadside after they were evicted, but at best this meant only a small supply of bread, fat pork, and coffee. With milk and vegetables unobtainable, the usual fare for the highway strikers was hard tack and black coffee. Sam Armstrong, the *Post-Dispatch* reporter, in a hundred-mile tour up, down, and across Highways 60 and 61, counted forty infants, most of whom were without milk.[66]

Lack of milk for the children was only one of many problems which began to plague the roadside dwellers. Protection from the elements, as already indicated, had been one of Whitfield's main concerns from the beginning because the croppers would be living outside in the open. The only campers who had anything at all which resembled permanent dwellings were those fortunate few who had driven to the highway in dilapidated automobiles or open trucks.

Those who had vehicles took turns sleeping in them; usually women, children, and the aged were given these accommodations. The open trucks were converted into sleeping quarters by filling them with bedding or corn-shuck mattresses. All of the other demonstrators simply threw mattresses or blankets on the ground. This afforded little protection, however, from the damp earth, and as a result these campers spent most of their hours huddled around the campfire, sleeping only after they were exhausted.[67]

The campfire was usually the center of activity in every encampment. A few croppers had iron stoves, but most cooked over the open fire. The fire also blazed through most of the night, with the croppers gathered around it, talking, praying, or singing spirituals in an effort to keep up their courage. Some of the leaders of the demonstration were concerned that the croppers might lose faith quickly and abandon the camps because Whitfield was not with them on the roadside.

The night before the demonstration took place, January 9, Whitfield had left the Bootheel for St. Louis, for fear that once the planters discovered he was behind the strike, they would try to lynch him. Whitfield later apologized to other union members for leaving the scene, but wrote that he would be of little help to the

66. *Post-Dispatch,* Jan. 12 and 13, 1939.
67. *Ibid.,* Jan. 10 and 11, 1939.

union "dead or in jail."[68] No doubt the Negro leader had again accurately gauged Bootheel sentiment. Indeed, Sgt. R. R. Reed of the Missouri Highway Patrol openly announced after the strike started that he had "been looking for Whitfield, who is the main squee-gee of this outfit."[69]

Whitfield had been careful, however, to designate camp leaders in each group to direct activities and to act as spokesmen in his absence. Many of these leaders were themselves ministers who held religious meetings around the campfire in the evening. A typical meeting, held at Sikeston, was described by Sam Armstrong of the *Post-Dispatch*. The meeting was under the direction of the Rev. S. J. Elliot, pastor of the St. James (Negro) Methodist Church in Sikeston. Although only a few white croppers were present, Armstrong reported, they joined in the evening services and knelt and prayed with their Negro brethren. "The Lord will take care of you," Elliott promised the campers. "He was able to deliver the children of Israel, to save Daniel in the lion's den and to rescue the three Hebrew boys from the fiery furnace. He will not forget you."[70] Many of the campers had guitars and banjos, which provided accompaniment for the hymns which were always sung following every service. The *Post-Dispatch* reported that "On Jordan's Stormy Banks I Stand" could be heard in many of the camps far into the night.[71]

Wednesday night, January 11, temperatures dropped into the thirties, and by Thursday, a cold rain had set in. When a committee representing a camp of over two hundred persons located between New Madrid and Marston appealed for supplies at New Madrid one of the surplus commodities depots, they were denied. O. E. Wright, in charge of the depot there, told the committee that each applicant had to make a personal appearance, since regulations required those persons receiving aid to fill out "complicated questionnaires covering detailed past personal histories." When the committee objected on the ground that it would take weeks to obtain information from all the needy croppers because of the limited personnel at the relief offices, Wright said he "could do nothing but follow regulations."[72]

68. Whitfield to All Locals, STFU, Feb. 5, 1939, STFU Papers; Mrs. Zella Whitfield, interview with author, Dec. 19, 1965.
69. Quoted in *Daily Worker,* Jan. 13, 1939.
70. *Post-Dispatch,* Jan. 11, 1939.
71. *Ibid.*
72. *Ibid.*

Surplus commodity offices were located at New Madrid, Sikeston, Charleston, Benton, Caruthersville, Kennett, Bloomfield, and Poplar Bluff. Since there was no means of getting to the warehouses from the camps, spokesmen for the croppers suggested that trucks be sent to carry supplies to those on the road, but V. S. Harshbarger of Sikeston, the district supervisor for relief in the Delta counties, said that this was also out of the question because of the regulation requiring individual application.[73]

The St. Louis Industrial Union Council tried desperately to help the croppers during the first few days. Wednesday night they held a special meeting in the city. After sending a telegram to President Roosevelt requesting him to send word to the War Department to release army tents, they collected thirty-seven dollars for the needy campers. The council also made a truck available to collect any contributions of food or clothing from those who would call its headquarters. The distribution of the supplies, however, was a more difficult task than their collection. When representatives of the Industrial Union drove down to the Bootheel, along with members of the Greater St. Louis Lodge of Colored Elks, to distribute the supplies, four members of the union were arrested by deputy sheriffs for "impersonating government officials."[74]

A. F. Kojetinsky, a spokesman for the union, said a deputy sheriff told the group: "We don't have any use for people like you in this area." The four men were taken to a highway patrol office in a patrol car and held there for questioning. Afterward, their automobile was brought back to them, and they were told: "You'd better go on ahead."[75] One newspaper reported that the Highway Patrol and the planters "complained that the distribution of relief made it hard to drive the croppers back to their farms. . . ."[76]

In spite of the harassment, the supplies were distributed. Most of the food was prepared and cooked in a Negro cafe in Charleston. On their way back home, the CIO representatives stopped at a camp to hand out the few remaining supplies they had and "in half a minute," to use the union leaders' words, "two deputized planters, brandishing blackjacks, ordered us to move on."[77]

73. *Ibid.*, Jan. 16, 1939.

74. *Ibid.*

75. *Ibid.*

76. *Southeast Missourian,* Jan. 23, 1939.

77. Quoted in *ibid.,* Jan. 23, 1939; Charleston *Enterprise Courier,* Jan. 19, 1939; Mrs. Sarah Howard, a participant in the demonstration, interview with author, March 16, 1966.

A group of students from Eden Theological Seminary in St. Louis attempted to distribute food and clothing to the campers, and they also were stopped by deputy sheriffs who told them that "relief makes the situation worse."[78] STFU at first had no better luck. When J. R. Butler attempted to come into the area along with several other STFU officials, he was stopped by the State Police, and held on the grounds that the police "were fearful of violence by local planters."[79]

Butler later recalled that he was "verbally lashed with charges of 'enciting to riot,' giving Missouri a 'black eye,' violating 'accustomed usage,' and what have you."[80] The STFU President was then escorted to the Arkansas line by the state police, told to leave the state of Missouri and not to return. Despite state police orders to keep out union officials, Butler and other STFU leaders made constant trips into the Bootheel with supplies under cover of darkness.[81]

One or two other attempts were made to get supplies to the campers during the first week. A few of the croppers drove to surplus areas in rickety autos, and residents of Kinlock Park, a St. Louis County Negro community, formed an "emergency club" and delivered an automobile full of food and clothing to some. One motorist with a Michigan license plate reportedly gave one group enough money to buy ten pounds of pork chops. But most of the campers continued to get by on what they had.[82]

On Thursday night, January 12, snow started falling, and before it stopped the next morning, an inch and a half was on the ground, with temperatures near freezing. Despite persistent pleas to General Means for National Guard tents, none ever appeared. Without tents, the croppers protected themselves as best they could. Many improvised windbreaks of quilts or sheets thrown over poles; oil drums were converted into stoves, and corncobs or whatever else was available was used for fuel. The snow heightened the drama on the roadsides. Mendicant croppers, hungry and shivering in the snow and ice, stirred even the most unsympathetic souls, and local pres-

78. *Post-Dispatch,* Jan. 23, 1939.

79. Press release, STFU, Jan. 14, 1939, STFU Papers.

80. J. R. Butler, letter to author, Jan. 7, 1966.

81. *Post-Dispatch,* Jan. 16, 1939; press release, STFU, Jan. 14, 1939; Butler to Oliver Hotz, Dec. 2, 1939; Butler to STFU locals and members in Southeast Missouri, March 31, 1939, STFU Papers.

82. *Post-Dispatch,* Jan. 13 and 15, 1939.

sure began to build to do something about an increasingly difficult situation.[83]

Coverage of the demonstration had now become nationwide, with newspaper reporters from all over the country, as well as representatives of government and private agencies on the scene. The *Post-Dispatch* reported that by Thursday there were, on hand in the Bootheel, officials from the AAA, the FSA, the Social Security Administration, the State Labor Department, the State Highway Patrol, the CIO, the STFU, the Red Cross, and the Communist party.[84] Undoubtedly all of the excitement and news coverage of the event forced state officials to find a means of ending the demonstration.

By the end of the week, an order from the President to the National Guard in Jefferson City had started trucks, loaded with tents, field kitchens, and other equipment rolling toward Southeast Missouri. They never arrived. State officials had at last found a means of removing the ugly spectacle from the highway.[85]

83. *Ibid.*; New York *Times,* Jan. 13, 1939; *Daily Worker,* Jan. 13, 1939. The *Daily Worker* charged that one person died on the highway from "exposure," although this was not mentioned in any of the other papers at the time, which probably meant that the actual cause of death was uncertain. See *Daily Worker,* Jan. 14 and 15, 1939.

84. *Post-Dispatch,* Jan. 13, 1939.

85. Mitchell, "Oral History," pp. 111–112; Butler to Harry H. Woodring, Feb. 20, 1939; Mitchell, undated memo for Burgess; Mitchell, "Workers in Our Fields," p. 14, STFU Papers; Mrs. Zella Whitfield, interview with author, Dec. 19, 1965; Mr. John Stewart, interview with author, May 1, 1966.

7 Dispersal

On Friday, January 13, the state health commissioner, Dr. Harry Parker, toured the campsites and decided they were a menace to public health. The lack of sanitary facilities and good drinking water, he said, caused him to fear a possible outbreak of epidemic meningitis. The next day, the state police, enlisting the aid of county sheriffs and deputized citizens, began to move the croppers from the roads. Those who decided to leave, returned to their farms if they could. Most planters announced that they did not want to take the demonstrators back, although a few offered to hire them, not as croppers, but as day laborers.[1] The remainder who chose to leave looked elsewhere for work, or merely drifted.

A large number, however, objected to leaving, and in several instances camps had to be broken up by police. STFU charged that the camps were "forcibly broken up with violence, threats and intimidations at [the] instigation of plantation interests."[2] The union dispatched telegrams to President Roosevelt, Secretary Wallace, and Attorney General Frank Murphy, appealing for an immediate

1. *Post-Dispatch,* Jan. 14, 1939; Report of Herbert Little, dictated over the telephone, Jan. 16, 1939, *Selected Documents,* Roosevelt Library; *Post-Dispatch,* Jan. 15, 1939.

2. Executive Committee, STFU to Roosevelt, Jan. 21, 1939, STFU Papers.

investigation by the Justice Department of denial of civil liberties of the campers.[3]

The evidence seems to suggest strongly that STFU's charges were at least in part true. Federal officials, after their investigation, reported that there were "numerous violations of civil liberties." As one example, they mentioned the action of the State Highway Police in forcing J. R. Butler and other STFU officials to leave the state. As another, they cited "the forcible removal of the demonstrators from the public highways," by the State Police and the special role played by Sheriff A. F. Stanley of New Madrid County.[4]

The investigators' report was extremely critical of Sheriff Stanley's handling of the sharecroppers' firearms. Since the campers had burned their bridges behind them, they had their entire belongings with them on the highway. It was not uncommon for a poor sharecropper to possess a shotgun or hunting rifle in order to add rabbits, squirrels, and other wild animals to his meager diet. Thus, many had weapons in their possession while on the roadsides. The arms were confiscated by Sheriff Stanley. All together, forty-nine shotguns and rifles and four pistols were taken by Stanley's men. The owners were told they could get them back at the county jail only after the camps were broken up.[5]

Stanley told local reporters that he had "no trouble at all getting these guns" and that most of the campers had turned them over willingly, suggesting that the dispersal of the camps had taken place without incident.[6] The government investigation, however, reported otherwise. It defined the seizure of weapons as another violation of civil liberties. It was during this seizure that some violence erupted. One Negro was clubbed and cut in the face and gashed by blows from a pistol and a cane.[7]

Herbert Little's eyewitness account is also decidedly contrary to Stanley's report: Sheriff Stanley's "men invited us to watch [the dispersal of the highway camp]. He claimed the negros were armed." Little said Stanley's deputies "then forced all the Negro

3. Press release, STFU, Jan. 23, 1939, *ibid.*
4. Wallace to Murphy, Jan. 24, 1939, *Selected Documents,* Roosevelt Library.
5. *Southeast Missourian,* Jan. 17, 1939.
6. *Ibid.*
7. Wallace to Murphy, Jan. 24, 1939, *Selected Documents,* Roosevelt Library.

men across the Highway while some of them made a careful search of all the thirty or forty make-shift tents" the Negroes had occupied on the other side of the road. "One of our party," Little reported, "saw a negro struck in the face by one of the citizens. Another negro was put in handcuffs."[8]

Those campers who chose to remain in the demonstration were now removed from the highway in twenty-four highway department trucks. Whites and Negroes were purposefully placed in separate groups. The largest group—about a hundred families, comprising approximately five hundred campers—was taken to an area in the Birds Point–New Madrid Spillway in New Madrid County. The land—a forty-acre tract—was owned by the county and was located not far from the LaForge Project.[9] Others were put in much smaller groups in an obvious effort to scatter the demonstrators. One group of whites was taken to the River Levee in Dorena, in Mississippi County. Other Negroes were put in empty barns or shacks. One sizeable group was taken to the Sweet Home Baptist Church, between Wyatt and Charleston, Missouri. The FBI later reported that one group was placed in a Negro cabaret.[10]

Sheriff Stanley and six of his deputies were put in charge of the big camp at New Madrid. The description of the New Madrid Spillway strongly suggests that the decision to move the campers was determined more by a desire to get them out of the public eye than by the fear of a health menace. The area—later dubbed "Homeless Junction" by the croppers—was a swampy, uncleared region that had been covered with water in the 1937 floods; there were no sanitary facilities and no means of obtaining drinking water, save from open ditches and rivers. The conditions in the spillway, government investigators later reported, were "as conducive to serious

8. Herbert Little, memo to Aubrey Williams, "Subject: Eyewitness accounts of dispersal of roadside camps of farmers by Sheriff in New Madrid County near Sikeston, Missouri, Sunday, Jan. 15, 1939," *ibid.* Later, Little interviewed the Negro who was struck: "This fellow has two wounds on his forehead," he reported, "and one on his right cheek which, he says, were inflicted by the sheriff's deputy on Sunday, January 15" (Case No. 45, Aubrey Williams to Roosevelt, Jan. 19, 1939, *ibid.*).

9. *Southeast Missourian,* Jan. 16, 1939; *Post-Dispatch,* Jan. 25, 1939; *Daily Worker,* Jan. 16, 1939; see Will Alexander to Henry Wallace, with attached memo for Mr. Henry Kannee, Jan. 19, 1939, NA, RG 16.

10. FBI Report, *Post-Dispatch,* March 13, 1939; see also Will Alexander to Henry Wallace, with attached memo for Mr. Henry Kannee, Jan. 19, 1939, NA, RG 16.

epidemic sickness, if not more so, than [the] highway camps."[11] The state police, government officials, and local newspapers openly referred to the croppers new home as a "concentration camp."

A letter-writer in the *Post-Dispatch* reflected the opinion of those who were critical of the decision to move the croppers when she said: "The State Police, like embarrassed housewives, snatched the laundry from the roadside and hustled to the spillway, hoping the Father of Waters would wash it next spring."[12] Whitfield, upon being told that the croppers had been removed for reasons of health, replied: "Do they think those shacks my people have been living in are any healthier?"[13] A *Post-Dispatch* editorial aptly concluded: "There is no difference between this and the previous camps, except that the present one is off the highway."[14]

Once again the sharecroppers constructed makeshift protection of sheets, canvas, oilcloth, tarpaulin, and boards in the timberless flats. But, with temperatures near freezing, the conditions remained essentially the same, and so did the attitude of the state officials. J .V. Conran, the prosecuting attorney of New Madrid County and the prime mover in passing the planters' resolution, said: "We're not going to do anything for them. It's up to the Federal Government." Still convinced that the presence in the area of the LaForge Project was the cause of all the Bootheel's troubles, Conran asserted: "They [the federal government] put that damn thing down here."[15]

Local authorities did provide one service—a police guard at the concentration camp, who checked all who entered, and apparently only those on official business were permitted to do so. Government investigators reported that Captain A. D. Sheppard, the head of the Highway Patrol, told them that "no one would be allowed in or out of the camp."[16] When one government investigator appeared at the camp to interview some of the participants in the demonstration, the State Highway Patrol permitted him to enter, but made it obvious that he was not welcome. Captain Sheppard is reported to have

11. Aubrey Williams, memo to Roosevelt, Jan. 16, 1939; Wallace to Murphy, Jan. 24, 1939, *Selected Documents,* Roosevelt Library; *Southeast Missourian,* Jan. 17, 1939.

12. *Post-Dispatch,* Jan. 22, 1939.

13. *Ibid.,* Jan. 15, 1939.

14. *Ibid.,* Jan. 16, 1939.

15. Quoted in *ibid.,* Jan. 17, 1939.

16. Report of Herbert Little, dictated over the telephone, Jan. 16, 1939, *Selected Documents,* Roosevelt Library; see "Report of Contact Men in Missouri," STFU Papers.

said that the government man "did not appear to be a southerner and might not understand what was necessary in 'handling niggers.' "[17]

Federal officials were apparently uncertain both about the legality of the action of the state police and the status of the croppers while in "Homeless Junction." Indeed, they were not even sure if the campers were being held forcibly. "It is believed the individuals in [the concentration camp] have been placed under technical arrest," the government report later said, although it indicated that its information on this point was still indefinite. "It was stated that no one would be permitted to visit them," the report pointed out, "but that they would be permitted to leave under certain conditions."[18]

Undoubtedly the state authorities were operating under the expectation that all the campers would shortly abandon the idea of continuing the demonstration, and "go back where they came from." One government official reported: "Captain Sheppard said that from his knowledge of Negroes, he expects the . . . camps to be dispersed and the occupants to return to their former farms in a few days."[19]

Most of the other smaller groups—apart from the New Madrid camp—did gradually disperse, although some remained for months in the locations where they had been placed.[20] The five hundred at "Homeless Junction," however, were determined to continue the vigil. The state officials seemed equally determined to disperse them completely.

On January 19, J. V. Conran announced that the croppers at "Homeless Junction" were "being moved to the houses they left when they started this silly demonstration." Conran said Sheriff Stanley had guaranteed safety for the campers only until January 21. He further reported that many residents of the area around the temporary site at "Homeless Junction" had complained to the

17. Wallace to Murphy, Jan. 24, 1939, *Selected Documents,* Roosevelt Library.

18. Aubrey Williams to Roosevelt, Jan. 16, 1939, *ibid.*

19. Report of Herbert Little, dictated over the telephone, Jan. 16, 1939, *ibid.*

20. It is difficult to determine precisely what happened to all of the other groups, because after they were scattered, the newspapers concentrated their coverage almost entirely on the largest camp at New Madrid. The camps at Dorena and the Sweet Home Church apparently remained together until April. See *Post-Dispatch,* April 28, 1939.

county authorities "in a way that we knew they meant business." Conran said the sheriff's deputies had informed him that "the Negro sharecroppers had virtually taken charge of a white school and had frightened the teacher and her pupils away." The prosecuting attorney did not bother to identify the school or the teacher, which raises doubts about the authenticity of the allegation, especially because of his otherwise openly hostile attitude toward the croppers. Only two days before, for example, Conran had said of the sharecroppers that somehow they had obtained the notion that they were "the most important [people] in the world." This same condescending attitude was expressed by Sheriff Stanley, the croppers' official watchguard at the camp. Referring to the croppers' motives in the strike, he told one reporter: "They apparently want to stay up there and wait for some guardian angel to come and take care of them."[21]

On the day Conran made his decision to move the croppers, the FSA announced that tents had already been ordered to the New Madrid site to "provide at least temporary shelter." Since the FSA representative at Sikeston had used the telephone to inform his field agent of the decision to send the tents, the federal agency immediately charged that the phone conversation was overheard, and as a result, state officials had decided to remove the campers in an effort to frustrate FSA efforts to help.[22]

Whether the charge was true or not, the New Madrid authorities removed the croppers in six county-owned trucks just before the FSA equipment was to arrive. Indeed, R. G. Smith, the regional director of the FSA, was already on his way to New Madrid from his home office in Indianapolis to take charge when he received word that the croppers had been removed. So sudden was the decision of the New Madrid officials that Smith said it would now be necessary to change the plans he had made to "provide food, a pure water supply and sanitary facilities, in addition to shelter."[23]

There is no doubt that because the campers were now scattered in four or five counties, the problem of assistance offered by FSA was greatly increased.[24] The majority of those who sought to con-

21. *Ibid.*, Jan. 17–19, 1939.

22. *Ibid.*, Jan. 20, 1939.

23. *Ibid.*, Jan. 21, 1939.

24. *Ibid.*, Jan. 20, 1939. See Josephine Johnson, "New Year for the Sharecroppers," *The American Teacher* (Feb. 1939), pp. 22–23, Josephine (Johnson) Cannon Papers. These papers are in the possession of Mrs. Josephine (Johnson) Cannon. I am indebted to her for their use.

tinue the demonstration now asked to join those at the Sweet Home Baptist Church near Wyatt, rather than return to the shacks state officials found for them. "It is reported that a good many of the families did not want to move into the houses that were provided," Will Alexander, the FSA head, wrote, "apparently thinking this was not a solution of their problem."[25]

Of the 134 men, women, and children who remained, one in every ten, the *Post-Dispatch* estimated, was ill from the ordeal. Most of them, the paper reported, had colds obtained in the two weeks' exposure to the elements. A potbellied stove in the middle of the Sweet Home church provided some warmth from the freezing temperatures for those fortunate enough to be inside. About one third of the campers were not so lucky and lived in makeshift shelters of bed clothing pitched in the tiny churchyard until a week later when FSA tents finally arrived at the church at the end of January. There were eleven infants in the group, and five of the women were expecting babies within the next two months.[26]

One observer estimated that there were thirty families living in the tents surrounding the church. "Tents with room for two beds and a stove and nothing more," the writer noted. "In the raw spring air and the cold mud, the families cook on stoves outside the tents, with windbreaks of sacking tied to poles." Those inside the church, were not much better off. It was "filled with makeshift bedding piled on boards and springs between the pews." Food consisted of "a little salt pork, beans and bread. Oatmeal for the children, but hardly ever milk." Yet, not surprisingly, state health officials inspected the Sweet Home Church and declared its conditions to be "passable."[27]

Twice the State Highway Patrol visited the church group and made an effort to get them to disband. They refused, arguing that they were members of the congregation, and had received permission to stay from their pastor. The croppers remained there for some time, continuing to experience various types of harassment. Members of the St. Louis American Civil Liberties Union com-

25. *Post-Dispatch,* Jan. 23, 1939; Will Alexander to Henry Wallace, with attached memo for Henry Kannee, Jan. 19, 1939, *Selected Documents,* Roosevelt Library.

26. *Post-Dispatch,* Jan. 24 and 25, 1939; Mrs. Sarah Howard, interview with author, March 16, 1966.

27. Josephine Johnson, "What Became of the Sharecroppers," *Post-Dispatch,* April 3, 1939; Charleston *Enterprise Courier,* Jan. 26, 1939.

plained that a number of croppers, all qualified voters, were not permitted to vote in a school election at nearby Wyatt. A spokesman, who declined to use his name, said the apparent reasons for the refusal were "resentment over the recent demonstration and fear that the Negroes would vote for a school director opposed by many white residents. . . ."[28]

The croppers remained in the church—despite sporadic efforts to move them—until April, when the owner of the land on which the church was located sued the church trustees who had allowed the campers to occupy the building and grounds. He sued for fifty dollars damages and a retroactive monthly rental of five dollars from the time the church had been occupied.[29]

It seemed as though the long trek which started back on Missouri's highways on January 10 had finally come to an end, and the campers once again would be permanently without a roof over their heads. Their long suffering had not been in vain, however. For although Whitfield had not been with them during their ordeal, he had been working for the homeless campers all along.

When Whitfield returned to St. Louis on January 10, he immediately sought out those individuals who had first expressed a desire to help him in 1938. From this group, he helped to organize the St. Louis Committee for the Rehabilitation of the Sharecroppers.[30] Working closely in St. Louis with this committee, Whitfield had managed to raise enough money to purchase a ninety-acre tract of land at Harviell, fifteen miles southwest of Poplar Bluff, Missouri, which was to serve as a permanent home for those participants in the demonstration who were still without a place to live.

Since the middle of January, the St. Louis Sharecropper Committee had been requesting the Congress of the United States to provide money for additional resettlement projects in the Bootheel similar to LaForge. One committee resolution calling for Congress to provide the funds was sent to the FSA at the end of January, but was immediately referred to the Senate Committee on Agriculture and Forestry, and there it remained.[31]

When the federal government refused to take action immediately,

28. *Post-Dispatch,* Jan. 26, April 6, 1939.
29. *Ibid.,* April 28, 1939.
30. Al Murphy to T. J. North, Jan. 18, 1939; Mitchell, "Report of the Secretary, 1939," STFU Papers.
31. *Post-Dispatch,* Jan. 23 and 31, 1939.

the St. Louis committee began to raise contributions to purchase land which might serve as a permanent home for the campers. Ninety acres—sixty-five acres of timber and twenty-five acres of cleared land—was purchased with funds raised by private contributions. The announcement of the purchase of the ninety acres was made simultaneously with the news of the court action ejecting the squatters from the church property near Wyatt, so the campers never had to disperse.[32] In addition to the church group, many others who were still without a place to live were now to have a permanent home at Harviell.

At the time the purchase of the ninety-acre tract was made, Whitfield estimated that there were about a hundred families who had participated in the demonstration who were still without homes. The smaller groups of campers who had decided to remain together, apparently had faired little better than the largest faction which had been taken to "Homeless Junction." The families who were taken to the abandoned dance hall near Charleston, had unlighted and unventilated rooms barely large enough for one person and certainly not adequate for an entire family.[33] "How they keep alive is a miracle," Fannie Cook of the St. Louis Sharecropper Committee, wrote after visiting the Charleston camp. She saw eight families living "in a series of stalls," which she described as "partitions of old, dirty, corrugated boxes nailed to uprights." Approximately forty-five people lived there, without access to outhouses, "except those whose use they could beg." There were two pregnant women in the abandoned dance hall, who had to walk several blocks just to get the use of a privy. Miss Cook visited other camps, and found conditions equally deplorable. "Four births have occurred in one camp without medical assistance," she wrote. "Two will occur soon in the camp without outhouses."[34]

In addition to the hundred homeless families who had participated in the demonstration, Whitfield estimated that at least three hundred families in the Bootheel were still "in dire need of better dwelling quarters." The Negro leader openly announced that all refugees would be welcomed to the new Harviell camp, which was

32. *Southeast Missourian,* June 15, 1939.

33. Press release, STFU, June 15, 1939, STFU Papers; Josephine Johnson, *Post-Dispatch,* April 3, 1939.

34. Fannie Cook to Edna (last name unknown), April 17, 1939, Fannie Cook Collection.

to be open to both white and Negro families.[35] On June 17, 1939, eighty Negro and fifteen white families moved into the camp.

Local hostility to the croppers' presence was so strong that the first group of settlers decided to move in at night. Indeed, because of the fear of hostile whites, the purchase of the land and the transfer of title of ownership was carried out secretly by Bill Fischer, a white participant in the demonstration, who then transferred the title to the Sharecropper Committee.

During the first few weeks, the croppers found it necessary to post a guard at the camp at night "to ward off attack from local vigilante groups who hoped to drive out the unwanted newcomers."[36] Many brought their tents from the Sweet Home Church with them and others constructed barrel-stave shacks. Food came mostly from relief. One author described the regular allotment as "four pounds of corn grit (chicken feed looks more appetizing) four pounds of meal and two pounds of beans," which was a month's supply for one family, often as large as ten. The same author charged that doctors refused to treat the sick in the camp, though several women and children were seriously ill. He claimed that the county doctor was a brother of a large planter in Mississippi County, who reportedly said "he'd 'be damned' if he'd ever help the camp in any way."[37]

By spring forty acres were cleared, and FSA grants started coming in regularly. The St. Louis Sharecropper Committee continued to send assistance, and a few lucky campers were able to earn a little cash by picking cotton. Some of the boys were later admitted to the CCC camps, and a few found jobs with WPA.[38] The American Friends Service Committee, an organ of the Society of Friends, came to assist the campers in the summer of 1941. They reported that most of the white families had "found better opportunities outside and moved off, as did a few colored families. . . ." By this time,

35. *Southeast Missourian,* June 15, 1939.

36. See "Report on Cropperville by the 1941 Summer Work Camp of the American Friends Service Committee at the Sharecropper Camp near Harviell, Missouri" (Confidential), Fannie Cook Collection.

37. See Mildred G. Freed, "Ten Million Sharecroppers," *The Crisis* (Dec. 1939), Fannie Cook Collection, pp. 367–368. See also *UCAPAWA News,* I, No. 3 (Sept. 1939), 6 (microfilm, State Historical Society of Wisconsin, Madison, Wis.).

38. See *UCAPAWA News,* I, No. 7 (April 1940), 5; and "Copy of Petition sent to President Roosevelt, Dr. Alexander, Mr. Beck, Harviell, Missouri, July 9, 1939," Fannie Cook Collection.

there were seventy-two families—about three hundred people—all but one of whom were Negro.[39]

A school was later established by the St. Louis committee. Josephine Johnson and Fannie Cook helped raise most of the funds to defray the cost of erecting the school building. Whitfield continued to assist at Harviell by working with the campers, the Friends and the St. Louis committee.[40] Over the years the area came to be known as "Cropperville," and a number of the people who participated in the demonstration still live there today.[41]

Whitfield's escape to St. Louis did not distract from the effectiveness of his demonstration in any way. The Negro farm leader had already made preparation long beforehand to have his lieutenants take over on the roadside, while he was away, and they served admirably, as evidenced by the orderliness of the entire affair. His presence once again in St. Louis, however, was to have much greater significance in his relationship with STFU, because once again he became the center of the union's internecine struggle, a struggle which grew to a new intensity after his flight to St. Louis, and was to end finally in the union's complete annihilation.

39. "Report on Cropperville by the 1941 Summer Work Camp. . . ," Fannie Cook Collection; and *Post-Dispatch,* Aug. 9, 1942.

40. Whitfield to Fannie Cook, Oct. 23, 1944; Otto Aldrich, Butler County Superintendent of Schools, to Mrs. Jerome Cook, Sept. 11, 1940; Zella Whitfield to Fannie Cook, Nov. 19, 1945; Otto Aldrich to Fannie Cook, July 17, 1940, Fannie Cook Collection; Clarence Yarrow to Josephine Johnson and Fannie Cook, July 8, 1942; Fannie Cook to Josephine Johnson, Jan. 23, 1949; Homer C. Bishop to Mrs. Grant (Josephine Johnson) Cannon, Dec. 20, 1956, Josephine (Johnson) Cannon Papers.

41. Mrs. Sarah Howard, interview with author, March 16, 1966. See also Belfrage, "Cotton-Patch Moses," *Harper's Magazine*; *Post-Dispatch,* Aug. 9, 1942.

8 The Mitchell–Whitfield Feud

The focal point in the controversy between Whitfield and the STFU was the St. Louis Committee for the Rehabilitation of the Sharecroppers. This committee, headed by Josephine Johnson and Fannie Cook, two prominent St. Louis writers, was composed of about thirty persons, the majority of whom were sympathetic liberal-minded people who wanted to do something to aid the Southeast Missouri demonstrators. There were also in the ranks of the committee at least a few Communists.[1]

Members of the committee who actually belonged to the Communist party were Lief Dahl, a representative of UCAPAWA, William H. Senter, vice-president of the St. Louis CIO Electrical Workers Union, and Al Murphy, who later ran for governor of Missouri on a Communist party ticket. Others who helped organize the committee but were not associated with the party, were members of the St. Louis Urban League, church leaders—many of whom were from Eden Theological Seminary in St. Louis—and officials of the St. Louis Industrial Union Council.[2]

From the start, Mitchell was convinced that the Communists in St. Louis were out to embarrass STFU in retaliation for the expulsion

1. Josephine (Johnson) Cannon, letter to author, Oct. 29, 1967.

2. See Al Murphy to T. J. North, Jan. 18, 1939; Mitchell, "Report of the Secretary, 1939," p. 3, STFU Papers.

of Claude Williams and E. B. McKinney. He felt that those Communists who had helped organize the sharecroppers' committee were exploiting Whitfield and the other members of the group, without regard for the best interests of the Missouri croppers. Many members of the committee met Mitchell's approval. Earlier, he had had contact with some of them, and had even requested the support of Josephine Johnson, one of its key figures, in helping to raise money for National Sharecropper Week. Although Mitchell realized that the sharecropper committee contained "a lot of good friends of the STFU," and while he approved of their efforts, the union secretary felt that they did not understand the political implications of the STFU-UCAPAWA split.[3]

STFU's executive committee sent a letter to John L. Lewis, head of the CIO, immediately after the demonstration started, accusing UCAPAWA of trying to "inject [the] communist issue into the struggle" in Southeast Missouri. Mitchell specifically charged that Whitfield had "been led to believe that no help will be given by [the] CIO unless he follows [the] direction of St. Louis," and UCAPAWA leadership.[4] The executive committee requested the CIO to help directly through STFU. The CIO refused to take sides in the dispute, however, insisting only that STFU had the right to act officially in Southeast Missouri. After this, Mitchell claimed UCAPAWA "faded out of the picture officially," but he believed that the union's voice continued to be heard through the Communists who were members of the St. Louis Sharecroppers Committee.[5]

Once the demonstration started, Mitchell was certain that the Henderson faction was "frankly out to seize the opportunity to take over and disrupt the STFU in Missouri."[6] Looking back on the event in later years, Mitchell was convinced that Henderson thought that STFU's preoccupation with the demonstration would make an opportune moment to take over the control of the union.[7]

3. Josephine Johnson to Mitchell, Dec. 21, 1938; Executive Committee, STFU, to John L. Lewis, undated, Jan., 1939; Mitchell to Harriet Young, Feb. 17, 1939; Butler to Josephine Johnson, Dec. 11, 1939; Howard Kester to Mitchell, Jan. 27, 1939; Kester to Mitchell, May 10, 1939, *ibid.*

4. Executive Committee, STFU, to John L. Lewis, undated, Jan. 1939. Mitchell also sent word to the CIO in St. Louis. See Mitchell to Bert Tavender, CIO Regional Director, St. Louis, Jan. 14, 1939, *ibid.*

5. Telegram, John Brophy to J. R. Butler, Jan. 17, 1939, *bid.*

6. Mitchell, "Report of the Secretary, 1939," p. 4, *ibid.*

7. Mitchell, "Oral History," p. 113, *ibid.*

Henderson's efforts to control Whitfield, Mitchell further believed, were part of a sinister plot by UCAPAWA to establish dual unions in each state, and thereby usurp control. This plan, Mitchell felt, had started in the summer of 1938, when Henderson tried to set up a dual organization in Oklahoma under Odis L. Sweeden, the organizer for STFU in that state.[8] The Sharecroppers' Committee in St. Louis, according to Mitchell's way of thinking, was nothing more than a facade for the party's conspiracy. The Communists have "set up a Committee to Rehabilitate Sharecroppers composed of interested liberals under their direction,"he wrote, "and have tried to use it to stir up dissention among the people." Furthermore, the union Secretary said, the Communists hope to "break the Mo. locals off and establish a separate organization chartered direct with [UCAPAWA]."[9]

Mitchell sent Howard Kester to St. Louis to try to bring Whitfield back to Memphis, where, hopefully, he would be out of UCAPAWA's grasp. For a while it worked, and Whitfield temporarily got back into STFU's good graces. After talking to Whitfield in St. Louis, Howard Kester wrote to Mitchell that the Negro leader now felt UCAPAWA was a "botheration" to him and he would soon "decide to 'get out.' "[10]

Mitchell then sold Whitfield on the idea of capitalizing on the demonstration by making a speaking trip around the country. Mitchell hoped to use the event in Southeast Missouri which had captured the nation's headlines to try to raise money for STFU, and also to help publicize National Sharecroppers Week, which was scheduled for the last week in March. Whitfield spoke in Chicago, New York and Washington at the end of January and early February. The trip culminated in Washington with a visit to the White House where Whitfield talked privately with government officials and on one occasion directly with the President.[11]

Whitfield was fond of telling the story of his experience with Roosevelt at the White House. When the President asked him if he

8. An Open Letter to Friends of STFU, Oct. 1, 1939, p. 5; Mitchell to Philip Murray, March 14, 1939; Mitchell to Butler, Feb. 4, 1939; Mitchell to J. B. Nathan, Feb. 15, 1939, *ibid.*

9. Mitchell to J. B. Nathan, Feb. 15, 1939, *ibid.*

10. Kester to Mitchell, Jan. 27, 1939, *ibid.*

11. "Minutes, National Executive Meeting, Memphis Tennessee, Jan. 21, 1939"; Mitchell to Butler, Feb. 4 or 5, 1939; Mitchell to J. B. Nathan, Feb. 15, 1939, *ibid.*

were a Communist, the Negro minister asked Roosevelt to define what he meant. FDR said a Communist was someone who wanted to overthrow the government, and take something that did not belong to him without paying anything for it. Whitfield then replied that he recalled reading in his McGuffey's Reader how the white man took the Indian's land and overthrew his government when he came to this country. Thus, he suggested to the President, the white people are the real Communists. Whitfield liked to end the story by saying that Roosevelt later recalled that this was one of the few times that someone had thought faster than he did in the White House. "Anytime a Negro goes to Washington," Whitfield said, "he's going to have to out-think everyone else."[12]

Mitchell felt the speaking trip around the country did a great deal to "open Whitfield's eyes" to the danger of UCAPAWA, and by the time it was over it looked as though the Negro leader had seen the light. On February 5, Whitfield wrote a letter to all STFU locals urging them to forget about UCAPAWA and to work for STFU.[13]

Nevertheless Whitfield had not been completely willing to break his relationship with, or his belief in, UCAPAWA. Indicative of his mixed feelings at the time was the fact that he crossed out much of the harsh language written about UCAPAWA before the letter was sent out to the locals. In the first draft, for example, Whitfield had said UCAPAWA was "mostly all communists and reds and we don't want to get mixed up with any radical bunch," but decided to mark this out before he mailed the letter. In his final draft, his strongest statement was nothing more than a mild rebuke for the International UCAPAWA. He said that in his travels around the country he had found that "people don't like the UCAPAWA," and urged all members to "build up our own STFU union and make it the greatest organization in the United States."[14]

Although Whitfield's letter was a clear rejection of UCAPAWA and an endorsement of STFU, his heart was not in it. Indeed, his return to the STFU fold was extremely short-lived. By the middle of February, he was back in St. Louis in an office in the Urban League, and this time he was there to stay. Mitchell had planned

12. Mrs. Zella Whitfield, interview with author, Dec. 19, 1965; see also *Southeast Missourian,* Feb. 8, 1939.

13. Mitchell to J. B. Nathan, Feb. 15, 1939; Butler to Mitchell, Feb. 4 or 5, 1939; Whitfield to All Locals in Missouri, Feb. 5, 1939, STFU Papers.

14. Whitfield to All Locals in Missouri, Feb. 15, 1939, *ibid.*

to appear with Whitfield in Washington before the Senate Committee on Unemployment at the end of February, but Whitfield refused to leave St. Louis.[15] He had now joined forces completely with the Henderson faction.

On February 24, Whitfield wrote from St. Louis to all STFU locals saying that letters from croppers were pouring into his mailbox complaining about the shabby relief job STFU had done in Southeast Missouri. He called for a separate state convention of Missouri STFU locals to decide whether to support STFU or join with UCAPAWA and the CIO.

Whitfield now claimed that his earlier letter appealing to croppers to leave UCAPAWA and stick with STFU had "bounced like a rubber ball," to use his phrase, and people everywhere were turning to Henderson and the CIO for help. "The people, in so many words," he said, "told me to go to hell. . . ."[16]

Mitchell wrote to Whitfield, pleading with him to come to Memphis, reminding him that the Communists in St. Louis were using him and "other good people [there] for their own ends." Mitchell specifically accused the St. Louis committee of using funds raised ostensibly to help the croppers for the purpose of taking over the Missouri locals of STFU.[17]

Whitfield replied to these charges in strong language, and severely criticized Mitchell for his accusation. By this time, both men were openly opposing one another, their differences now due to a number of factors. Recalling the event later, Mitchell felt that Whitfield chose to side with UCAPAWA in the dispute because he was given special treatment. "Whitfield abandoned the STFU," he insisted, "because the top officers of the CIO opened an office for him in St. Louis and gave him a secretary."[18]

Undoubtedly, Whitfield welcomed the chance to obtain a private office and personal secretary, but it is highly unlikely that the Negro farm leader left STFU—an organization for which he had suffered much and about which he had earlier been so enthusiastic—for such a small and transient reward. The more likely explanation is that the differences between Whitfield and the STFU leadership were

15. Lawrence Westbook to Mitchell, Feb. 20, 1939; Mitchell to Harriet Young, Feb. 24, 1939, *ibid.*

16. Whitfield to All Locals, Feb. 24, 1939; Whitfield to F. R. Betton, Feb. 27, 1939; Mitchell to Kester, Feb. 26, 1939; *ibid.*

17. Mitchell to Whitfield, Feb. 26, 1939, *ibid.*

18. Mitchell, letter to author, Jan. 21, 1966.

deep seated, and the events in recent weeks in the demonstration had brought these differences to a dramatic, and at times, rather emotional culmination.

No doubt Whitfield was quite disturbed by the fact that STFU's relief office had closed in Blytheville February 18, while many of the campers were still without jobs and in desperate condition. Mitchell decided to close the Blytheville office after the Farm Security Administration had indicated that needy campers would be given rehabilitation grants.[19] FSA had increased its funds and sent additional personnel into the Bootheel immediately after the demonstration, with orders to make subsistence grants wherever required.[20] Moreover, at the end of January, when R. G. Smith, the regional director of the FSA, announced that tents were being sent to the Sweet Home Church, he also pointed out that work on allocating the emergency grants was being speeded up. Smith estimated that those families who were eligible might receive grants as high as ten to twenty-four dollars a month.[21]

Theoretically, most of the homeless campers could now expect to get at least some government relief. Yet, because of the criticism expressed by Charleston planters and businessmen, the FSA, on February 8, stopped all relief checks in Mississippi County, where the Sweet Home Church group was located, until applications could be investigated. Members of the Charleston community had charged duplication in the granting of relief checks, and insisted that the emergency grants, which had started after the demonstration, should be stopped because they felt an emergency no longer existed.[22]

A "protest telegram" was sent in early February to FSA headquarters, recommending that all grants be stopped pending an immediate investigation of the relief program. The Charleston planters estimated that FSA grants would soon total $40,000 per month to 2,000 heads of families in Mississippi County. Moreover, the planters pointed out that beside the FSA resettlement grants, the county had 480 heads on direct relief and 670 working on WPA. The

19. Mitchell, "Report of the Secretary, 1939," p. 4, STFU Papers.

20. Will Alexander to Henry Wallace, with attached memo for Mr. Henry Kannee, Jan. 19, 1939, NA, RG 16.

21. R. G. Smith to J. R. Butler, Feb. 27, 1939; Mitchell to James Myers, Feb. 10, 1939; Mitchell to John Herling, Feb. 10, 1939, STFU Papers; *Post-Dispatch,* Jan. 25, 1939.

22. *Southeast Missourian,* Feb. 2 and 3, 1939.

telegram estimated that if aid to the aged, blind pensioners, and dependent children were added, 10,000 to 12,000 would be getting public aid in Mississippi County.[23]

An investigation of what was termed a "disgraceful" situation was demanded to determine specifically who in the FSA office arranged "to make indiscriminate payments to all askers." The planters insisted that they did not mind "helping [the] deserving needy" but were vehemently opposed to "reckless giving to [the] undeserving." Since no emergency existed in Mississippi County, the telegram concluded, "indiscriminate wasteful giving is bringing numbers of undesirables to this county to get easy money and threaten to overwhelm us."[24]

One of the landlords in Mississippi County said most of those who were receiving grants of four dollars a month for each member of the family "have no earthly need of them, just use the money to buy trinkets." The granting of relief checks, he argued, only "tends to demoralize our tenants."[25]

Congressman Zimmerman also put pressure on the FSA to withhold additional assistance until an investigation could be made. By this time, Zimmerman apparently was also convinced there had been a conspiracy in the demonstration. It was "secretly organized" by certain "social leaders" in St. Louis, he later told a House committee, a "diabolical effort of a certain group there."[26]

Never popular in the Bootheel, the FSA undoubtedly came under fire at this time because of the embarrassment and resentment many planters and officials still felt over the recent demonstration. Actually, the FSA was already having a reappraisal of its whole program in the Bootheel when the Mississippi County investigation was requested. The national office had already announced at the end of January that the tremendous number of applications for rehabilitation grants since the demonstration had "taxed to capacity" the county offices in the Bootheel. Will Alexander, the FSA head,

23. Henry Wallace to Orville Zimmermann, with attached telegram from Charleston, Mo., Feb. 16, 1939, NA, RG 16.

24. *Ibid.*

25. Quoted in Charleston *Enterprise Courier,* Feb. 9, 1939.

26. Mitchell to James Myers, Feb. 10, 1939, STFU Papers; Zimmerman, U.S. Congress, House, Select Committee of the House Committee on Agriculture, *Hearings to Investigate the Activities of the Farm Security Administration,* 78th Cong., 1st Sess., 1943, pp. 691–692.

announced that over 4,000 relief grants, averaging about twenty dollars each were made to about 3,500 tenant farmer families in four Southeast Missouri counties during the month of January. "We are robbing other parts of the country of funds they should receive," Alexander said, "in order to make grants to the Southeast Missouri families."[27]

When the FSA announced that the investigation would take place in Mississippi County, it emphasized that emergency grants would be continued to those deserving families who had established their need. A large number of croppers in Mississippi County, however, had their grant checks stopped by this action. To compound the woes of the Sweet Home Church campers, this happened at the same time that the St. Louis Sharecroppers' Committee announced that it was out of funds. Once again, these croppers were without aid of any kind.[28]

Mitchell was aware of this at the time the decision was made to close the relief center at Blytheville, but he had little choice. Union funds were exhausted, and "nothing was coming in" by way of relief. Perhaps most importantly, the Church Emergency Relief Committee, the chief fund-raiser for the Bootheel demonstrators, had indicated that money had stopped coming in to its headquarters.[29] Moreover, by the middle of February, Mitchell was becoming preoccupied with plans for National Sharecropper Week (NSW).

NSW was a highly important occasion for Mitchell because this was one of the few times during the year that STFU launched an all-out campaign to raise union money. The event, first held in 1937, was sponsored by STFU in conjunction with the Socialist party's Workers Defense League. In 1939, NSW was scheduled for the last week in March and was thus beginning to take up a large part of the union secretary's time. Furthermore, the activities of the Southeast Missouri demonstration were beginning to conflict directly with NSW. For example, in order to obtain additional funds for the Missouri sharecroppers at this time, Mitchell would have had to launch a new appeal for individual contributions, something

27. Quoted in *Southeast Missourian,* Jan. 25, 1939, Feb. 8, 1939.

28. *Post-Dispatch,* Feb. 9 and 11, 1939. See Peter Wilderness, president of Marston, Missouri, local, to Butler, Feb. 10, 1939, STFU Papers.

29. Mitchell to All Locals, Feb. 21, 1939; Mitchell to Savannah Warr, Feb. 24, 1939; Mitchell to Ike Tripp, Feb. 20, 1939; James Myers to STFU, Feb. 6, 1939, *ibid.*

he did not warmly welcome, since he would be shortly soliciting the same people for aid for NSW.[30]

Mitchell was now beginning to think of the value of Whitfield and the publicity from the demonstration in terms of possible help for raising additional funds for STFU during NSW. As already indicated, Whitfield's speaking trip was designed for that purpose. Gardner Jackson, STFU's representative in Washington, wrote to Mitchell on February 1, 1939, that it was "too late to utilize [Whitfield] on the current relief situation [in Congress], but it is entirely possible that he can be of value in anticipation of the next relief appropriation."[31]

This by no means meant that Mitchell had forgotten about the Bootheel croppers. Though outside contributions had come to a virtual standstill by the middle of February, Butler and other STFU officials continued to make clandestine trips into Southeast Missouri to take what few supplies they received at the Memphis office, even after the Blytheville headquarters closed. Moreover, the union constantly wrote letters to the secretary of war, Mrs. Roosevelt, and other government officials to try to obtain aid for the Sweet Home Church campers, and Butler relentlessly requested the FSA to continue grants to those who were needy.[32]

Whitfield, however, bitterly resented Mitchell's efforts to raise funds for the union and to promote NSW while his people were still hungry and homeless. Whitfield felt Mitchell was more concerned about the status of the union than he was about getting relief to the campers. Whether or not Whitfield's resentment was justified is debatable; his appraisal, however, was quite correct, for at this point, Mitchell's prime concern was the continuation of the union.

Mitchell's concern was not entirely without justification because at that moment the union was on shaky financial ground. It would have made little sense to continue aiding the campers if in the

30. National Advisory Committee on Farm Labor, *Farm Labor Organizing 1905–1967* (July 1967), pp. 24–25; Harriet Young to Butler and Mitchell, Jan. 19, 1939, STFU Papers.

31. Gardner Jackson to Mitchell, Feb. 1, 1939, STFU Papers.

32. Butler to W. B. Lloyd, Jr., Feb. 28, 1939; Butler to Harry H. Woodring, secretary of war, Feb. 20, 1939; Mitchell to Mrs. Roosevelt, undated; Butler to Mrs. Roosevelt, Feb. 20, 1939; Malvira C. Thompson (secretary to Mrs. Roosevelt) to Butler, April 27, 1939; Butler to R. G. Smith, regional director, FSA, Feb. 20, 1939; Butler to R. C. Smith, March 27, 1939, *ibid.*

process the union would have collapsed economically. The union obviously could not provide relief indefinitely, and the government's promise to increase its assistance seemed to Mitchell a logical clue to terminate STFU's aid. Thus, the decision was made to close the Blytheville office. Whitfield, however, saw the action as a sellout, and the entire affair further widened the gap between STFU and the UCAPAWA. Butler best summarized the problem when he wrote: "Our inability to give unlimited relief . . . has complicated the situation in Southeast Missouri beyond what the UCAPAWA difficulty would have been."[33]

The closing of the Blytheville office seems to have been the turning point in Whitfield's decision to abandon STFU. It is certainly more than coincidental that Whitfield returned to St. Louis and joined the Henderson group immediately after February 18, when the Blytheville relief center closed. This action on the part of STFU apparently confirmed Whitfield's growing suspicions of the union's relief role in the strike. There had already been various charges that STFU's relief was not getting to everyone on the roadside, and UCAPAWA had specifically accused the union of mishandling union funds. UCAPAWA's accustations were no doubt politically motivated, and there is no evidence to support them. Anticipating trouble, Mitchell was careful to have union relief funds itemized by an independent auditor, and he made them available for inspection at the time. As already indicated, virtually all of the money raised for the croppers was used for their relief.[34]

There was some validity to the charge, however, that the relief was not getting to all of the campers, but this seems to have been largely beyond STFU's control. The problem was a physical rather than a political one. Union headquarters, located at Blytheville, was over fifty miles away from Charleston, the approximate location of the largest group of campers at the Sweet Home Church. The difficulty in getting supplies over that distance was compounded by the fact that state police had orders to keep union officials out of the area.

The head of the STFU local at Wyatt—outside Charleston—

33. Butler to Kester, Feb. 18, 1939, *ibid.*

34. W. R. Fischer and Whitfield to Henderson, March 20, 1939; Kester to Mitchell, Jan. 27, 1939; Mitchell, "Report of the Secretary, 1939," p. 4, *ibid.*

wrote to the Memphis office that "the temporary relief in Blytheville is good. . . . Tho most of our members have no way to get to Blytheville." He then requested that the union establish an office at Charleston, or somewhere closer.[35] Howard Kester had already written to Mitchell on January 27, after visiting St. Louis, that if STFU did not get help to Charleston immediately, "there is going to be a severe kick back from the people in St. Louis and maybe elsewhere."[36]

STFU never established an office at Charleston or anywhere else in Missouri. The difficulty of working unharmed in Missouri was the main reason the relief center had originally been established in Arkansas. Perhaps another important reason STFU was reluctant to establish a relief site as far north as Charleston, though, was the fear that UCAPAWA might be able to control it, because of its being closer to St. Louis.

Already the St. Louis Sharecroppers Committee had requested a Charleston office. Sidney Williams, president of the St. Louis Urban League, and the representative for the sharecroppers' committee, had sent a letter to STFU headquarters on February 8, saying he had "been informed that [the] croppers around Charleston [are] in serious need of relief." The "distance of Blytheville from [the] needy area," Williams said, "apparently makes a station further north necessary. PLEASE WIRE IMMEDIATELY IF YOU WILL SET UP RELIEF CENTER IN THAT DISTRICT."[37]

Whatever the reason, STFU, rather than set up a northern relief site, decided instead to turn over funds to committees representing the groups still in the camps, and rely on them to pass the help along to their own people. "Since it was dangerous, in fact well nigh impossible, for cars or trucks from Arkansas to go into the area," J. R. Butler later wrote, "we were compelled to furnish money to committees of the various groups" who in turn would then "come into Blytheville in their own cars and get the things we provided for them."[38]

Whitfield later claimed that STFU leaders made "us pay our own

35. H. Turner to Butler and Mitchell, Feb. 17, 1939, *ibid.*

36. Kester to Mitchell, Jan. 27, 1939. See also Sam Romers to Mitchell, Feb. 13, 1939; telegram, Kester to Mitchell, Jan. 24, 1939, *ibid.*

37. Sidney Williams to STFU, Feb. 8, 1939, *ibid.*

38. Butler to Oliver Hotz, Dec. 2, 1939, *ibid.*

gas and oil money to get a little relief" in Blytheville, but STFU maintained that Howard Kester had gone "to every camp and left money with which to buy medicine and with which to pay expenses of cars to go to Blytheville. . . ."[39]

Butler insisted that F. R. Betton, a union officer, "made several trips into the Charleston area to take food," but there is strong evidence to indicate that very little, if any, STFU relief got that far north.[40] STFU answered the allegation that relief did not reach some of the croppers in the camps with the explanation that some of the committee heads must have been unscrupulous and failed to pass the assistance along. "We later found," Butler wrote, "that some of these committees were lacking in honor and honesty."[41]

Whitfield did not accept this explanation, and later he accused STFU of using the relief as a tool in its feud with UCAPAWA, since both organizations were now jockeying for support of the Missouri locals. Whitfield claimed STFU gave help only to those who would "support them," and not "for relief of those that really needed it."[42]

Part of Whitfield's growing resentment must be in part attributed to the fact that he was frustrated by his own economic plight. He received very little pay for his work in STFU. After his speaking engagements following the demonstration, his economic condition was worse than ever because he received little monetary benefit from his speaking trip, except reimbursements for expenses.[43]

He was obviously disturbed that he now lacked funds to help his campers, and especially bothered by his struggle to obtain enough money to bring his family to St. Louis. Mrs. Whitfield and the children had had to flee from the LaForge Project at the beginning of the demonstration, without any of their possessions. His family was then "in as bad a shape as the people out on the road," Whitfield wrote to F. R. Betton, "or worse because the people out on the road

39. W. R. Fischer and Whitfield to Henderson, March 20, 1939; Butler to the STFU Locals and Members in Southeast Missouri, March 31, 1939, *ibid.*

40. Butler to the STFU Locals and Members in Southeast Missouri, March 31, 1939, *ibid.* The author interviewed a number of the participants in the demonstration who were located in this region, and without exception, they claim they received no relief from STFU.

41. Butler to Oliver Hotz, Dec. 2, 1939, STFU Papers.

42. W. R. Fischer and Whitfield, to Henderson, March 20, 1939, *ibid.*

43. "Annual Report for STFU for year Dec. 30, 1939," p. 10; Mitchell to Purnell Benson, Feb. 21, 1939; Whitfield to F. R. Betton, Feb. 27, 1939; Whitfield to Mitchell, Feb. 28, 1939, *ibid.*

will get govmt help soon but the govmt will be afraid to help me until the political fire cools down which will take some time."[44]

Whitfield's family at first had sought refuge in Cape Girardeau, but were still in danger until they could be moved further north to St. Louis. Since Whitfield himself had escaped public attack by fleeing to the north during the demonstration, many frustrated lynchmen had vented their spleen by harassing his family. Despite efforts to hide out in Cape Girardeau, Mrs. Whitfield later recalled, there were several incidents of midnight riders passing in front of the house, tossing rocks and hurling choice expletives.[45]

Whitfield's letters during this time constantly speak of his lack of funds and the accompanying futility he felt because he and his family had had to abandon LaForge. He wrote Mitchell that he had lost everything important to him. "My family was moved out . . . and put in a little shack in cape girardeau with[out] any household goods, which means that i have lost the good home and security of my family and everything they had."[46] Whitfield complained to his friends that he was practically penniless. "O. H. [Whitfield] is in need," J. F. Moore, a union leader and close friend, wrote at the end of February. "His family has been moved from the LaForge Project. He says just 5 cts from each local would do him lots of good."[47]

Whitfield—already philosophically inclined toward UCAPAWA and already disturbed over STFU's relief role in the demonstration—undoubtedly drew closer to Henderson because of his own economic frustration. Henderson was able to offer the Negro leader a regular salary in UCAPAWA, no doubt a strong enticement for a man who saw no immediate way out of his sad financial predicament.[48]

Although Mitchell was not oblivious to Whitfield's problem, STFU could hardly compete with Henderson and the financial resources available to him. Howard Kester later pointed out that it was not difficult to understand why Whitfield was strongly attracted by what UCAPAWA had to offer. "Henderson had money and prestige. The future seemed bright and promising," Kester recalled.

44. Whitfield to F. R. Betton, Feb. 27, 1939, *ibid.*
45. Mrs. Zella Whitfield, interview with author, Dec. 19, 1965.
46. Whitfield to Mitchell, Feb. 28, 1939, STFU Papers.
47. J. F. Moore to Rev. R. H. Bradford, Feb. 28, 1939, *ibid.*
48. Mitchell, "Oral History," p. 114, *ibid.*

"Why not? STFU was getting on on virtually nothing—dues coming in a little bit, hardly enough to keep it alive, and here was an organization [UCAPAWA] with all kinds of means, status and prestige."[49]

Early in February Mitchell expressed concern over Whitfield's economic plight. He wrote to Jim Meyers, the prime figure in the Church Emergency Relief Committee, on February 10, complaining that most of STFU's funds were being sent into Missouri because of the exigency of the situation there, and expressed the hope that some of the money raised for the campers might be used for families of the organizers. "The most pressing need is that of Rev. O. H. Whitfield . . .," Mitchell wrote. "He is now a refugee from Missouri and his family is being threatened."[50]

Nevertheless, Mitchell could not help Whitfield a great deal. After all, STFU's funds were still exhausted, and Mitchell had no immediate way of getting more, though he tried. He again went to the CIO in an effort to obtain help, but failed.[51] Mitchell's mistake, however, was not his inability to raise funds, but his seeming willingness—in Whitfield's eyes—to abandon the Bootheel campers' cause in his efforts to do so.

As already indicated, Mitchell's efforts to exploit the demonstration by using it to publicize NSW were in part justified because of the union's desperate financial condition. Despite the handicap under which he was working, however, Mitchell's preoccupation with plans for NSW at the expense of both Whitfield's and the sharecropper's welfare was a tactical error, but only because Mitchell misjudged Whitfield's true feelings.

Mitchell thought his differences with Whitfield only a passing misunderstanding, vividly evidenced by the fact that he continued making plans to use Whitfield to help raise funds for NSW right up until the end of February, when it finally became obvious to some of the other STFU leaders that Whitfield was "irrevocably lost" to UCAPAWA.[52] Indeed, Mitchell fully expected Whitfield to

49. Howard Kester, interview with author, Aug. 7, 1966. Actually Whitfield's condition improved little after he joined UCAPAWA. Kester saw Whitfield in May in St. Louis and wrote to Mitchell that the Negro leader "seemed to be having considerable difficulty in maintaining himself and his family as funds seemed to be very low" (Kester to Mitchell, May 10, 1939, *ibid.*).

50. Mitchell to Meyers, Feb. 10, 1939, *ibid.*

51. Mitchell to John L. Lewis, Feb. 25, 1939, *ibid.*

52. Evelyn Smith to Harriet Young, Feb. 28, 1939; Harriet Young to Whitfield, Feb. 26, 1939; Mitchell to Harriet Young, March 14, 1939, *ibid.*

return to Memphis and STFU long after the Negro minister had chosen to remain with UCAPAWA and the split between Mitchell and Henderson had disrupted the union. Mitchell later wrote that he "did not abandon hope that Whitfield would return to the STFU until the spring of 1941 when [F. R.] Betton met him at Mr. [Thad] Snow's plantation."[53]

It was unfortunate that the otherwise well-intentioned Mitchell did not accurately sense the extent of Whitfield's alienation and growing resentment. In the final analysis, the explanation for this can only be attributed to the fact that neither man—Whitfield nor Mitchell—was entirely candid with the other. Had they been, much of their difficulty it seems, could have been eliminated.

This was especially unfortunate for Mitchell because his alienation of Whitfield lost him enormous political capital in the struggle with UCAPAWA. The Communist faction in St. Louis was undoubtedly able to exploit Whitfield's increasing unhappiness, and apparently made even greater capital of it because of his race.

Although Mitchell and STFU seem to have been innocent of any real racial prejudice, the union's inability to do more to help Whitfield and the Negro campers in Southeast Missouri permitted charges of discrimination by those who opposed its efforts. Officially stated STFU policy was biracial. Realistically, however, the union frequently left the decision of whether to have races mixed or segregated to the individual local.

Evelyn Smith, the STFU Memphis secretary, in a letter to a potential local organizer who had inquired about the problem, stated quite clearly STFU's position. "The decision as to whether or not your local shall have both races represented in it rests entirely with your members," she wrote. "Many locals are mixed. Some are not. The national office," she said, indicating the union's official stand on the issue, "leaves that matter entirely up to the locals. Certainly, it is all right to mix the races in your locals."[54]

Howard Kester, STFU's unofficial theoretician, described himself as one who was "very sensitive to any kind of discrimination." Kester later recalled that if there was any discrimination in STFU at this time, he must have been "blind to it." Union leaders, white and black, traveled together, ate together, and invited each into the other's homes. There were instances, however, Kester later recalled, when realistically it was politically advantageous for STFU to em-

53. Mitchell, undated memo to Burgess, General Histories Folder, *ibid.*
54. Evelyn Smith to J. A. Learue, March 9, 1939, *ibid.*

ploy either a white or a Negro organizer in a particular area. Sometimes, Kester said, "a job demanded a white person," or a Negro.[55] Indeed, the union's decision to use Whitfield as an organizer in the Bootheel, was no doubt motivated in part by the fact that the majority of the sharecroppers and farm workers in this area were Negro. Though the records do not specify, most Missouri locals were probably segregated, and since Whitfield was a Negro, he was a logical choice to be the Missouri organizer.[56]

Although these STFU tactics demonstrated more political realism than flagrant discrimination, they nonetheless were fuel for the fire for STFU critics, and they provided an open target for the more militant faction who sought to embarrass the union in whatever way it could.

Claude Williams, bitter over his ejection from the union, was convinced that STFU was a "sectarian, splinter racket of a few whites."[57] Williams was with Whitfield in St. Louis at this time and no doubt tried hard to convince the Negro Bootheel leader that race was a factor in guiding STFU policy. Whitfield himself seldom expressed his views on race. He always liked to think of himself as one concerned with the plight of the economically deprived—a condition, to his way of thinking, that transcended race, color, or creed. He was, nonetheless, conscious of his color. One of the things that had helped change some of his ideas about STFU during his speaking trip following the demonstration was a talk with Roy Wilkins of the NAACP in Chicago. Presumably, Wilkins convinced Whitfield that UCAPAWA was hurting the cause of unionism by exploiting STFU's race policy. Mitchell later wrote that Whitfield's talk with Wilkins "put the finishing touches to the change in his attitude" about UCAPAWA.[58]

Apparently Claude Williams succeeded in communicating at least some of his ideas to Whitfield while the two men were together in St. Louis. After his return there, Whitfield became much

55. Howard Kester, interview with author, Aug. 7, 1966.

56. See, for example, Mitchell to W. B. Moore, Feb. 26, 1939; and F. R. Betton to Mitchell, Feb. 24, 1939, STFU Papers. In both letters, references are made to efforts at organizing "white" locals in Southeast Missouri.

57. Claude Williams, tape recording to author, March 25, 1966.

58. Josephine (Johnson) Cannon, letter to author, Oct. 29, 1967; Mitchell to Butler, Feb. 4 or 5, 1939, STFU Papers. For a thorough discussion of the efforts of the Communist party to exploit Negro discontent, see Wilson Record, *The Negro and the Communist Party* (Chapel Hill, 1951).

more race conscious. The year after the demonstration, he wrote that the STFU-UCAPAWA split was "not a battle between two unions, but simply a feud between a few white men in both unions." Moreover, after his return to St. Louis, Whitfield began thinking of his union accomplishments in terms of how much the Negro, specifically, was helped—something he had not done before.

After some success in getting Negroes on local county committees in Missouri, Whitfield was quite pleased. "I worked hard to get such a committee with a man of our race on it in each county," he wrote, "because it meant so much to us." Whitfield wrote that it did not matter "whether he belonged to the UCAPAWA [or] the STFU or whether he belonged to any union or not just so there was a Negro on it."[59]

Perhaps indicative of the influence Claude Williams had on Whitfield was the fact that the Negro leader quit union organizing later in his life to work and travel with Williams. And perhaps indicative of the effect that UCAPAWA's charges of discrimination had on STFU was that after the union split with UCAPAWA, it sent in a white man, W. M. Tanner, as the new organizer for Missouri.[60]

Thus, race played a role in the feud between Mitchell and Whitfield. But it was only a minor role. The most significant issue dividing the Negro and the union secretary, and the real irreconcilable factor in the STFU-UCAPAWA split, was not race, but communism. Mitchell was convinced that Whitfield was being lured into the Communist camp unknowingly. "Those of us who had known and respected him" Mitchell later recalled, "were inclined to believe that [Whitfield] was merely a victim of sinister forces working against the interests of . . . STFU, which he did not recognize until he was trapped." After the struggle was over, Mitchell wrote to other members of the union: "We should not be vindictive—Whitfield is only a weak man and a victim of circumstances."[61] Actually, Whitfield was fully aware of the Communist element in St. Louis, but was not especially worried about it. Whitfield wrote Mitchell and criticized him for categorizing as a Communist any-

59. Whitfield to F. R. Betton, undated, 1940, STFU Papers. Negroes had long been excluded from representation on AAA Committees. See Myrdal, *An American Dilemma,* pp. 258–259.

60. Mrs. Zella Whitfield, interview with author, Dec. 19, 1965; Whitfield, undated and unpublished article, Owen Whitfield Papers; STFU *News,* April 27, 1939, STFU Papers.

61. See Mitchell, "Report of the Secretary, 1939," p. 4, *ibid.*

one who "doesnt suite [*sic*] the fancies or comply with the wishes of some other person or group of persons."[62]

Whitfield was an aggressive union organizer, but he was no revolutionary. He "got his ideas from the Bible," Claude Williams later said, "rather than from the Russians."[63] Completely committed to a doctrine of nonviolence, Whitfield once said: "We have a more better and more peaceful way to work out our program and obtain our object than resorting to violence." Indeed, the Negro leader was convinced that unless a more aggressive attitude was taken by union organizers, the cause would be lost to the more militant factions. The reactionism on the part of the planters, he wrote in 1937, made farm workers "more and more susceptible to radicalism and communism and all the other 'isms.' We must stop it and nip it in the bud."[64]

Whitfield opposed Communist methods, but he did not fear Communist aid and support. In fact, he welcomed it, primarily because he felt he had very little to lose. "No one can loose something he or she haven't got," he wrote to Mitchell. Since his people were in desperate condition, he accepted help where he could get it. "Must I ask every person i meet what his politic are?" Whitfield asked.[65] To him a person's politics mattered little as long as that person wanted to help. As a perceptive observer of the incident noted, Whitfield "did not take blood tests" when he appealed for aid.[66] The Bootheel minister had an absolute confidence in his own ability to lead his people; he therefore never feared usurpation by Communists or anyone else.

Mitchell, on the other hand, as a confirmed Socialist, could not afford such a liberal political attitude. Mitchell was dedicated to building a strong union and was convinced that this could not be done with Communist interference.[67] Already Norman Thomas

62. Whitfield to Mitchell, Feb. 28, 1939, *ibid.*

63. Claude Williams, tape recording to author, March 25, 1966. The idea of taking the planters' possessions and dividing them among the tenants, for example, was foreign to Whitfield's way of thinking. "We wish to make it plain," he once wrote, "that we are not organizing to come [into] posesion of the big mans wealth and land" (Whitfield to Editor, Charleston *Enterprise Courier,* Oct. 16, 1938, Thad Snow Papers).

64. Whitfield to Editor, Charleston *Enterprise Courier,* Dec. 23, 1937, Oct. 20, 1938.

65. Whitfield to Mitchell, Feb. 28, 1939, STFU Papers.

66. John Stewart, interview with author, May 1, 1966.

67. Mitchell, "An Open Letter to Friends of the Sharecroppers from the STFU," March 1939, STFU Papers.

had expressed concern to Mitchell over Communist influence in UCAPAWA. "We as friends of the STFU and as Socialists," Thomas later wrote, "must see that our house is put in such order that we can present no unexposed places for successful Communist attack."[68]

When Whitfield insisted on staying on in St. Louis, he sealed his fate with STFU, because Mitchell was ready now for a complete break from Henderson and UCAPAWA. By the middle of February, Mitchell was writing that he was hoping Henderson would sever ties with STFU once and for all. "Some of our folks are sending up prayers," he wrote, "in hopes that he [Henderson] will kick us out so we will be thru with the damn mess."[69] Henderson apparently had already heard STFU's prayers.

68. Norman Thomas to Messrs. Kester, Mitchell, McCallister, April 7, 1939. See also Ward Rodgers to J. R. Butler (personal and confidential), March 3, 1939; Norman Thomas to Frank McCallister, April 5, 1939; and Mitchell to Norman Thomas, April 10, 1939, *ibid.*

69. Mitchell to J. B. Nathan, Feb. 15, 1939, *ibid.*

9 The STFU–UCAPAWA Split

At the end of January, Henderson sent out letters ordering STFU locals to disregard the action of the Cotton Plant meeting and directed that they pay dues directly to UCAPAWA. On February 14, the STFU national executive council countered this action by passing a resolution saying that dues would be paid only through the STFU Memphis office.[1]

By this time the argument between STFU and UCAPAWA had reached the emotional stage, and both sides had dipped their pens in vitriol. Henderson was accusing Mitchell of "red-baiting," while Mitchell consistently argued that Henderson followed a "Communist rule or ruin policy."[2] Mitchell charged that UCAPAWA wanted to use STFU for political, rather than for economic, purposes. "Mitchell and Butler, in their charges of communism," Henderson wrote bitterly, "are speaking the language of the Southern landlords and the Dies [Un-American Activities] Committee."[3]

1. Henderson to Mitchell, Jan. 28, 1939; Mitchell to International Executive Board, UCAPAWA, Feb. 14, 1939, STFU Papers.

2. Butler to Whitfield, March 28, 1939; Henderson to Butler and Mitchell, March 1, 1939; press release, STFU, March 12, 1939, *ibid.*

3. Henderson, quoted in *Daily Worker,* March 16, 1939; Mr. Howard Kester, interview with author, Aug. 7, 1965. See also Vera Rony, "Sorrow Song in Black and White," *New South* (Summer, 1967), Southern Regional Council publication.

UCAPAWA accused Butler of being a reactionary and alleged that he worked "in the interests of the rich planters" against the croppers. Al Murphy charged that Butler tried to encourage croppers to go to Mississippi, where they would have to "work for plantation owners under worse conditions" than those in Missouri.[4] Actually Butler and W. M. Tanner had gone into the Bootheel at the time of the demonstration and, according to Herbert Little's account, "advised the campers to accept accommodations offered to them by farm owners and to leave the Highway if the accommodations were liveable."[5] But this action hardly represented "reactionism."

Both Butler and Mitchell were justifiably cautious at the beginning of the demonstration, primarily because STFU had never employed the protest demonstration as a tool in dealing with the Southern planters. Moreover, Butler had personally experienced violent reactions by planters in Arkansas previously, and since he was personally unacquainted with the attitudes of Southeast Missouri planters, his action was understandable in the early days of the demonstration. The suggestion that the croppers leave the highway and accept a better offer if a landlord made it was no doubt motivated by an honest concern about the safety and welfare of the union members in the Bootheel. After the demonstration proved to be successful, both Butler and Mitchell became quite enthusiastic about it, and there is no evidence to indicate that STFU ever entertained the notion of persuading the Missouri croppers to move to Mississippi and accept worse working conditions.

When UCAPAWA charged that Butler and Mitchell mishandled union relief funds collected to help the Missouri croppers, STFU countered with the charge that Henderson and UCAPAWA had not spent a single penny on the demonstration.[6] Although mixed with emotion, Mitchell's charges seem to have been authentic. Apparently Henderson gave no direct financial support to the demonstration.

4. Al Murphy, *Daily Worker,* March 15, 1939.

5. Herbert Little, memo to Aubrey Williams, "Subject: Eyewitness accounts of dispersal of roadside camps of farmers by Sheriff in New Madrid County near Sikeston, Missouri, Sunday, Jan. 15, 1939," *Selected Documents,* Roosevelt Library.

6. Whitfield and W. R. Fischer to Henderson, March 20, 1939; Mitchell to Philip Ham, Feb. 24, 1939; Butler and Mitchell to all locals, Feb. 18, 1939; statement issued by Butler and Mitchell in behalf of the Executive Committee of the STFU, March 11, 1939, STFU Papers.

He did endorse the work Whitfield and the St. Louis Sharecroppers' Committee were doing, and he did advocate that the federal government not only assist the Bootheel croppers, but that it also do something about correcting the injustices of the farm program throughout the country. Henderson also sent telegrams to the AAA, FSA, WPA, and Governor Stark demanding immediate action to assist the homeless campers in Southeast Missouri.[7] But Henderson, like Brophy and the CIO, never ventured beyond the role of political gadfly—sending hotly worded telegrams demanding governmental action. Neither provided direct financial assistance, and neither chose to become actively involved in the physical problem of aiding the croppers on the highways. Mitchell labeled UCAPAWA's charge that STFU had misappropriated relief funds as "an effort to cover up their own mishandling of relief and at the same time stir up distrust of the STFU among its members in Missouri."[8]

The final crisis started on February 23, when Henderson sent out letters to several STFU organizers announcing that a reorganization of District IV was about to take place.[9] The UCAPAWA head suggested that those locals that wanted to follow Mitchell and Butler and try to "do better alone" could do so. If they wanted to desert the International, they could remain independent. All the rest, he said would be organized into state groups chartered directly by UCAPAWA. State conventions, Henderson said, would be held immediately in all states in District IV—Arkansas, Oklahoma, and Missouri. Those organizers who helped in the preparation of the state conventions, he said, would be given jobs by UCAPAWA. Henderson's announcement pointed out that Whitfield had already decided to stand by UCAPAWA and was in the process of preparing a state convention to be held in Missouri.[10]

STFU reacted immediately. Mitchell called a special meeting of the executive council. On March 1, the council met and decided to ask all locals to determine by vote whether to affiliate with STFU or UCAPAWA. On the same day, Henderson sent word to Butler and Mitchell that all executive officers of District IV were sus-

7. See *Daily Worker,* Jan. 15, 1939.

8. Mitchell, "Report of the Secretary, 1939," p. 4, STFU Papers.

9. An Open Letter to Friends of STFU, Oct. 1, 1939, p. 7, *ibid.* Identical letters were sent to J. F. Hynds, D. A. Griffin and W. B. Moore, all members of the STFU executive council.

10. Henderson to D. A. Griffin, Feb. 23, 1939, *ibid.* This same letter went to Hynds and Moore.

pended, and that the first state convention, designed to reorganize the union would be held in St. Louis on March 12.[11]

After quickly making copies of Whitfield's letter written February 5 in which he was critical of UCAPAWA, Mitchell circulated them among the STFU locals, hoping to capitalize on Whitfield's popularity in the Bootheel prior to the vote.[12] The union secretary then sent J. R. Butler and a STFU delegation to Washington to try to talk directly with John L. Lewis in an effort to obtain CIO support in the showdown fight.[13]

Lewis himself was busy negotiating with the mine workers and the AFL; thus, STFU officials once again talked to John Brophy who, although trying to continue to maintain neutrality in the dispute, ardently refused to accept STFU's charges that UCAPAWA and CIO held allegiance to communism. "The CIO is not in the habit of guiding its policy by the familiar accusations of 'allegiance to an outside political group,' " he said. Moreover, the "newspaper and other attacks on the CIO have dulled whatever edge this weapon once possessed." Brophy echoed Henderson's charges that STFU was "red-baiting," and he was joined by others who had previously been sympathetic with STFU.[14]

Perhaps the most significant switch occurred when Gardner Jackson, STFU's representative in Washington, turned on Mitchell. Jackson resented Mitchell's charges of Communist domination in UCAPAWA, and thought STFU did not have "a leg to stand on" in its dispute with the parent labor organization. "I am profoundly disillusioned," Jackson wrote to Mitchell, "to find the leadership of [STFU] unable to adjust itself so as to play according to the rules of the trade union game, which it voluntarily chose to accept when it voted to become a part of the UCAPAWA."[15]

In a letter to Henderson, Jackson indicated his support of UCAPAWA in the dispute dispite the differences he had had in the

11. Mitchell to All Locals, March 1, 1939; Henderson to Butler and Mitchell, March 1, 1939, *ibid.*

12. At the top of the statement, Mitchell had printed in capital letters: "HERE ARE SOME OF THE THINGS THAT O. H. WHITFIELD SAID IN A LETTER WHICH HE SENT TO ALL THE MISSOURI LOCALS A FEW DAYS AGO WHILE HE WAS IN NEW YORK" (Mitchell to All Locals, March 1, 1939, *ibid*).

13. Mitchell to John L. Lewis, March 6, 1939; press release, STFU, March 8, 1939, *ibid.*

14. Mitchell, "Report of the Secretary, 1939," p. 5; Brophy to the Editors of *Nation,* March 21, 1939, *ibid.*

15. Gardner Jackson to Mitchell, March 13, 1939, *ibid.*

past with the UCAPAWA president, and pointed out that the CIO was "one of the few hopes in this country" for helping the working man. The STFU leadership, he continued, "must know that the CIO movement is greater than the Southern Tenant Farmers Union." In conclusion, he accurately predicted that "this move taken by their officers is bound to lead to the ultimate smashing of the STFU as such."[16]

In an effort to avoid an open split, John Brophy proposed a compromise between the two dissident factions. The compromise was a threefold plan: (1) that STFU conform to the UCAPAWA constitution; (2) that STFU be guaranteed its autonomy; and (3) that UCAPAWA lift the suspension of the executive officers of STFU.[17]

Mitchell and the other STFU officers were willing to accept the compromise only if Henderson called off the proposed state conventions.[18] When Henderson went ahead with his plans to hold the conventions, the executive council of STFU called a special convention on March 19. At this convention, Mitchell announced that the voting returns from the locals indicated overwhelming support for STFU, and complete rejection of UCAPAWA. Mitchell pointed out that of 200 locals, the vote was 138 for withdrawal from UCAPAWA, and 2 against. Sixty locals either did not vote, or failed to turn in their results.

After the results were announced, the union officially voted to withdraw from UCAPAWA, a "funeral" was held, and the UCAPAWA, Mitchell said, was "officially buried. The members have plainly shown that they are through with Henderson and his crowd and want to be left alone."[19] Whitfield was suspended as vice-president of STFU, and a new white minister, W. M. Tanner, was given the job of Missouri organizer for STFU.[20]

One can only speculate whether STFU would have split with

16. Gardner Jackson to Henderson, March 31, 1939. See also Mitchell to Gardner Jackson, Feb. 27, 1940, *ibid.*

17. John Brophy to Mitchell and Butler, March 9, 1939; "Chronology of Events in STFU-UCAPAWA Dispute," March 11, 1939, *ibid.*

18. Mitchell to Brophy, March 11, 1939, *ibid*; *UCAPAWA News*, I, No. 1 (July 1939), 12.

19. Butler and Mitchell to All Locals, STFU, March 23, 1939; Mitchell, "Report of the Secretary, 1939," p. 6. See also statement issued to the membership of the STFU by Butler and Mitchell in behalf of the Executive Committee, March 11, 1939, STFU Papers.

20. Butler to Whitfield, March 28, 1939; Mitchell, "Oral History," p. 117; STFU *News,* April 27, 1939, *ibid.*

UCAPAWA had it not been for the Bootheel demonstration. Looking back on the event later in life, Mitchell was convinced that Henderson had already decided to destroy STFU, and had considered the latter's preoccupation with the demonstration an opportune moment to take over. Indeed, so decisively divided were the two camps, that a final split seems to have been unavoidable; the demonstration merely brought the smoldering conflict to a head. "The STFU knew before it affiliated with UCAPAWA," Mitchell wrote after the split, "that Henderson was a Communist but we affiliated anyway." Mitchell claimed he had no objection to Communists but only to "destructive trade union tactics." Mitchell maintained that STFU abandoned UCAPAWA not because it was Communist controlled, "but because that Communist control has made it impossible for us to carry on our job as a union."[21]

After the break, STFU sent a letter to the AFL-CIO peace committee, warning them of the prevalence of Communists in UCAPAWA. Mitchell had maintained all along that his quarrel was with UCAPAWA, and not the CIO. However, despite Mitchell's constant affirmation that STFU welcomed support from either the AFL or the CIO, the union never affiliated with either national organization.[22]

Immediately following the split with UCAPAWA, STFU applied to the CIO for a separate charter, but Brophy flatly refused. The National Director said that he believed that the CIO's compromise proposal had been "an honorable settlement," and one which, had it been "accepted by the officers of the STFU, would have settled the present differences satisfactorily." The CIO, Brophy concluded, "believes that the interests of the members of the STFU would be best served by them remaining with the UCAPAWA," and for that reason he refused to issue a separate charter. STFU also made an application to join the AFL, but they were turned down, according

21. "An Open Letter to Friends of the Sharecroppers," March, 1939. See also Mitchell, "Oral History," p. 113, *ibid.*

22. "We will leave the door cracked," Mitchell said. Mitchell, "Report of the Secretary, 1939," p. 20. See also press release, STFU, "STFU warns Communist Destructive tactics in letter to CIO-AFL peace committees," March 24, 1939; Mitchell to Gardner Jackson, Feb. 27, 1940; Mitchell to John L. Lewis, March 6, 1939; Mitchell, "The STFU in 1938," unnumbered page at end; Evelyn Smith to Savannah War, March 8, 1939; Mitchell to *Nation,* March 30, 1939, p. 5; Mitchell to Philip Murray, March 14, 1939; Butler and Mitchell to Matthew Woll, March 22, 1939; Arthur G. McDowell to Butler, March 27, 1940; Mitchell to Butler, March 23, 1939, *ibid.*

to Mitchell, because "they could see no value in having a union of sharecroppers."[23]

STFU's break with UCAPAWA was disastrous. Mitchell later admitted that after it was over, he "didn't have much of a union left." He estimated that he lost three-fourths of his membership and ended up with less than forty active locals, and fewer than one thousand members. Henderson fared little better, although his union survived. UCAPAWA remained a part of the CIO until it was expelled by that organization in 1950 because of "Communist domination."[24]

"The other side," Mitchell later wrote, "had less than we did." Many members had abandoned the union in confusion. "This does not mean that Henderson and his crowd have succeeded in capturing the other locals," Mitchell wrote to Norman Thomas. "The situation has been so confused to the people, they have just shut down and quit for the time being, many of them just disgusted. . . ." There was no doubt in Mitchell's mind that it was primarily STFU's preoccupation with the internecine struggle that sapped its energy and caused its downfall. "You know, when you get into a union fight," Mitchell later recalled, "you don't pay attention to anything else except the fight."[25]

Although the demonstration was fatal for STFU, it proved to be quite worthwhile to Owen Whitfield and his people in Southeast Missouri. The Negro minister had succeeded in his immediate goal of focusing national attention on the plight of the cropper. Southeast Missouri's sharecropper demonstration was front page news from New York to California. Although the croppers were quickly removed from the highway and taken out of the public view, the mass exodus remained in the minds of the Bootheel citizens for some time to come, and this, as we shall now see, was the most significant part about it.

23. Mitchell to John Brophy, April 4, 1939; Mitchell, "Workers in Our Field," p. 15, *ibid.*; *Daily Worker*, March 19, 1939; *UCAPAWA News*, I, No. 1 (July 1939), 12.

24. Mitchell, "Oral History," p. 118; Mitchell to Norman Thomas, March 5, 1939; Mitchell, "Workers in Our Field," p. 12, STFU Papers.

25. Mitchell, "Oral History," p. 118; Mitchell to Norman Thomas, March 5, 1939, *ibid.*

10 Aftermath: Thad Snow's "Confession," Trotsky, and the FBI

After the STFU-UCAPAWA split, Whitfield, under the direction of Henderson, led the reorganization meeting in St. Louis on March 12, 1939. UCAPAWA later claimed that there were fifty-two delegates from twenty-one locals representing four thousand Missouri sharecroppers at the gathering.[1] Whitfield helped establish a new union at this meeting, the Missouri Agricultural Workers Council, which was chartered directly by UCAPAWA. William Fischer, a white sharecropper, was named president, and Whitfield was appointed secretary-treasurer of the new organization. Whitfield was also one of a delegation of six elected to go to Washington to deal with the problem of those campers still without homes in Southeast Missouri.[2]

It was through the Missouri Agricultural Workers Council that Whitfield worked when he rallied the support of the St. Louis Sharecroppers' Committee in the summer of 1939 in order to obtain the ninety-acre tract near Poplar Bluff as a refuge for the families at Wyatt. The Negro leader remained with the Agricultural Workers

1. See *UCAPAWA News,* I, No. 1 (July 1939), 12; *Daily Worker,* March 15 and 16, 1939; and *Post-Dispatch,* March 13, 1939.

2. Mitchell, "Report of the Secretary, 1939," p. 6, STFU Papers; Owen H. Whitfield, "The Missouri Agricultural Workers Council and What It Stands For," Fannie Cook Collection; *Daily Worker,* March 15, 1939; St. Louis *Star Times,* March 11, 1939; *UCAPAWA News,* I, No. 6 (Feb. 1940), 4.

Council until 1944, at which time he quit the union to travel with Claude Williams in an organization called the People's Institute of Applied Religion.[3] During this time Whitfield made his home in Kirkwood, near St. Louis. He tried to bring his family to live with him, but as was the case with STFU, he was not making much money with the new union, and living expenses were high. Thus, Mrs. Whitfield and the children moved to Cropperville.[4]

STFU meanwhile continued to concern itself with the Bootheel croppers who had participated in the demonstration, but by now it was Owen Whitfield's name that had become synonymous with the strike, and it was he who was to continue the momentum it had begun.

The Negro minister's single purpose of dramatizing the condition of Southeast Missouri's sharecroppers had already been achieved by the publicity given to the demonstration during the four days the croppers remained on the roadside. What was to happen to them afterward was something that Whitfield had not carefully planned. The forces unleashed by the dramatic event, however, did not dissipate when the demonstrators left the highway. Although Whitfield had not counted on it, additional stories relevant to the demonstration had already begun to appear in the papers even while the small group at the Sweet Home Church sat huddled around their tiny potbellied stove, seemingly reconciled to the idea that once again they had been forgotten.

Toward the end of January 1939, the story of the demonstration was beginning to fade from the front pages of most of the Bootheel newspapers. With the croppers safely removed from the highways and out of sight, coverage of the event became sparse, and it seemed certain that the news about it would soon stop completely. "Here in the heart of the cotton country," the *Southeast Missourian* happily reported on January 21, "the matter is slowly slipping away as the chief topic of discussion. . . ."[5] Just as the story threatened to slip

3. *Post-Dispatch,* June 15, 1939. One of Claude Williams's pamphlets described the goals of his organization. "The work of the Institute is not 'interracial.' It is a program of the people—'all the people.' It is not theological but religious; not political but democratic; not sectarian but partisan—partisan to the broader interests of the people" (Claude Williams, "People's Institute of Applied Religion" [Evansville, Indiana], Fannie Cook Collection).

4. Mrs. Zella Whitfield, interview with author, Dec. 19, 1965; Whitfield to Fannie Cook, March 25, 1943, Fannie Cook Collection.

5. *Southeast Missourian,* Jan. 21, 1939.

away all together, it was given a new impetus by Thad Snow's so-called confession.

Since January 10, Snow had been nothing more than an avid spectator of the demonstration, thoroughly enjoying all of the activity from the sidelines. He busied himself, as usual, by writing cogent letters to the *Post-Dispatch*, giving its readers the essential background information leading to the great event.[6] All the while, he had suffered nothing more than minor abuse from his colleagues for not having shared his early knowledge of the demonstration with them. "He knew what was brewing," one local paper chided, "and instead of him doing a neighborly act and telling landowners what was going on, [he] stood with the negro Whitfield in getting the roadside setters going."[7]

As yet, however, Snow had not become an actual participant in any of the activity. His role as an "outside observer," though, was to be short-lived. An opportunity to become a protagonist in the sensational Bootheel drama was something that a soul like Thad Snow could not resist. The opportunity came quickly.

Most residents of Southeast Missouri were quite reluctant to accept the idea that the demonstration could have been planned and executed so perfectly by Owen Whitfield, a poor Negro sharecropper. The intricate planning and tactical maneuvering necessitated by such an event was obviously beyond the scope of a lowly cropper's mentality. "After all," Snow wrote in jest, "black brains could hardly have handled anything so big and spectacular."[8] So, according to Snow, people in the Bootheel began looking for a scapegoat almost at once. Even while the clarion call went up for Whitfield's hide, the "real" culprit in the sordid affair was being sought.

"Mass hysteria," Snow later recalled, "requires a Devil." As a student of "social phenomenon," the Bootheel philosopher was convinced that society dictated that all great historical movements had to have a prime mover. Since most people in Southeast Missouri were convinced that the roadside demonstration was the result of a vile conspiracy, it needed a conspirator—a single individual who

6. Snow also wrote a series of articles for the *Post-Dispatch*, giving readers a general history of the problems in Southeast Missouri, which led to the 1939 exodus. See especially Jan. 22, 1939, March 5, 1939, April 30, 1939, and March 1, 1940.

7. Sikeston *Standard*, Jan. 17, 1939.

8. Snow, *From Missouri*, p. 254.

would serve as a kind of original sinner. Thus, Snow was certain that the Bootheel would not be content until it found the one man who had been the sole cause of the ugly event on January 10 which had exposed Southeast Missouri's sharecropper problem to the nation.[9]

Since Whitfield was ruled out, Delta citizens began to look elsewhere. At first, there was an attempt to place the guilt on Hans Baasch, the head of the LaForge Project. Baasch was a foreigner, and therefore immediately suspect. One local newspaper speculated that Baasch's ideas were as foreign to the Bootheel as his origin: "Whether he did any farming in Denmark," it reported, "or devoted his time to socializing the people is debated."[10] Although he was never completely exonerated, Baasch was soon forgotten, however, for the finger of suspicion began to point naturally toward Thad Snow. Since Snow was already a pariah to most Bootheel residents, he was a logical choice. He had the reputation of treating his croppers fairly, and it was a well-known fact that he was a good friend of Owen Whitfield's.

After some reflection, Southeast Missouri's most famous citizen concluded that he would indeed make the perfect scapegoat, and so he decided to cast himself in the role of the "devil." Snow hit upon the idea of writing a "confession," that would be "so absurd," to use his own words, "that even the most hysterical reader might entertain doubt on a second perusal or after some hours of deliberation and discussion." According to Snow's way of thinking, the story might be accepted at first, but upon sober reflection, its ridiculous details would appear to most readers to be ludicrous and the idea would pass finally into limbo. Meanwhile, the "spiritual need" for a devil would be satisfied, Southeast Missouri would have its catharsis, and once again all would be sweetness and light.[11]

Just prior to the demonstration, Snow had taken a trip to Mexico for his health, and so he decided to use that event as a point of departure for his story. He then wrote a confession for the papers, detailing how the demonstration was actually a vile conspiracy of

9. *Ibid.,* p. 256.

10. *Southeast Missourian,* Jan. 17, 1939. The New Madrid County planters' resolution, it will be recalled, had asked for a government investigation of Baasch along with Whitfield.

11. Snow, *From Missouri,* p. 262.

a number of people, the most important of whom was Leon Trotsky. Snow confessed that he had met Trotsky via Diego Rivera, whom he had encountered on his trip to Mexico. Snow was pleasantly surprised, the confession went on, to find that the great Russian revolutionary leader was quite conversant with the problem of the Bootheel sharecroppers. Together they sat down and worked out the details for the strike, even locating each campsite on a hand-drawn map of Southeast Missouri.[12]

Final plans were made only after discussing the matter with fellow conspirators, President Cardenas of Mexico, Ambassador Daniels, Secretary Hull, President Roosevelt, Upton Sinclair, Tom Mooney, Al Smith, Norman Thomas, Dorothy Thompson, Tom Girdler, and Frank Hague. Some thought Hitler and Mussolini "ought to be consulted by cable," Snow confessed, but this was decided against. The confession first appeared in the Sikeston *Standard* on February 2, 1939, and the immediate reaction to it was precisely as Snow had anticipated it would be.[13]

The absurdity of the confession ultimately accomplished Snow's purpose of converting hysteria into laughter, but for some time after it was published, many Bootheel residents believed it. One newspaper editor suggested Snow should be "horsewhipped," and at least one local leader proposed a resolution in a Kiwanis meeting "condemning Thad Snow for his subversive conspiracy with the Red Revolutionary, Trotsky, to undermine American institutions."[14]

Snow, of course, delighted in the whole business. Later recalling his role as the "devil," he said: "I have served creditably, I think, and have got an enormous kick out of it." The only "public disavowal" he ever made of the confession was in the *Post-Dispatch*. He later wrote, with a seemingly never-ending consistency for whimsical remarks, that he "had less to do with it [the demonstration] than the man in the moon; because undoubtedly some of the union meetings were held on moonlight nights."[15] By now, however, many had learned not to take Snow seriously at all times. On another occasion, for example, when a local reporter asked him if he planned

12. *Ibid.*, p. 263.
13. The entire confession may be seen in the Appendix, pp. 183–185.
14. Snow, *From Missouri*, p. 265. The resolution did not come to a vote.
15. *Ibid.*, p. 274; *Post-Dispatch*, March 10, 1939.

the demonstration, he replied that he would deny nothing, but then quickly added : "I also admit that I planned and executed the now famous Munich pact."[16]

The Bootheel iconoclast later paid another visit to Mexico, actually met Trotsky this time, and when he informed the former Russian leader that "many good people had swallowed the absurd tale whole," Trotsky "laughed and chuckled," Snow reported, and said "he thought he and I had made a fine team of 'devils' in the cropper road-side affair."[17]

Snow's "confession" and the furor that followed it added an unexpected amount of publicity to the demonstration. The croppers received further publicity in March 1939, when the FBI's "findings" were released.[18] As indicated, the Department of Agriculture had immediately conducted an investigation in the Bootheel while the demonstrators were still on the highways to determine if the AAA program was in any way responsible for the exodus. Afterward, Henry Wallace wrote Attorney General Frank Murphy and strongly suggested that the FBI conduct its own investigation.[19]

Wallace expressed the hope to Murphy that the Justice Department "would be more effective" in conducting an investigation than a congressional committee. Since planters had sent resolutions to the Dies Committee, arguing subversive elements were behind the demonstration, Wallace was apparently anxious to keep the investigation out of Congress's hands.

An investigation by the Justice Department, Wallace felt, ought to be conducted in order to clear up the charges that had been made on both sides.[20] On the one hand, the planters consistently maintained that outside radicals were responsible for the demonstration. When the Bootheel planters' resolution drew no response from government officials, J. V. Conran, the New Madrid County spokesman, reiterated the demand for an investigation in an open letter to Congressmen and Washington officials. "We are not going to be satisfied here in New Madrid County without a complete official investigation of this thing," the prosecuting attorney said. "It looks

16. Charleston *Enterprise Courier*, Jan. 19, 1939.
17. Undated letter to *Post-Dispatch*, Thad Snow Papers.
18. See *Post-Dispatch*, *Southeast Missourian*, Memphis *Commercial-Appeal*, *Daily Worker*, all March 13, 1939.
19. Wallace to Murphy, March 13, 1939, NA, RG 16.
20. *Ibid.*; Wallace to Roosevelt, Jan. 21, 1939, *ibid.*

like [the federal government is] trying to smooth this thing over, but we want action."[21]

On the other hand, STFU had been joined by many other civic organizations in demanding the FBI look into the charges of violations of civil rights and liberties. The American Civil Liberties Union, the Socialist party of America, and the party's Workers Defense League had all complained to Frank Murphy of alleged violations of civil liberties.[22] Moreover, there were also allegations being made at the state level. The St. Louis branch of the American Civil Liberties Union had asked Governor Stark for a "thorough investigation of several alleged violations of civil rights of citizens of Missouri and other states by the State Highway Police and local officers. . . ."[23]

Of particular concern to the national office of the ACLU was the interception of several telegrams intended for Whitfield. In addition to Mitchell's wire to Whitfield from New York at the start of the demonstration, STFU had sent other telegrams from the Memphis headquarters to him in care of Hans Baasch at the LaForge Project. The telegrams, STFU later charged, were turned over by the telegraph company to the Missouri State Police, and later broadcast over Radio Station KMOX in St. Louis. Whitfield, STFU alleged, first received the information contained in the telegrams when they were broadcast over the radio.[24]

Murphy had responded to Wallace's request to clear the air of all these charges by conducting an FBI investigation in the Bootheel late in January 1939. In essence, the FBI report was a complete refutation of the planters' allegations. Despite the more militant faction's charge that Hoover and the FBI "whitewashed" the landlord's conduct in the demonstration and, in the words of the *Daily Worker* "absolved the planters of any guilt," the report was almost a total condemnation of that group's role in the dispute.[25]

Instead of being an uprising promoted by outside agitators, as the

21. Quoted in *Southeast Missourian,* Jan. 18, 1939.

22. Telegram, David Clendenin, Workers Defense League to Frank Murphy, Jan. 18, 1939; Mitchell to Roger Baldwin, ACLU, Jan. 24, 1939; Julia Verner, Sec., Branch I, SPA to Gov. Stark, Jan. 30, 1939, STFU Papers.

23. Cited in *Post-Dispatch,* Jan. 27, 1939.

24. Mitchell to Roger Baldwin, ACLU, Jan. 24, 1939; Mitchell, undated memo to David S. Burgess, STFU Papers.

25. See *Daily Worker,* March 13, 1939.

landlords had charged, the investigators found that the demonstration was a protest of a "disadvantaged group," the great majority of whom were actually residents of the state.[26] While many non-sharecroppers participated in the demonstration, these people—mostly day laborers—made "no claim or pretense," the report said, of being sharecroppers, as alleged by the landowners. Although the movement was planned and not spontaneous, the landowners' lack of knowledge of the plans, the investigators said, "was to a certain extent due to their own apathy."[27]

The report was critical of the planters for their lack of understanding of the activities surrounding the demonstration. "The great majority of land owners had no conception whatever as to who was behind the movement," it stated, and practically all of them "based their complaints entirely upon rumors and gossip which came to them." Furthermore, the investigators reproached the planters for their failure to comprehend the conditions which led to the movement to the highways. Most landowners "apparently did not understand," they pointed out, "nor have they yet been able to grasp that the demonstration was against the economic system prevailing in the area."[28]

This economic system, the report went on, was a result of a number of factors: "It arose in part from a new system of absentee landlordism," which had developed relatively late in Southeast Missouri. Other causes were "the rapid elimination of small holdings in favor of farms of thousands of acres, the power mechanization of farm operations," and finally a general "speculation in land and cotton. . . ." Without making a total condemnation of all the Bootheel planters, the report was critical of "a large group of landlords," who it said were "interested only in speculative profits from the sale of land or from the production of cotton or both. This

26. *Post-Dispatch,* March 13, 1939. This appraisal was confirmed by Herbert Little, who estimated in his report to Aubrey Williams that two thirds of the demonstrators were from Missouri, with the largest percent of others originally from Arkansas. See Report of Herbert Little (dictated over the telephone) to Aubrey Williams, Jan. 16, 1939, *Selected Documents,* Roosevelt Library.

27. *Southeast Missourian,* March 13, 1939. Since the report was not published, the information given here is taken from what the various papers reported that the FBI document said.

28. *Ibid.*

group," it concluded, "is alleged to have contributed materially to the social and economic instability of the area."[29]

The income of the tenant farmer in the Bootheel, the report pointed out, was ordinarily too low to provide "a decent standard of living." This problem was compounded by the fact that many planters were reducing tenants to the bottom of the wage scale. Thus, the immediate or direct cause of the demonstration, the FBI investigators said, was "a policy recently discovered by landlords under which the sharecropper, whose lot was already degraded, has been further reduced to the status of a day laborer. . . ." The landlord was tempted to make this reduction, it said, because it relieved him of the most grievous burden a planter carried, the "responsibility for [the tenants'] existence between crops. . . ." Instead many Bootheel planters chose to shift this responsibility "to relief agencies of the Government. . . ."

The "decisive factor" in determining the landlord's decision to reduce croppers to day laborers, the report stated, in what was undoubtedly its most important conclusion, was "the Department of Agriculture's 1938 program, which provided that the farm tenant should receive 50 per cent of Government subsidies to cotton growing, instead of 25 per cent as under the 1937 program." There was no doubt at all, the investigators concluded, that some landlords had attempted to "chisel" and keep the entire parity payment for themselves.[30]

The FBI acquitted the croppers of any violation of federal law and exonerated those campers who had been accused—mostly by the local press—of inciting violence by their possession of firearms on the roadside. The only individuals the FBI found guilty of any disorder or violence were the law enforcement officials. As a final reprimand, the report specifically mentioned that J. R. Butler was unfairly "induced" by the Missouri Highway Patrol to leave the state, and cited that Robert Haynes, a Negro, was beaten with a stick and revolver butt by deputies from the office of the Sheriff of New Madrid County.[31]

After the findings of the report were made public, Attorney General Murphy announced that the only matter the Justice Department was continuing to consider after its investigation was whether to

29. *Post-Dispatch,* March 13, 1939.
30. *Ibid.* 31. *Ibid.*

bring criminal prosecutions against individuals alleged to have held up telegrams during the demonstration. Murphy said this was the only instance found by the FBI which "might come within the Federal criminal statutes." The real reason for the Bootheel protest demonstration, he said, was a social problem in Southeast Missouri, and thus not within the jurisdiction of the Justice Department.[32]

The findings of the FBI, coupled with Thad Snow's confession, kept the story of the highway exodus before the eyes of Bootheel residents for several months after it ended. Although group attitudes are a very difficult quality to measure accurately, it is safe to say that the publicity attending the demonstration undoubtedly helped to change at least some of the attitudes of the power structure in the Bootheel, as was evidenced vividly the next year. Whitfield's most practical gain came not from the 1939 demonstration, but from the threat of a repeat performance in 1940.

32. *Ibid.*, March 9, 1939. Action was never taken against the individuals alleged to have violated the federal law, either because no one ever made formal charges, or because criticism died down after the findings of the report were made public. Whatever the reason, the matter was finally dropped.

11 Homes for the Homeless

At the end of 1939 Whitfield announced that there were more evictions in the Bootheel than there had been the previous year. It was estimated that about fifteen hundred persons were to be evicted from their farms in January of 1940. Landowners argued that large-scale evictions were occurring because a bumper crop in 1939 enticed buyers from a wide area, and as a result, big landholders from all over were coming into the Bootheel to purchase the land, and most had their own workers.[1]

It is true that the sale of land often led to the removal of tenants on farms because, in many instances, the sale itself evicted them. "The tenant does not know how long he may be on the farm," a government report stated at the time, "because leases usually provide for eviction in case of resale or transfer of the land."[2]

Whatever the reason, when Whitfield learned of the evictions set for 1940, he informed Governor Stark that unless something was done immediately, another demonstration similar to the one which had occurred in 1939 seemed highly likely. In contrast with January

1. See "Survey of evictions for 1940," Dec. 1939, STFU Papers; Charles S. Hoffman and Virgil L. Bankson, "Crisis in Missouri's Boot Heel," *Land Policy Review,* III (Jan.–Feb. 1940), 1; *Southeast Missourian,* Jan. 6 and 10, 1940.

2. *Southeast Missouri: A Laboratory for the Cotton South.*

of 1939, Stark acted quickly. Apparently determined to avoid the adverse publicity which had accompanied the 1939 strike, the Governor called a special conference in St. Louis on January 6, 1940, and invited landowners, sharecroppers, and officials of both state and federal government.

He summoned Whitfield from Washington to St. Louis to be the spokesman for the sharecroppers. Perhaps of greatest significance was the fact that the FSA, previously anathema in the Bootheel, was now invited to attend the meeting. The Governor sent a wire to Will Alexander, FSA head in Washington, saying: "The situation is urgent and we need your advice and assistance immediately."[3] Alexander did not attend the conference, but R. W. Hudgens, the assistant administrator of the FSA, came to St. Louis from Washington to represent the agency on the committee, along with Phil Beck, the regional director for FSA.[4]

In marked contrast to 1939, when he had looked upon FSA projects in the Bootheel as troublesome, the Governor now requested the agency to expand greatly its whole rehabilitation program in the area. Hudgens met with Stark the afternoon before the conference was to open, somewhat surprised by the willingness of the Governor to have the federal government assist in the Bootheel. "All he [Stark] wanted to know," Hudgens wrote, "was how much money the Farm Security Administration would contribute."[5]

In fact, FSA was already convinced of the necessity of governmental action to head off a new demonstration. Phil Beck, the regional director, had written to Alexander at the end of November 1939, reminding him of the 1939 highway exodus, and said he was convinced that a similar situation would develop in 1940 unless a program could be created which would "provide for at least partial rehabilitation for many families which we are unable to help under our standard loan program."[6]

FSA envisaged not only increasing its own efforts in the Bootheel, but also leading a massive campaign in cooperation with the Social Security administration, the WPA, and other state organizations and

3. Cited in the *Southeast Missourian,* Dec. 29, 1939.

4. *Post-Dispatch,* Jan. 5 and 6, 1940; C. B. Baldwin, memo for Henry Wallace, Feb. 2, 1940, NA, RG 96.

5. R. W. Hudgens, memo for Will Alexander, Jan. 19, 1940, *ibid.*

6. Phil Beck, memo for Will Alexander, Nov. 19, 1939, *ibid.*

local civic groups. Beck had been bothered at the end of 1939 because an early cotton crop meant many in the Bootheel would be unemployed again before Christmas. In addition, Social Security funds for Southeast Missouri were low, so he had already been making plans for a program in which FSA would get together with the Social Security office in an effort to pool their resources.

Now that the Bootheel's attitude about FSA had changed, Beck was quite enthusiastic about the possibility for success. FSA would be perfectly willing to carry the brunt of the program if necessary, he wrote to Alexander, but because of "the interest of the Governor and local citizens of the area, together with the splendid spirit in which other agencies are willing to cooperate," he expected the full support of everyone.[7]

At the same time that Governor Stark announced the special conference, he also appealed to all landowners to delay evictions that were set for January 10 until February 1, to "enable state and federal agencies to carry out relief measures" and try to remedy conditions. Stark also requested that landowners try, if at all feasible, to "retain present tenants and sharecroppers for the coming season."[8]

The change in the Governor's attitude was no less evident than the change in the thinking of the Bootheel landowners. Landlords met with the Governor in several sessions at the end of 1939, prior to the proposed January conference. These *ad hoc* meetings were held as soon as the first rumblings of a new demonstration were heard. At the close of these meetings, the Governor announced that a "concrete proposal" to solving the sharecropper problem was arrived at in cooperation with the planters.[9]

The fact that the Bootheel landowners were willing to discuss the problem of their farm tenants with government officials represented in itself a transformation. Thad Snow, who always had his finger on the pulse of planter sentiment, said the change in the attitude of the landlord class could only be described as "amazing." Unlike 1939, Snow wrote, "this year they [the planters] seemed to look

7. Phil Beck to Will Alexander, Nov. 2, 1939; Phil Beck, memo for Will Alexander, Nov. 19, 1939; C. B. Baldwin, memo for Henry Wallace, Feb. 2, 1940, *ibid.*

8. *Post-Dispatch,* Jan. 6 and 8, 1940; *Southeast Missourian,* Jan 6, 1940.

9. Phil Beck to Will Alexander, "Subject: Southeast Missouri," Feb. 12, 1940, NA, RG 96.

at it quite differently, and held meetings in December ahead of the dreaded walkout, admitted the problem, and deliberated earnestly on what to do about it."[10]

C. B. Baldwin, a representative of the FSA, also sensed the conversion which had taken place in Southeast Missouri, and he expressed his feelings in a memorandum to Henry Wallace. "One important development has occurred in the area recently," he wrote, "which offers a ray of hope that something constructive may be done" in the Bootheel. The complete change in the attitude of "landowners, merchants, local officials, and other leading citizens of the area," Baldwin wrote, indicate that now "there is an honest and sincere desire on the part of many citizens of the area to approach the problem in an objective and sympathetic manner." This attitude was practically the antithesis of 1939, he noted, when "for a few months after the demonstration, feelings ran so high and the general situation was so tense that it was difficult to promulgate a constructive program of action."[11]

In essence, the proposals agreed upon at the Governor-planter sessions had two goals. First, to solve the immediate short-range problem of providing housing facilities for the tenants who would be without homes on January 1, 1940. Second, a long range objective was sought which would solve the cropper problem permanently. The latter called for a resettlement program to place homeless croppers on small tracts of unused land, and have the FSA assist them in building homes and purchasing equipment.[12] The most popular plan was one offered by Edward P. Coleman, a large landholder from Sikeston.

According to this plan, small tracts of land—perhaps five or ten acres—might be leased to the FSA, who would then in turn build the houses for the tenants. An alternative plan, Coleman suggested, would be to have the landlord build the house and lease it along with a small tract to the FSA, who would then in turn provide low cost rental to the tenant. All plans envisaged the FSA increasing its standard loan program in the area to permit tenants to purchase equipment, work stock, and other materials needed to farm.[13]

10. Thad Snow, unsent letter to *Post-Dispatch*, Thad Snow Papers. An abbreviated version of this letter appears in the *Post-Dispatch*, March 1, 1940.
11. C. B. Baldwin, memo for Henry Wallace, Feb. 2, 1940, NA, RG 96.
12. *Southeast Missourian*, Jan. 6, 1940.
13. *Post-Dispatch*, Jan. 6, 1940.

At the Governor's conference in January, Stark announced the establishment of a special landlord-sharecropper committee, to study the problems of evictions in the Bootheel, and as a first step toward solving the problems, ordered the State Employment Service to work with this committee as well as state and federal agencies, and attempt to register all tenants and sharecroppers who had been unable to find places to live.

It was hoped that landowners would supply the State Employment agency with the names of families they planned to evict and also a list of land available for rent or lease in the hope of resettling the displaced workers.[14] Questionnaires were sent out by the State Employment Service to three thousand landowners in the Bootheel to determine job openings, and also to find out precisely how much land was available for providing small tracts of five to ten acres for the possible establishment of subsistence farms.[15]

The Governor ordered the Employment Service to expand its branches in the Bootheel to facilitate its work on the survey. When its findings were completed, it would turn them over to the landlord-sharecropper committee, who would then have on file at all times any information which might be needed regarding the status and location of tenant and sharecropper families as well as the availability of land opportunities.[16]

The six-man landlord-sharecropper committee appointed by the Governor consisted of Jewell Mayes, the Missouri commissioner of agriculture, who served as its chairman, J. W. Burch, director of the extension service of the Missouri College of Agriculture, E. P. Coleman and Sam L. Hunter of New Madrid, representing the landowners, and Whitfield and Charles E. Underhill of near Sikeston representing the tenants. This committee was to work closely with R. W. Hudgens and Phil Beck of the FSA, and Bishop William Scarlett of the Episcopal Diocese of Missouri. Scarlett had been in on the earlier conferences the landlords had had with the Governor, and it was he who first proposed the schemes later put forth by the landlords for the cropper problem.[17]

Whitfield claimed his presence on the committee was as a repre-

14. *Ibid.*; Phil Beck to Will Alexander, Jan. 15, 1940, NA, RG 96.
15. *Post-Dispatch*, Jan. 11, 1940.
16. R. W. Hudgens, memo for Will Alexander, Jan. 19, 1940, NA, RG 96.
17. *Post-Dispatch*, Jan. 6, 1940; *Southeast Missourian*, Jan. 6, 1940; Mr. E. P. Coleman, interview with author, Dec. 31, 1966.

sentative of the Missouri Agricultural Workers Council. When the Governor's conference was called, J. R. Butler wrote to Stark, requesting that STFU be represented. Claiming "over 5,000 members in Southeastern Missouri," Butler argued that his union was the official spokesman for most of the tenant farmers in the Bootheel. STFU was conducting its own survey at the time to determine the number of its members who would be evicted in 1940, and it reported to the Governor that the situation was "particularly acute in Missouri. . . ."[18] Moreover, the union had been working late in 1939, trying to force Washington to provide assistance for those croppers then located at the colony at Harviell, near Poplar Bluff, on one occasion sending a delegation to Washington to appeal directly to Will Alexander of FSA to help. Specifically, STFU proposed to Alexander that the FSA construct a permanent labor camp in Southeast Missouri, similar to the LaForge Project, to provide facilities for one hundred to three hundred families.[19]

Governor Stark, however, denied STFU representation at the conference in St. Louis, apparently because the union's headquarters were still located out of the state in Memphis, Tennessee. In reply to STFU's request, Stark pointed out that the conference was limited to a group from Southeast Missouri, and made it clear that organizations from outside the state were not welcome.[20]

Whitfield was convinced that CIO power, via UCAPAWA, was the decisive factor in the Governor's decision to select him to serve on the landlord-sharecropper committee. "With the assistance of the UCAPAWA-CIO," he wrote, after the choice was made, "I licked the doggone Governor. . . ." The Governor's choice, Whitfield was certain, was completely unprecedented. "For the first time in the history of this state," he said, "a Negro has been appointed on a level with landlords to represent all of the sharecroppers and tenants and day laborers in the state. . . ." Whitfield was convinced

18. Butler to Governor Stark, Dec. 29, 1939; press release, STFU, Dec. 29, 1939, STFU Papers. STFU later reported that three hundred families in five Southeast Missouri counties were without homes for 1940. Butler to Stark, Feb. 1, 1940, *ibid.*

19. Butler to Josephine Johnson, Dec. 11, 1939; Butler to Oliver Hotz, Dec. 2, 1939; press release, STFU, "Submitted to FSA from STFU concerning Farm Labor Homes for Displaced Tenant and Farmers and Sharecroppers in Southern States," undated, 1940, *ibid.*

20. Butler, night letter to Stark, Dec. 29, 1939; Stark to Butler, Jan. 3, 1940; Butler to Stark, Jan. 10, 1940; Butler to Bishop William Scarlett, Jan. 10, 1940, *ibid.*

that Stark was opposed to unions in general; therefore, the Governor's decision, he felt, could only be explained by his fear of the powerful organization the Negro leader represented. "Think of an anti-union governor appointing a union man—Ha! Ha! *But it wasn't me that he feared but the organization behind me.*"[21]

Whatever the reason for Whitfield's appointment, his presence, along with several other Negro tenants in the midst of the white landlords and government officials at the "swanky" Park Plaza Hotel in St. Louis caused some of the Bootheel papers to express amazement. "There was something ironic about the conference," one local paper reported, "with at least one man in overalls and high state and federal officials" fraternizing with Negro sharecroppers "whose clothing bill for a lifetime wouldn't cost much more than some of the jewelry that adorns the ritzy society leaders, who grace the highly decorated cocktail bars of the hotel."

When Whitfield walked around the plush hotel "carrying an important looking brief case," he was constantly pursued by newsmen, and thus received enough attention, a local paper decided, "to delight any No. 1 politician. . . ."[22] Many Bootheel papers carried a picture of Whitfield, flanked by Governor Stark on one side and R. W. Hudgens of FSA on the other. Thad Snow savoring the incident, wrote with typical sarcasm what the poor croppers' reaction to Whitfield's mingling with the white power structure must have been like: "Then when the Governor allowed himself to be photographed with their great negro leader Whitfield, each smiling cordially upon the other—why that was like giving them a look into the promised land."[23]

Most landlords heeded Stark's pleas for a postponement of evictions until February 1, and the action, temporarily at least, headed off a new demonstration on January 10. Whitfield claimed that the croppers did not want another protest strike. "We don't want to demonstrate in the cold and snow," he said, "and our organization won't sponsor any."[24] The Negro minister reported that he was encouraged by the Coleman plan presented to the St. Louis con-

21. Italics are mine. Whitfield to F. R. Betton, undated 1940, *ibid.* See also *UCAPAWA News,* I, No. 6 (Feb. 1940), 5.

22. *Southeast Missourian,* Jan. 6 and 8, 1940.

23. Thad Snow, unsent letter to *Post-Dispatch,* Thad Snow Papers. An abbreviated version of this letter appears in the *Post-Dispatch,* March 1, 1940.

24. Quoted in *Post-Dispatch,* Jan. 10, 1940; Phil Beck to Will Alexander, Jan. 15, 1940, NA, RG 16.

ference, but added, "we will have to work and work fast" in order to head off a new strike. "A demonstration may become a racket," he pointed out, "and that we do not want. We want no violence. I prevented violence last year although some of my people were ready for it, and I will do so again." Whitfield concluded that if there was another demonstration, it would be caused by the inaction of the landowners themselves.[25]

While Whitfield was undoubtedly quite sincere in his efforts to head off a new demonstration, at the same time he made it very clear that the union was determined to obtain a "fair solution" to the sharecropper problem in the Bootheel, and he did everything in his power to lead the dignitaries at the Governor's conference to believe that unless action was taken, a new demonstration would indeed take place.[26]

While the conference was in session, for example, croppers appeared on the campsites of the 1939 demonstration bearing signs carrying the name of the Missouri Agricultural Workers Council, calling attention to the fact that the first year's anniversary of the exodus was close at hand. Handbills were also printed and handed out to passersby. Both the signs and the handbills bore the caption, "Lest you Forget," and were directed toward President Roosevelt and Secretary Wallace. One of the signs read:

> One year ago sat on this roadside 1500 sharecroppers, shelterless for days in snow and freezing cold. The planters' abuse of New Deal cotton control drove us to this roadside in mid-winter. To hide our wretched plight from public view, the State police moved us off this road. The abuses remain and grow. The planters grow rich on cotton control. We croppers do the work and grow poor. Henry Wallace! President Roosevelt! You saved the planters by cotton control! Don't you want to save us, too?[27]

The handbills reminded readers that the 1939 demonstration was a peaceful yet strong protest against the New Deal's farm policy. "Again we protest," the handbills said, "the increasing defeat of labor policy in cotton control." The circulars pointed out that there had been no major change in the farm control law, and that "the abuses that drove us to the highways a year ago remain and grow." Specifically, the handbills called for a law that would "make the

25. *Southeast Missourian*, Jan. 6 and 8, 1940.
26. *Ibid.*
27. *Post-Dispatch*, Jan. 8, 1940.

labor payment accrue only for labor performance. . . ." The planter who is honest and obeys the intent of the law, it was suggested, gets exactly half as much of the government subsidy as the planter who turns his croppers out on relief. "Is it right," the handbills asked, "to give double payment to the planter who kicks his croppers out and lets them have no part of the cotton subsidy? Is that a New Deal? We croppers call it a Raw Deal."[28]

Immediately after the Governor's conference came to a close on January 8, 1940, the FSA accepted the Governor's new invitation and sent additional personnel into the Bootheel, with instructions "to increase the number of loans of new applicants as rapidly as possible."[29] This action, FSA hoped, would suffice until the survey of the State Employment Service could be completed.

Meanwhile, during the middle of January, Whitfield made another trip to Washington, joining UCAPAWA representatives from six other states to attend a national cotton conference. Having now another chance to talk with FSA officials in Washington, Whitfield charged that local AAA committees were still controlled by landowners who were capable of denying benefit checks to sharecroppers. AAA officials asked him to provide specific examples of those croppers who had been denied benefit payments, but the Negro leader objected, arguing that if he did, he would "put individuals 'on the spot' and subject them to further acts of discrimination."[30] STFU had long contended that union members were discriminated against and were always the first to be evicted in order that planters might be rid of the troublemakers.[31]

Whitfield suggested that the real problem was the farm law and asked that it be amended so as to require the landlord to pay minimum wages as a prerequisite for receiving federal payments. Before leaving Washington, Will Alexander assured him that steps would be taken "to secure bonafide sharecropper and working tenant farmer representation on all county committees."[32]

28. Undated circular, Thad Snow Papers.

29. Phil Beck to Will Alexander, "Subject: Southeastern Missouri," Feb. 12, 1940, NA, RG 16.

30. Quoted in *Southeast Missourian,* Jan. 16, 1940. See also *Daily Worker,* Jan. 10 and 16, 1940; and *UCAPAWA News*, VI, No. 6 (Feb. 1940), 4.

31. J. R. Butler, letter to author, Jan. 7, 1966. See also Blackstone, "Minority Report," U.S. Congress, House, *Farm Tenancy*. . . . 75th Cong., 1st Sess., 1947, House Doc. 149, p. 26.

32. Quoted in *Daily Worker,* Jan. 25, 1940. See also *Southeast Missourian,* Jan. 16, 1940.

While in the nation's capital, Whitfield also used the opportunity to request officials of the WPA and the United States Housing Authority to provide a work program for farm tenants which would be put into effect during the slack seasonal periods. Before he departed, Whitfield and his delegation were again invited to the White House, this time by Mrs. Roosevelt. There he found the First Lady "very sympathetic" to the problem of tenancy reduction in the Bootheel. Whitfield later said: "She was deeply interested in our educational situation, and the trouble we have getting schooling for our children."[33]

All together, Whitfield's sojourn was a profitable one, and his continuous activities no doubt helped to keep pressure on Governor Stark, and other leaders of the state, who were still trying to find a permanent solution to Southeast Missouri's sharecropper problems. On February 2, 1940, Stark asked landowners for another reprieve on the threatened evictions. The Governor requested that Bootheel planters delay once again the time set for evictions until the findings of the Employment Service could be obtained.[34] Again, most landowners complied.

On February 15, Carl Wedeking, the head of the District Employment Service, announced that the registration of jobless tenants in Southeast Missouri was complete. The survey found that 925 farm families in the seven Delta counties who had been on farms in 1939 were "not yet placed" and were still "looking for other farm locations."[35] Indicative of the work instability in the area was the fact that this extremely large registration occurred, a government report later stated, "even though the registration day was cold and rainy and the registration was given inadequate publicity."[36]

According to the Governor's request, landlords turned over job openings and land available for tenants to the Employment Service, but by February 15, there were orders for only ninety-eight "desirable" tenant families, and even most of these were merely offers for clearing leases on new land. "If the land is heavily wooded," Wedeking pointed out, "it is well nigh impossible for a man to clear a sufficient amount of land in the short time that remains before planting season."[37]

33. Quoted in *Southeast Missourian*, Jan. 23, 1940. See also *Daily Worker*, Jan. 25, 1940; and *UCAPAWA News*, I, No. 6 (Feb. 1940), 4.

34. *Post-Dispatch*, Feb. 2, 1940.

35. Governor Stark, press release, Feb. 15, 1940, STFU Papers.

36. *Report to the Tolan Committee*, Pt. II, p. 7.

37. Carl Wedeking to Jewell Mayes, Feb. 13, 1940, STFU Papers.

At the time the figures on the survey were released, Wedeking wrote to the landlord-sharecropper committee and emphasized that governmental action would be necessary to head off a new demonstration for 1940. The employment service chief said he had talked with various leaders around the Delta counties, and "those who should know" were of a rather firm opinion that there would be no new demonstration only if "the survey is followed quickly by some action on the part of the Farm Security Administration or some other agency that may be able to give assistance." Wedeking stated that most of the Bootheel landowners were anxious to cooperate with the Governor thus far "in trying to avoid evicting families if possible," as was evidenced by the fact that very few families had been evicted at that date. He did stress, however, that he was certain that "evictions will increase in number during the next three weeks," and suggested that unless something was done before then, there could be trouble. "Among the sharecroppers especially," he affirmed, "I find a deep seated belligerent attitude."[38]

Stark was already aware of the ill feeling among the sharecroppers sensed by Wedeking, and he had already made the decision to take positive action in order to head off a possible new demonstration. When the Governor made public the Employment Service's survey on February 15, he also announced that the landlord-sharecropper committee had approved a five-point program for the Bootheel drawn up by Phil Beck, the regional director for the FSA.[39]

In essence, the program worked out by the FSA was a compromise between the planters and the landless croppers in Southeast Missouri. Most of the croppers who had participated in the demonstration, especially those who were then living on the open tract near Poplar Bluff, expressed the hope that the FSA might make arrangements to establish housing and farm units similar to the LaForge Project.[40]

As far as the FSA was concerned, there was no doubt but that the LaForge experiment had proved successful. Farm families who entered LaForge in 1937 with possessions averaging $28, had an average gross worth estimated by government officials in 1940 at

38. *Ibid.* See also J. Truman Carter to Jewell Mayes, Feb. 13, 1940, *ibid.*

39. Governor Stark, press release, Feb. 15, 1940, *ibid.* See also *An Area Adjustment of People to Land and Farm Labor Requirements: The FSA's Program in Southeastern Missouri* (FSA, Indianapolis, Indiana, 1940), Fannie Cook Collection.

40. David S. Burgess (Highly Confidential), "Basic Facts about Delmo Labor Homes Project. . . ," June 25, 1945, STFU Papers.

$1,400. In addition, each family on the project at the beginning of 1940 had, after all costs, an average of $377 in surplus cash. Moreover, not only were payments on all the five-year loans made in 1937 on schedule in 1940, but government officials reported that they felt certain the entire amount would be repaid with interest in the very near future.[41]

Despite the government's optimism about the LaForge experiment, projects similar to it were not to be built in Southeast Missouri, primarily because of continued local opposition. Although the political climate in Southeast Missouri had changed since 1939, there was still considerable opposition to any kind of "communal" living plan, similar to that which existed at LaForge. One Bootheel paper probably reflected local feeling when it cried out against "the socialistic scheme of putting the farm families in [either] large or small colonies."[42] The planters themselves favored a government program to provide some kind of housing, but they felt it best to leave the families "in the communities where they now reside," rather than to have them "unified" in a project like LaForge.[43]

The five-point program finally outlined by the FSA included the following:

1. An acceleration of the FSA standard rural rehabilitation loan program in the Bootheel. This would mean an increase in the conventional FSA rehabilitation loan offered to tenants for the purchase of teams, tools, seed and other farm equipment. FSA was then serving approximately 1,300 to 1,400 families in the seven Delta counties. It was now hoped to increase this to nearly 2,000 families. More workers were to be brought in to meet the increased load, and it was estimated an extra $100,000 would be needed to service the additional families just for the first two months of the program.[44]

2. A housing and labor rehabilitation program, designed to give

41. "LaForge Project Review," Farm Security Administration, October 5, 1940, NA, RG 96. See also *Southeast Missouri: A Laboratory for the Cotton South*; and Carey McWilliams's chapter, "A Kick from the Boot Heel," in *Ill Fares the Land* (Boston, 1942), pp. 292–295.

42. *Southeast Missourian*, Jan. 10, 1940. See also Phil Beck to Will Alexander, Jan. 15, 1940, NA, RG 96.

43. See Burgess, "Basic Facts about Delmo Labor Homes Project. . . ," June 25, 1945, STFU Papers.

44. Governor Stark, press release, Feb. 15, 1940, STFU Papers; Phil Beck, memo for Will Alexander, Nov. 19, 1939; C. B. Baldwin to Phil Beck, Jan. 16, 1940; telegram, Phil Beck to C. B. Baldwin, Jan. 31, 1940; R. W. Hudgens, memo for Will Alexander, Jan. 19, 1940, NA, RG 96, and RG 16.

laborers a subsistence living during the slack seasons and to provide a steady work force during the busy chopping and picking seasons. Under this plan, hopefully 1,500 to 2,000 laborers and croppers might be able to obtain small tracts of rent-free land. The FSA would work with those landlords willing to sublease tracts to their tenants. In essence, the government would serve as a broker permitting the cropper to lease the land from the owner, usually on a sharecrop basis. The government would further help the tenant by providing grants and loans for the purchase of subsistence gardens and livestock for the improvement of housing facilities.[45]

3. A scattered labor homes program to provide two hundred to three hundred homeless families with a place to live rent-free. Farm families would lease or purchase small tracts of land—perhaps five to ten acres—and then obtain ten-year loans from FSA to help build their own homes. During the ten years, farm families would pay their landlords no rent, but "in the case of leased lands," the proposal suggested, "the improvements would revert to the landowner at the end of the lease period in lieu of rent."[46]

4. Construction of a number of farm worker homes to be built on tracts owned by the FSA. This plan would provide low rental homes to day laborers. FSA would also furnish subsistence gardens as a means of supplementing their seasonal wages.

5. Government financing to groups who would form associations and then purchase or lease underdeveloped lands. The associations, assisted by a forty-five year FSA loan, would develop the land, subdivide and then sublease to its members. The rent from members of the association would be used to pay off the loan.

In announcing approval of the five-point program, the Governor also reported that he was establishing local county committees throughout the Bootheel to work with the FSA and help implement the program. The committees would be composed of four people—two landowner representatives and two persons representing tenants, sharecroppers and farm laborers. Representatives for the seven Delta counties were to be chosen at meetings called by the county agricultural extension agents.[47]

Within a year, all of the programs outlined by FSA and approved

45. *Southeast Missouri: A Laboratory for the Cotton South*; C. B. Baldwin, memo for Henry Wallace, Feb. 2, 1940, NA, RG 96.

46. *Ibid.*; Governor Stark, press release, Feb. 15, 1940, STFU Papers.

47. *Ibid.*

by the Governor's committee were working effectively in the Bootheel. Although FSA still had many problems in Southeast Missouri, the project that proved to be the most successful and the most long lasting was the pilot labor homes program to provide low rental housing to farm workers. The program—called the Group Workers Homes Project and later more popularly known as the Delmo Homes project—permitted the FSA to purchase land, build homes—complete with individual garden plot—and then rent them to farm families for low monthly rates. For all practical purposes, the government took the place of the landlord. There were ten housing units subsequently built, each unit consisting of about fifty to seventy-five dwellings.[48]

The idea behind the Delmo Homes project was that the planters and farm laborers would help one another. The presence of the farm laborers in the homes would insure planters a constant labor supply, while at the same time the farm laborers would be provided with adequate housing and garden facilities. In order to be eligible to be accepted in the homes, one had to be a farm worker and agree to make himself and his family available for work during the peak seasons. Later, during World War II, when there was no work available in the Bootheel, STFU recruited and transported hundreds of farm workers from the Delmo project to Arizona, New Mexico, Texas, California, and Florida to help harvest farm crops during the peak seasons.[49]

Although the LaForge Project had been integrated (sixty white and forty Negro families), the Delmo Homes were to be segregated, no doubt in deference to the continued hostility toward LaForge. While Bootheel residents had labeled LaForge "socialistic," much of the resentment toward the communal project seems to have been largely because both Negro and white farmers lived together on it.[50]

The fact that the facilities were to be segregated at Delmo seemed

48. See Carey McWilliams's chapter, "A Kick from the Boot Heel," in *Ill Fares the Land*, pp. 293–295; Nancy Elliott, "Delmo Homes," in *Dunklin County Historical Society*, I (Kennett, Mo., 1948), 351–357; Snow, *From Missouri*, pp. 319–333; Mr. John Stewart, interview with author, May 1, 1966; Lowell C. Carpenter to P. G. Beck, June 12, 1943; John Stewart to P. G. Beck, July 14, 1942, NA, RG 96.

49. Elliott, "Delmo Homes," p. 354; H. L. Mitchell, letter to author, Jan. 21, 1966.

50. Frank Hancock, Administrator, FSA, to Orville Zimmerman, April 10, 1945, STFU Papers. Forty per cent of the Delmo Homes were alloted for Negroes. Phil Beck to Will Alexander, May 5, 1940, NA, RG 96.

to matter little to the occupants, who enthusiastically welcomed their new homes. The first tenants moved in early in 1941, and their feelings were typified by one "barefoot housewife," who told a reporter: "Its the first decent [house] ever I lived in, 'cept mebbe one year when my husband he got us a farm place, but 'course it wasn't nothen like as nice as this here one, and . . . we couldn't hold on to that there place for long."[51]

The homes had electric lights and running water—novelties for most of its new inhabitants—"three small bedrooms, a closet, some cellar storage shelves and a screened porch." Each tenant had an acre of ground for his own garden and an "outhouse with a concrete vault and dual vent." The government furnished each occupant "a stove, a table, four chairs, two metal chests, three wide mattresses, as well as a rake, plow, hoe and a pressure cooker for preservation of garden products." Each of the ten units, moreover, was supplied with a utility building which included bathrooms, laundry rooms, and a doctor's office.[52]

The Delmo Homes remained in the area under the control of the government until 1946, when the FSA was abolished. Just before its death, the government agency put the Delmo Homes up for sale. Most of the residents were unable to purchase their own homes at the time, and undoubtedly would have lost them had it not been for the organization of a private corporation, which helped the residents finance their purchase. The Delmo Housing Corporation was created late in 1945 by the same interested citizens in St. Louis who had been aroused by the demonstration. This group, working with Mitchell and other STFU leaders, helped raise enough money at the eleventh hour to purchase the homes from the government, and then resold them to the residents on a long-term, low-interest basis.[53]

The Sherwood Eddy Foundation of New York helped finance the initial down payment for the St. Louis group, with later contri-

51. Quoted in *Post-Dispatch*, Feb. 28, 1941.
52. *Ibid.*; Elliott, "Delmo Homes," p. 354.
53. C. B. Baldwin, memo to Henry Wallace, Feb. 2, 1940; press release from Gov. Stark, Feb. 15, 1940, NA, RG 96; Burgess, "Basic Facts about Delmo Labor Homes Project. . . ," June 25, 1945; Sherwood Eddy to Frank Hancock, Nov. 1, 1945; Mitchell to STFU "Sirs and Brothers," Nov. 19, 1945; statement by Frank Hook before Sub-Committee of House Committee on Agriculture, July 10, 1945; statement by David Burgess before Sub-Committee of House Committee on Agriculture, July 10, 1945, STFU Papers.

butions coming from the Episcopal Diocese of Missouri, Marshall Field, and Alfred Baker Lewis. During this time Whitfield was in Chicago, working with Claude Williams and the People's Applied Religion. When he received word that the FSA was going to put Delmo up for sale, he rushed back from Chicago to help. Although he did not work directly with Mitchell and STFU, ironically enough, both Whitfield and his former union joined forces with the St. Louis group to assist those people in the Bootheel who had once been indirectly responsible for the split between the Negro and the top leadership in the union.[54] Thus, it was a fortunate ending for what had been a rather unpleasant experience for both. Fate was kind in having it that way because, although Whitfield and Mitchell did not see eye to eye in their political philosophies, both spent the greater part of their lives working tirelessly to improve the condition of the lowly tenant farmer.

54. Elliott, "Delmo Homes," p. 356; Memphis *Press-Scimitar*, Nov. 29, 1945; Mrs. Zella Whitfield, interview with author, Dec. 19, 1965.

12 The More Things Change, the More They Stay the Same

While the federal government ultimately made landowners of many people in the Bootheel who would not otherwise have had a home, it did not radically change its farm tenancy program after the demonstration. Although the FSA greatly increased its assistance in the Bootheel—FSA grants, for example, totaling over a half million dollars were made to eleven thousand farm families in Southeast Missouri in 1939—the government failed completely to eliminate the loophole in the farm law which had been the major cause of the demonstration.[1] The administration's failure to remedy the defect in the law obviously did not stem from any apparent lack of knowledge. Very little was done to change the law, despite the fact that both Roosevelt and Wallace were made acutely aware of its inadequacies.

The FSA investigation, for example, had stated quite clearly that the principal reason for the switch from cropping to day labor in the Bootheel was "to enable the land-owner to retain all of the AAA benefit money."[2] Moreover, as already indicated, Whitfield and Mitchell made numerous trips to Washington and talked at length to government officials about the loophole in the law.[3]

1. Phil Beck, memo to Will Alexander, Nov. 19, 1939, NA, RG 96.
2. Henry Wallace to Frank Murphy, Jan. 24, 1939, *Selected Documents*, Roosevelt Library.
3. They, of course, were not the first to bring the matter to the attention of the President. As early as 1935, Norman Thomas had visited Roosevelt

Perhaps the best indication the administration received of the farm law's failure to protect tenants adequately came as a result of Thad Snow's efforts to get a new law enacted which would correct what he called the "miscarriage" dealing with tenancy policy. In February of 1939, Snow, who had close friends in the Southern Division of the AAA, and who had known Henry Wallace since 1927, was brought to Washington by the Secretary of Agriculture. Snow actually drew up a bill which would guarantee tenants a fair share of the benefit payments.[4]

Snow's bill, which he said would "make it as difficult for ownership to gobble in the cropper's payments as it has been all along for the cropper to get hold of the ownership payments," called for a fundamental change in the AAA program because it prescribed a new method for making the benefit payment. Whereas in the past the AAA program had been based on the principle of land ownership, with the payment always going to the owner of the land, Snow's bill was based on the principle of labor performance and would have payments made directly to farm workers. Specifically, it stated that the portion of the parity payment "authorized by the statute for sharecroppers" should be considered a "payment for cotton crop" and should "be paid only to those who have done the bodily work of making the crop and are entitled to share in the crop or its proceeds. . . ."[5]

In essence, the bill provided that if sharecroppers worked the land, they should rightfully receive one half of the parity payment made on that land. This portion of the parity check, Snow said, should be considered the "labor" payment. It was hoped that AAA county committees would have little difficulty interpreting its precise meaning, and by prefacing the bill with the phrase: "Notwithstanding any other provision of the law," Snow insured that there could be no other interpretation read into it.[6]

Snow wrote to Henry Wallace, explaining why he considered the bill to be an honest and fair one, listing what he thought were its numerous virtues: (1) It would bother only those areas already

---

in the White House and tried to persuade him to do something about changing the farm law. See Frank Freidel, *FDR and the South* (Baton Rouge, 1965), pp. 65–66.

4. Sam Bledsoe, memo to Henry Wallace, March 9, 1939; Henry Wallace to Roosevelt, May 19, 1939, NA, RG 96.

5. Thad Snow to Henry Wallace, April 8, 1939, Thad Snow Papers. See also *Post-Dispatch,* April 30, 1939.

6. *Ibid.*

troubled. The localities where planter opposition would be greatest, Snow pointed out, "are already smouldering with labor revolt." Hopefully the bill would help quiet some of the labor unrest. (2) It would put into practice what had long been accepted as theory; i.e., that croppers should receive a fair share of the parity check. (3) Opponents of the bill would have to admit openly that they never intended for farm laborers to get the "labor" payment. (4) Planters would be likely to obey a bill "that meant what it said," Snow insisted, rather than one which permitted them to interpret it arbitrarily. "In spite of an impressive mass of supporting evidence in the hands of administrators at Washington," Snow said, still displaying his tender sardonic humor, all "planters are not rascals." (5) The bill would help planters as well as croppers by making "more secure the essential public support for future cotton legislation." (6) Finally, the bill's immediate effect, Snow believed, would be "to reabsorb many thousands of occasional day hands and give them a stake in the crop and a status in the law."[7]

Snow pointed out to Wallace that he realized that there would be one very important objection to the bill: "It violates our deep regard for property rights." He quickly added, however, that the logical alternative to it was "for the administrators at Washington to tell all county commissioners to do as they darned pleased about the labor provisions of the present law, since most of them were doing it anyway."[8]

Snow's bill never passed the Congress in 1939, nor did it pass the next year, when Snow made a return trip to Washington. At the end of 1939, the Charleston planter communicated to Wallace a resolution passed by a group of Mississippi County landowners, emphasizing their awareness of the present law's unfairness. Fearing another sitdown in January 1940, landlords had held several meetings in December 1939, and this resolution was one result of those gatherings. The statement urged both the Secretary of Agriculture and the Congress to pass a law in time to be effective for the 1940 crop which would "make it impossible for a landowner or tenant to receive that portion of Government payments set up for the sharecropper," unless the individual who received the parity payment had "done also the bodily work of making the cotton crop."[9]

7. *Ibid.*

8. *Ibid.*

9. See Resolution attached to letter, J. D. LeCron to Gordon McIntire, Dec. 20, 1939, NA, RG 96.

While Wallace recognized that Thad Snow's bill had "the merit of simplicity and brevity," and although he was "sympathetic" with Snow's objective, the Secretary was not yet convinced that either Snow or the Mississippi County planters who passed the resolution represented the "majority sentiment" of the landowners in the Bootheel.[10] It was doubtless presumed by the Secretary of Agriculture and his aides," Snow later wrote in less sophisticated language, "that these individuals [who drew up the resolution] were slightly cracked or at best quite unrepresentative of planters generally."[11]

Snow was also unable to arouse much support for the bill among the other members of the Agriculture Department. He had strong backing from Sam Bledsoe and I. W. Duggan in the Southern Division of the AAA, but even they felt the pressure of the lobbyists. Several powerful farm organizations, like the conservative planter supported American Farm Bureau Federation, fought the proposed change. Things were going well in the Agriculture Committee hearings, Snow wrote from Washington, but "then some of the high powered lobbyists rather overdid things."[12]

After Snow's departure from the capital, Sam Bledsoe wrote to him: "With you out of town, the sharecroppers are forgotten again." There was a great deal of talk about Snow's bill, Bledsoe said, "but talk is as far as it goes."[13] In the end, Snow later recalled, the Agriculture Department "held several post mortems over me. . . ."[14]

Although later farm bills continued to contain the admonition that the landlord would be denied his parity payment for changing the status of a tenant in order to increase his subsidy, Wallace consistently argued that because of the "wide variation in tenancy arrangements," it was necessary to give the county committee "considerable latitude and authority" in interpreting the change in status, so that "each individual case might be considered on its merit."[15]

10. Wallace to Morris Sheppard, June 12, 1939; Wallace to Roosevelt, May 19, 1939, NA, RG 16.

11. Snow, unsent letter to *Post-Dispatch*, Thad Snow Papers.

12. Thad Snow to Emily Snow, April 25, 1939, Thad Snow Papers. For a discussion of the role played by the various farm organizations during the New Deal, see Christiana M. Campbell, *The Farm Bureau and the New Deal* (Urbana, 1962), and Schmidt, *American Farmers in the World Crisis.*

13. Sam Bledsoe to Thad Snow, undated; Sam Bledsoe to Thad Snow, Sept. 25, 1939, Thad Snow Papers.

14. Thad Snow to Emily Snow, April 25, 1939, *ibid.*

15. Wallace to Morris Sheppard, Aug. 17, 1939; Wallace to Wright Patman, Nov. 1, 1939; NA, RG 16.

Wallace continued to take this position despite the fact that it was extremely apparent that the landlord-controlled committees afforded little protection for tenants, a fact that was particularly evident in the Bootheel.[16] The inability of the county committees to afford protection for tenants was dramatically demonstrated when the mass evictions occurred in the Bootheel in 1940, despite warnings by county committees after the 1939 demonstration. In February of 1939, the Mississippi County committee had sent a letter to all landowners in the county warning that payments would be withheld from landowners who sought to keep benefits rightfully due to tenants.[17] Yet, Mississippi County evictions in 1940 were as numerous as in 1939, and the situation there improved little thereafter.

Snow, testifying before a congressional committee as late as 1943, estimated that while 90 per cent of the cotton had been grown by sharecropping in Mississippi County in the early 1930's and 10 per cent by day labor, the figures had been completely reversed by 1943: 90 per cent of the cotton in that county was grown by day labor, and 10 per cent by croppers.[18]

County committees continued to afford little protection for the tenant primarily because the wording of the law was not changed, and thus local committees continued to interpret its vague meaning in any way they saw fit. Snow pointed out to the congressional committee that section 8 (f) of the 1938 law dealing with croppers and tenants was still applicable in 1943.

Testifying before the committee, the Southeast Missouri planter cited the fatal last line—"Such limitations [withholding the parity payment] shall apply only if the county committee finds that the change [in tenancy status] is not justified and disapproves of such changes." Snow caustically remarked to the committee that "that final, neatly emasculatory sentence" really makes the whole provision meaningless. In essence, he said, it "means exactly this: That no particular tenancy or worker policy is provided by law." Instead, the present law "affecting millions of farm tenants and croppers is turned over to 3 local committeemen in however many

16. See Sam Bledsoe, memo to Henry Wallace, March 9, 1939, NA, RG 96. STFU worked hard to get its members elected to county committees in 1939, but its victories were modest. Mitchell, "Report of the Secretary, 1939," p. 14, STFU Papers.

17. Charleston *Enterprise Courier*, Feb. 9, 1939.

18. Thad Snow, U.S. Congress, Senate, Subcommittee of the Committee on Appropriations, *Hearings*, 77th Cong., 2nd Sess., 1943, pp. 1086–1087.

farming counties there are in 48 States." What this amounts to, Snow observed, is that "we may have as many different tenancy or farm worker policies as we have counties." To make matters worse, he concluded, because county committees are frequently chosen each year "precisely for the purpose of changing tenancy policy," this means that "the number of different farm tenancy policies we have had or may have throughout our broad land is incalculable."[19]

Undoubtedly the conservative coalition in the Congress made the likelihood of radically altering the tenancy provisions slim.[20] Southerners held strategic places on many of the congressional committees. Already Roosevelt had vividly indicated his unwillingness to endorse legislation that might antagonize powerful southerners by refusing to support the antilynching bill in the Congress during the 1930's. "If I come out for the anti-lynching bill now," the President told Walter White of the NAACP, "they will block every bill I ask Congress to pass to keep America from collapsing. I just can't take that risk."[21]

Thus, Roosevelt, in working with the Congress, gave first priority to the legislation he considered the most important. "Even the bolder New Deal spirits," says William Leuchtenburg, one New Deal historian, "feared to jeopardize the rest of their program by antagonizing powerful conservative southern senators. . . ."[22] Roosevelt's position, in relation to legislation that might have substantially affected the South was, at best—another New Deal historian has observed—a "position of benevolent neutrality. . . ."[23]

Certainly, Roosevelt knew that the conservative mood of Congress was not susceptible to any sudden change in the farm law which might affect the planter-cropper relationship drastically. Indeed, in 1939 southerners were already trying to cut back on congressional programs designed to benefit the cropper. FSA cooperative farming projects were undergoing a thorough reappraisal by the Congress in the late thirties. Units such as LaForge

19. *Ibid.*

20. See James T. Patterson, *Congressional Conservatism and the New Deal: The Growth of the Conservative Coalition in Congress, 1933–1939* (Lexington, Ky., 1967).

21. Quoted in Freidel, *FDR and the South*, p. 86.

22. Leuchtenburg, *Franklin D. Roosevelt and the New Deal, 1932–1940*, p. 138.

23. Freidel, *FDR and the South*, p. 97.

were then under heavy fire from southern conservatives, who charged that their "communal" living arrangements were Soviet inspired. "I seriously doubt that the present Congress would authorize the acquisition of additional land for further projects of the LaForge type," Monroe Oppenheimer, the solicitor of the Agricultural Department, wrote to Fannie Cook, in February 1939, in answer to a request that FSA increase farming units in the Bootheel. Oppenheimer suggested to Miss Cook that persons interested in continuing government aid to the cropper urge their congressional representatives to expand the existing tenant purchase and rehabilitation loan program.[24]

In spite of the sentiment of the Congress, however, it seems certain that the chance of getting Thad Snow's bill passed would have been better had Wallace been more enthusiastic about it. Snow himself felt the bill was fairly innocuous. "Probably, Congress on the Secretary's recommendation," Snow speculated, "would pass quite in a routine manner a short, simple bill to make the 'labor' payment . . . accrue only for labor performance."[25]

Snow believed that most planters had no desire to violate the law, but each took advantage of it only because they thought all the other planters were going to also. Had the law been uniformly enforced, there was no need to change it. But since each local county committee was left to determine whether the change in the status of a tenant was justified, any committee could rationalize their failure to follow the intent of the law with the argument that if the others were going to take advantage of the loophole, why should they not do likewise. Moreover, the situation remained unchanged because no one wanted to take the initiative for fear of upsetting the others. "Thad Snow is by no means the only planter who feels as he does," Fannie Cook wrote in 1939, "but the others are afraid to speak out."[26] Thus, the only logical solution to the problem, as Snow saw it, was for the administration to try to close the loophole in the law.

Snow was convinced that the willingness on the part of at least

24. Monroe Oppenheimer to Fannie Cook, Feb. 7, 1939, Fannie Cook Collection.

25. Thad Snow, unsent letter to *Post-Dispatch*, Thad Snow Papers. An abbreviated version of this letter appears in the *Post-Dispatch*, March 1, 1940.

26. Fannie Cook to Edna (last name unknown), April 17, 1939, Fannie Cook Collection.

some planters to support the bill should have been sufficient cause for the administration to back it, since these same planters originally had been the worst violators of the farm law. Referring to the Mississippi County landowners' resolution, which called for a change in the farm law, Snow said it was passed "by our own Missouri planters, among whom were many of our most ambitious chiselers." To Snow, this indicated that "the trek on Washington of high powered planter lobbyists to oppose such a bill—a thing greatly dreaded by department executives—might not materialize at all."[27]

Snow was no doubt unduly optimistic, as was evidenced by the fact that these very lobbyists appeared at the time he presented his bill to the Congress. But by 1940, most planters were convinced of the necessity of cotton control. Thus the administration's failure to take the power out of the hands of county committees could no longer be justified as a necessary evil to induce planters to cooperate with the program. Its sole justification rested upon the assumption by Roosevelt that little could be done to change the farm law without upsetting southern congressmen, whose support he needed for the continuation of the AAA program as well as other New Deal legislation.

In the final analysis, the New Deal's pragmatic determination to make the AAA program a success at all costs blinded it to the program's most dramatic weaknesses. Its refusal to change the law to afford better protection for tenants, and its continued efforts to win planter support with the "bribe" of permitting county committees to interpret the law loosely was nothing more than political expediency. In acquiescing to political expediency, the New Deal shortchanged the landless farmer in the process. Although he probably needed more help than others, the poor tenant farmer—especially the Negro sharecropper—suffered more than most during the depression because of Roosevelt's acquiescence.

While it is true that Congress alone could change the law, much of the blame for the farm program's failure to help the tenant has to rest with the inaction of Roosevelt and his administration. After the Bootheel demonstration, there could be little doubt that the AAA program had worked to the detriment of the tenant farmer. The administration's failure to try to correct the farm law following the demonstration was a vivid testimony of its willingness to

27. Thad Snow, unsent letter to *Post-Dispatch,* Thad Snow Papers.

accept this striking inadequacy of its farm policy. Snow summed it up very well when he wrote: "So long as the Agricultural Administration marks time and acquiesces" in its refusal to change the existent farm law, "it assumes the grave responsibility for the forced demotion of a class, already, perhaps, the least privileged in our social scale."[28]

Henry Wallace was aware of the "social demotion" taking place in farming in the thirties, but felt this was beyond the scope of the AAA program. Wallace justified his inaction by arguing that the tenancy problem did not "arise as a result of the agricultural adjustment programs, but is one of long standing," and thus felt little compulsion to do anything for the tenant beyond the standard FSA assistance programs.[29]

Wallace, along with other advocates of the AAA program, could only rationalize their attitude toward tenants by arguing that farm mechanization would ultimately destroy the sharecropping system anyway, and perhaps the uncorrected farm law was the quickest, if not always the fairest, way to complete the process.

In March 1939, Wallace wrote to Thad Snow that "if there is any practical way to do it, I would like to correct any tendency the present program has to accelerate the change from sharecropper to day laborer."[30] Apparently, however, Wallace found no practical way to do it, because in later correspondence to the President and Mrs. Roosevelt, he took a somewhat different attitude, as indeed he did in the implementation of the farm program, which graphically continued to speed up the shift. In letters to President and Mrs. Roosevelt, written in June 1939, Wallace took the position that while the situation in Southeast Missouri was dramatized by the demonstration, the Bootheel was only a small percentage of migrant families who had no land and no prospects for obtaining land.

When Mrs. Roosevelt wrote Wallace inquiring about what was being done in Southeast Missouri, the Secretary replied by citing figures on farm population. "Few people are aware of or appre-

28. *Ibid.*

29. See Henry Wallace to Representative Sam Massingale, May 17, 1939; Wallace to Senator Tom Connally, Nov. 6, 1939; Wallace to Senator Morris Sheppard, Aug. 17, 1939; Wallace to Wright Patman, Nov. 1, 1939, NA, RG 16; U.S. Congress, Senate, Special Senate Committee to Investigate Unemployment and Relief, *Hearings, on Senate Resolution 36*, March 11, 1938.

30. Henry Wallace to Thad Snow, March 18, 1939, NA, RG 96.

ciate the importance of the basic population facts that bear on this question," he wrote to her. "There is a normal excess of births over deaths of from 400,000 to 500,000 on the farms of America every year." Wallace said that there was a time when the nation was young, when the surplus farm population would be absorbed on new land or in the cities. The closing of both of these, however, had "resulted in damning up on the farms millions of people who normally would have been taken care of elsewhere. . . ."[31]

The Secretary pointed out that the AAA program had done its job in increasing farm income, and argued that "any tendency implicit in the AAA program to increase technological efficiency," and thus eliminate farm jobs, "certainly has been fully offset by the increased income brought to farm people by the AAA." This tendency, Wallace said, "at best would only accelerate a normal economic tendency," and thus AAA should not be blamed. "To charge since this farmer has been displaced because of a landlord's reaction to certain AAA stimuli, that the AAA as a whole has tended to add to the displacement of farm people," he insisted, "is arguing from a particular to a general that is refuted by national statistics."[32]

In short, Wallace was arguing that there simply was not enough land for the huge farm surplus population, and thus all the government could do to "offset" this was to try to bring about an increase in overall farm income among those farmers who then held land. But the important point, easily overlooked, was the acceptance of the fact that ultimately the surplus population must be driven off the land. "Most of the surplus population can not hope to find place on the land," the Secretary wrote to the President on another occasion. "We must hope by general improvement in farm conditions to minimize the situation," he said, "but the solution is not to be found in making more farms and more farmers, but in making more city employment."[33]

In responding to Wallace's pessimistic figures on farm surplus population, Mrs. Roosevelt perhaps expressed the feeling of all those who felt more should be done for the landless farmer: "Your letter on farm population and conditions among the sharecroppers is most interesting," she wrote. "Thank you very much. Should we

31. Wallace to Mrs. Roosevelt, June 7, 1939, *ibid.*
32. *Ibid.*
33. Wallace to FDR, Jan. 21, 1939, *ibid.*

be developing more industries and services? Should we practice birth control, or drown the surplus population?"[34]

Sam Bledsoe recognized Wallace's conviction that what was taking place in agriculture was an inexorable process, but he felt that this was no justification for the AAA program accelerating the process. "Perhaps this program should not attempt to reverse or even interfere with a trend which may be inevitable," Bledsoe argued. "At the same time, I do not see how we can defend provisions in the program which stimulate the trend." Bledsoe wrote to Wallace that it would be feasible to defend the cotton reduction "as necessary for the welfare of all cotton growers," but this was hardly "a convincing argument for paying landlords subsidies to change the status of share tenants and sharecroppers to day laborers. . . ." Bledsoe acknowledged that a major factor for the change in tenancy status was the introduction of mechanization, but recognized that "undoubtedly, some of the displacement of tenants now going on in the South traces directly back to that part of this program which pays a landlord to make day laborers out of his tenants."[35]

Perhaps nothing better epitomized the Roosevelt administrations failure to include sharecroppers and tenants among the category of the "forgotten man" than its refusal to correct the farm law prior to World War II. It is true that the New Deal had not completely forgotten the landless farmer; the FSA was interested in him and was certainly sympathetic to his problems. FSA's relief program in the Bootheel following the demonstration, as indicated, did provide homes for some of the homeless. But the relief FSA brought the cropper was quite modest and only temporary; the permanent problem was still the loophole in the farm law. If the sharecropper was briefly remembered in the winter of 1939 because of the massive Bootheel demonstration, he was quickly neglected again shortly thereafter.

When the Japanese bombs fell on Pearl Harbor over two years later, he faded even further in the background, as the Roosevelt administration became preoccupied with foreign policy and winning the war. The cost of financing the war caused a drastic reduction in domestic spending, and one of the first agencies to be affected was

34. Mrs. Roosevelt to Wallace, June 15, 1939, NA, RG 16.
35. Sam Bledsoe, memo for Henry Wallace, March 9, 1939, NA, RG 96.

the FSA; weakened by the lack of appropriations during the war, its complete demise came in 1946.[36] During all this time, the landless tenant—if not totally forgotten—certainly remained a neglected stepchild of the New Deal.

36. Some of the functions of the FSA were transferred in 1946 to the newly created Farmers Home Administration. See Baldwin, *Poverty and Politics: The Rise and Decline of the Farm Security Administration.*

13 Conclusion

Although Owen Whitfield's roadside demonstration of 1939 was not primarily a Negro protest, but a protest against the economic deprivation and injustice of the sharecropping system, it was a vivid example of an early use of the nonviolent demonstration to dramatize human want and suffering.

It is easy to be skeptical of the overall effectiveness of the 1939 demonstration. Driving through the Bootheel some thirty years later, a cursory glance quickly indicates that many of the same conditions which plagued the lowly tenant farmer in 1939 still exist. The maldistribution of land ownership, the large cotton gins, the ubiquitous broken-down shacks, inhabited frequently by broken-down spirits, are vivid testimony to the fact that much remains the same. Indeed, one cannot help but conclude that Southeast Missouri might still be described—as it was by the FSA in 1938—as a region of rich land and poor people. Although sharecropping no longer exists, except on a diminutive scale, Negro day hands still toil from "can to can't" in the fields for wages only slightly higher than they were in 1939.

The demonstration's failure to alter conditions radically in the Bootheel is a story familiar to all those who today employ the protest demonstration with the hope of changing society radically. Today's protestors should not be shocked because the 1939 demonstration failed to make a sudden transformation in the Bootheel, for the limitation of the protest demonstration as a weapon for social change is as evident in 1969 as it was in 1939. Looking at the 1939 event from a long-range perspective of thirty years, a distinct pattern is clear—a pattern bearing a strong resemblance to the current protest movement.

The immediate reaction to the cropper's trek to the roadside in 1939 was that of shocked incredulity; many were horrified to see the farm workers' conditions dramatically exposed. The abominable conditions—the croppers' daily plight—were designed to stir the apathetic. It worked. The snow and ice on the highway actually helped the croppers' cause because they increased their difficulty and heightened their drama. The reaction was quick. The first thought of the public officials was to remove the croppers from the public view, lest they upset the sensibilities of fair-minded people everywhere.

Capitalizing on the initial shock, Whitfield aroused support for the croppers from sympathetic souls around the country and, a year later, wrested concessions from a governor heretofore virtually unsympathetic to the croppers' conditions. Still exploiting the initial reaction, Whitfield used the threat of a new demonstration in 1940 to help bring about increased activity in government programs in the Bootheel.

Yet these gains, seemingly large for their time, were only temporary accomplishments, with little of lasting consequence. It soon became obvious that the old attitudes, molded and hardened over a great many years, provided an inertial force that would be difficult to move. In many ways the Bootheel returned to its old habits. In 1942, for example, a Negro was lynched in Sikeston, Missouri. One investigation of the incident said that one of the main reasons for the tragedy was the feeling among many whites that the Negroes "were getting 'too cocky.' " Tension between the whites and Negro laborers had been running high, the report said, since the 1939 demonstration.[1]

1. "An Informal Report on Attitudes in Southeast Missouri Relative to the Lynching of Cleo Wright, Negro, January 25, 1942, for the National Association for the Advancement of Colored People by Mr. and Mrs. L. Benoist Tompkins, St. Louis, Missouri," Fannie Cook Collection. For a history of the previous lynchings in the Bootheel, see Wyllie, "Race and Class Conflict on Missouri's Cotton Frontier," pp. 183–196.

While the Bootheel returned to its old ways after the initial shock of 1939 wore off, the Congress of the United States, demonstrating its own legislative inertia, continued the status quo in farm tenancy by refusing to make any large-scale change in the farm law. Congress, in whose hands alone was the power to help correct some of the injustice of the sharecropping system, refused to change the farm law that had encouraged mass evictions and fraudulent swindling of parity checks. The refusal of Henry Wallace and the Department of Agriculture to do more permitted those congressmen who held control of the agriculture committees to keep the farm law intact. Thus, the real decision-making power dealing with farm tenancy was left in the hands of the AAA county committees, which were dominated by the large planter interests.

Roosevelt's sin was one of omission, rather than commission. At no time did the President capitalize on the publicity arising from the demonstration and attempt to galvanize support in the Congress to correct the farm law. In effect, he was oblivious to its injustice. Among the ranks of the lowest economic level of society—the sharecropper and the tenant farmer—the New Deal definitely preserved more than it changed.

It is easy to conclude, therefore, that although the demonstration brought some immediate gains for Whitfield and his people in Southeast Missouri, the roadside strike did little to alter the farm tenancy system or correct the abuses and injustices of economic servitude.

Yet, perhaps the significance of the Bootheel exodus lies not in its failure to bring about large-scale change, but in its success in producing some change, however limited. Although it is safe to say that no complete transformation occurred in Southeast Missouri after 1939 in the farm tenancy system, it is equally safe to say that had the strike not occurred, very little, if anything at all, would have been done to help alleviate the Bootheel croppers' burdens.

Because Owen Whitfield was willing to use what was then the more radical tool of the protest demonstration, he met with far greater success than STFU had had in the Bootheel prior to 1939. The union had never ventured beyond the trade union tactic of calling strikes in the fields to raise wages. This tactic had met with only partial success at best. After STFU's ruinous fight with UCAPAWA, even Mitchell became quite disillusioned with this method, and argued that "there is no basis for trade unionism in Southern agriculture with conditions such as prevail."[2]

Prior to 1939, Mitchell and STFU had never endorsed the protest demonstration as a method for improving conditions of the tenant farmer. Rather, Mitchell pursued what he considered to be a more practical course in order to build a firm foundation for a trade union. Whitfield, on the other hand, less concerned with the growth of the union and more interested in the specific problem of his people in Southeast Missouri, had less to lose than Mitchell by endorsing the more radical tactic. Whitfield thought specifically in terms of aiding the Bootheel croppers and only generally in terms of the union's welfare and the national problem of farm tenancy. Thus, his ultimate allegiance was not to STFU, but to whomever he felt offered the best hope for his people. "My sole interest," he once said during an interview, "is in my people and their welfare, and nothing else."[3]

If Communists were willing to assist Whitfield in obtaining this goal, he openly accepted their support. Mitchell, however, was convinced that his Socialist-inspired union had no room for Communists. Although never guilty of Henderson's charge of "red-baiting," he was nonetheless unwilling to work closely with the Communists in UCAPAWA, and the fatal union split was the result.

Although Whitfield got help from the Communists, he never endorsed their philosophy. At no time in his life did he ever advocate anything like a Marxist concept of public ownership of the means of production, nor did he ever advocate violence to achieve his purposes. Convinced that he had complete control of his people in Southeast Missouri, the Negro minister welcomed Communist support because he did not fear usurpation of his leadership. Unlike Mitchell, he saw in Communist support potential benefit rather than destruction. While Mitchell charged that the Communists in St. Louis were using Whitfield for their own ends, ironically enough, it seems as though Whitfield actually used the Communists for his own ends.

Though Whitfield's ultimate aim was the general improvement in the croppers' conditions, the only thing he specifically worked for, both before and after the demonstration, was federal housing

2. Quoted in Oren Stevens, "Revolt on the Delta: What Happened to the Sharecroppers' Union," *Harper's Magazine*, CLXXXIII (Nov. 1941), 664.
3. Quoted in Ridpath, "The Case of the Missouri Sharecroppers," p. 147.

for the tenants. He obtained this goal in part with Communist support. Only after the 1939 demonstration did the FSA expand its program in the Bootheel. Moreover, after the strike, sympathizers in St. Louis helped raise money for the camp at Harviell, and later helped finance the purchase of the Delmo Homes for their occupants. Thus, although he rejected Communist methods, he used their support to work for his own objectives.

Although its gains were modest, the 1939 demonstration had proven itself to be an effective weapon for social change. Had the fatal union split not occurred immediately thereafter, Whitfield and others might have been able to apply enough pressure—using other demonstrations—to achieve more meaningful gains from an otherwise largely unsympathetic administration. Indeed, A. Philip Randolph used the same tactic—a threatened massive protest march on Washington—only a few years later to wrest concessions for Negroes from Roosevelt during the early years of the war.

Therefore, although there was no immediate major alteration in the farm law following the roadside demonstration, it seems apparent that had it not been for Whitfield's more radical tactics, the political atmosphere in the Bootheel would never have changed enough to cause the FSA to expand its activity throughout the area, and the New Deal's very modest efforts to help the landless farmer would never have filtered down to the lowest field hand in the Bootheel of Southeast Missouri.

Appendix

Table 1. Dramatis personae

Titles and jobs of characters are those they held in January 1939

Will Alexander	Head of Farm Security Administration.
Sam Armstrong	St. Louis *Post-Dispatch* reporter who first broke the story of the demonstration in his paper January 8.
Hans Baasch	Supervisor of the LaForge Project.
Roger Baldwin	Head of the American Fund for Public Service, STFU's biggest contributor.
Virgil L. Bankston	Labor relations representative for FSA, sent to the Bootheel by Will Alexander to investigate STFU charges.
William M. Baxter, Jr.	Director of the midwestern branch of the American Red Cross.
Philip G. Beck	Regional administrator for FSA.
Walter K. Beck	Sheriff of Mississippi County.
F. R. Betton	STFU member who took over Blytheville relief office after Howard Kester left.
C. L. Blanton	Sikeston, Missouri, newspaper publisher.
Sam Bledsoe	Official in the Southern Division of AAA and close friend of Thad Snow.
R. H. Bradford	Negro minister in Mississippi County and close friend of Whitfield.
John Brophy	National director of the CIO.
J. W. Burch	Director of the extension department of the Missouri College of Agriculture.
J. R. Butler	President of STFU.
J. D. Byrne	Bird's Point landowner.
Colonel Marvin B. Casteel	Superintendent of the Missouri Highway Patrol.
John T. Clark	Executive secretary of the St. Louis Urban League.
David Clendenin	Head of the Socialist party's Workers Defense League.
E. P. Coleman, Jr.	Sikeston landowner who helped draft a proposal to give croppers land to live on.
Fannie Cook	Co-chairman of the St. Louis Committee for the Rehabilitation of the Sharecroppers.
Dr. Jerome E. Cook	Chairman of the St. Louis Civil Liberties Union.
J. V. Conran	Prosecuting Attorney of New Madrid County and leading figure in drafting the planter resolution in that county.

Malin Craig	Chief of Staff of the United States Army.
Robert Delaney	Charleston planter, son-in-law of Thad Snow.
I. W. Duggan	Official in the Southern Division of AAA and close friend of Thad Snow.
Clay East	One of the founders of STFU and its first president.
S. J. Elliott	Minister of St. James (Negro) Methodist Church in Sikeston and friend of Whitfield.
William Fischer	White participant in the demonstration who later was named president of the Missouri Agricultural Workers Council.
D. A. Griffin	Member of STFU executive council, invited by Henderson to organize for UCAPAWA.
V. S. Harshbarger	District supervisor for relief in the seven Delta counties.
George I. Haworth	State Social Security Administrator.
Robert Haynes	Negro who, according to the FBI report, was beaten by sheriff deputies with a stick and revolver butt.
Donald Henderson	President of UCAPAWA.
John Herling	Head of the League for Industrial Democracy, helped raise money for Bootheel campers.
James Horton	Minister of Sweet Home Baptist Church, Charleston, Missouri.
R. W. Hudgens	Assistant administrator for FSA.
Samuel Hunter	New Madrid County landowner and one of six-man landlord-sharecropper committee appointed by Governor Stark.
J. F. Hynds	Member of STFU executive council, invited by Henderson to organize for UCAPAWA.
Gardner Jackson	STFU's representative in Washington.
Josephine Johnson	Co-chairman of the St. Louis Committee for the Rehabilitation of the Sharecroppers.
Howard Kester	Early STFU organizer, sent to the union as Norman Thomas's personal representative.
A. F. Kojetinsky	One of three members of the St. Louis Industrial Union Council arrested while trying to assist Bootheel campers.
Herbert Little	Sent by Aubrey Williams into the Bootheel to investigate conditions.
Jewell Mayes	Missouri commissioner of agriculture.
James McDowell	Missouri state senator, critical of the demonstration.

William McKinney	STFU executive officer, expelled by the union along with Claude Williams.
Roy McKittrick	Attorney general of Missouri.
Lewis M. Means	Adjutant general of the Missouri National Guard, refused to supply tents to croppers.
Jim Meyers	Industrial secretary for the Federal Council of Churches, helped organize Church Emergency Relief Committee which raised money for Bootheel campers.
H. L. Mitchell	One of the founders of STFU, secretary, and the real policy-maker for the union.
J. F. Moore	STFU organizer.
W. B. Moore	Member of STFU executive council, invited by Henderson to organize for UCAPAWA.
Al Murphy	Head of the Alabama Sharecroppers Union, UCAPAWA worker, member of St. Louis Committee for Rehabilitation of the Sharecroppers, later ran for governor of Missouri on a Communist party ticket.
Frank Murphy	Attorney general of the United States, conducted an official FBI investigation of the demonstration.
Reinhold Niebuhr	Headed League for Industrial Democracy, helped raise money for Bootheel campers.
Monroe Oppenheimer	Solicitor of the Agriculture Department.
Dr. Harry F. Parker	State health commissioner, gave orders to disperse highway camps, fearing they were a health menace.
James Payne	One of three members of the St. Louis Industrial Union Council arrested while trying to assist Bootheel campers.
Sergeant R. R. Reed	Patrolman for the state highway police.
Morris Ridpath	Minister of Webster Hills Methodist Church.
Carl Ross	District supervisor for the FSA.
Robert K. Ryland	Director of the National Emergency Council of Missouri.
William Scarlett	Episcopal bishop of Missouri, largely responsible for drawing up a proposal later adopted by landlords as a solution for the Bootheel tenants' problems.
William Sentner	Communist party member and vice-president of the St. Louis CIO Electrical Workers Union.

Captain A. D. Sheppard	Head of Missouri Highway Patrol in the Bootheel.
Evelyn Smith	STFU Memphis secretary.
R. G. Smith	Regional director for FSA (office in Indianapolis).
Thad Snow	Charleston planter, Bootheel philosopher, and close friend to Owen Whitfield.
A. F. Stanley	Sheriff of New Madrid County, helped break up several camps of croppers.
Lloyd C. Stark	Governor of Missouri.
Frank Svoboda	One of three members of the St. Louis Industrial Union Council arrested while trying to assist Bootheel campers.
Odis Sweeden	STFU organizer in Oklahoma.
W. M. Tanner	White minister who replaced Whitfield as STFU organizer in Missouri after the union split.
Norman Thomas	Head of the Socialist party and unofficial "godfather" to STFU.
C. E. Underhill	Sikeston cropper, appointed with Whitfield to represent the tenants on the Governor's six-man landlord-sharecropper committee.
Dr. T. L. Waddle	District health officer for four Bootheel counties.
Carl Wedeking	Head of the district Employment Service for the Bootheel.
Owen Whitfield	Bootheel minister, STFU organizer in Southeast Missouri, and leader of the 1939 protest demonstration.
Zella Whitfield	Wife of Owen Whitfield, STFU organizer, and participant in the demonstration.
Claude Wickard	AAA North Central Division director.
Aubrey Williams	Head of the National Youth Administration and friend of STFU.
Claude Williams	STFU organizer, expelled by the union for allegedly sending a letter to Communist party headquarters requesting support to help win control over STFU.
O. E. Wright	In charge of the federal surplus commodities depot at New Madrid.
Harriet Young	STFU's eastern representative, located in New York.
Orville Zimmerman	Bootheel representative (Tenth Congressional District) in the U.S. Congress.

Table 2. Conditions of land before and after drainage in Southeast Missouri

	Acres		*Percentage*	
	Prior to drainage	*1930*	*Prior to drainage*	*1930*
Land unfit to raise any crop	1,301,071	42,320	71.4	2.3
Land fit to raise partial crop	205,969	162,284	11.3	8.9
Land fit to raise normal crop	315,570	1,618,006	17.3	88.8
Total	*1,822,610*	*1,822,610*	*100.0*	*100.0*

Source: Fifteenth United States Census, *FSA Report*, p. 15.

Table 3. Birthplace of heads of workers' families by tenure, 1940, New Madrid County, Missouri (preliminary)

	Share renters		*Sharecroppers*		*Laborers*		*Total*	
Birthplace	*Number*	*Percentage*	*Number*	*Percentage*	*Number*	*Percentage*	*Number*	*Percentage*
Southeastern Missouri	9	37.5	15	15.2	17	23.0	41	20.8
Elsewhere in Missouri	3	12.5	7	7.1	3	4.0	13	6.6
Arkansas	2	8.3	25	25.2	25	33.8	52	26.4
Kentucky	1	4.2	7	7.1	3	4.0	11	5.6
Mississippi	2	8.3	15	15.1	13	17.6	30	15.2
Tennessee	4	16.7	14	14.1	8	10.8	26	13.2
Other cotton states	—	—	8	8.1	4	5.4	12	6.1
Elsewhere in United States	2	8.3	8	8.1	1	1.4	11	5.6
Mexico	—	—	—	—	—	—	—	—
Not reporting	1	4.2	—	—	—	—	1	0.5
Total	*24*	*100.0*	*99*	*100.0*	*74*	*100.0*	*197*	*100.0*

Source: Report to the Tolan Committee, Pt. V, p. 26.

Table 4. Negro farm population in Southeast Missouri, 1935, by counties

Butler	729
Dunklin	413
Mississippi	4,102
New Madrid	4,777
Pemiscot	7,341
Scott	1,191
Stoddard	1,358
Total	*19,911*
Missouri	28,855

Source: United States Census of Agriculture, 1935, *FSA Report*, p. 19.

Table 5. Types of tenure among 1,097 farm families in Dunklin, New Madrid, and Pemiscot counties, by color

	Number		*Percentage*	
Tenure group	*White*	*Negro*	*White*	*Negro*
Owners	145	38	16.0	20.2
Renters	298	15	32.8	8.0
Croppers	181	56	19.9	29.8
Laborers	285	79	31.3	42.0
Total	*909*	*188*	*100.0*	*100.0*

Source: Survey of 1,533 households in Dunklin, New Madrid, and Pemiscot counties, *FSA Report*, p. 20.

Table 6. Gross income of 1,013 farm households in Dunklin, New Madrid, and Pemiscot counties in 1935, by color and tenure group

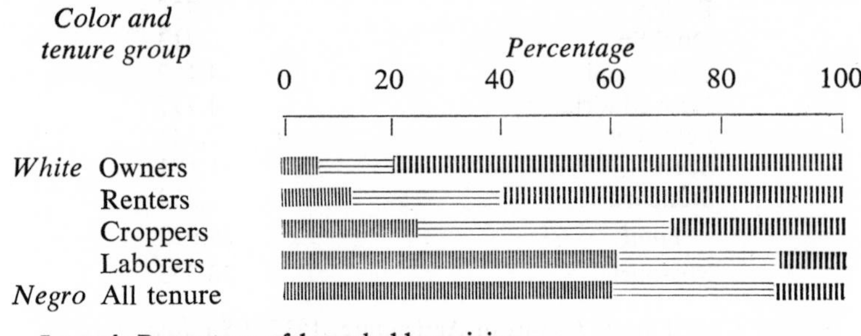

Legend: Percentage of household receiving
Less than $300
$300 to $599
$600 and over

Source: Survey of 1,533 households in Dunklin, New Madrid, and Pemiscot counties, *FSA Report*, p. 37.

Table 7. Infant mortality rate in Missouri and in Southeast Missouri, by color, 1934 (infant deaths per 1,000 live births)

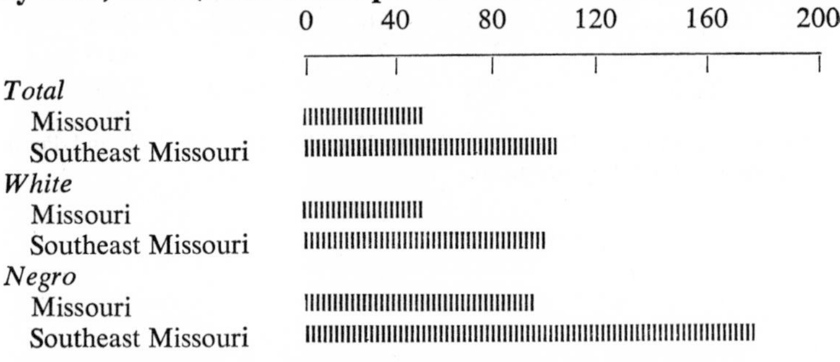

Source: Adapted from data furnished by the State Board of Health of Missouri, *FSA Report*, p. 53.

Table 8. Number of children under 5 years of age per 1,000 women 20–44 years of age in rural-farm population of Southeast Missouri, 1930, by counties

County	Number
Butler	941
Dunklin	932
Mississippi	840
New Madrid	922
Pemiscot	769
Scott	871
Stoddard	797
Missouri	657

Source: Special Tabulation from United States Bureau of Census, *FSA Report*, p. 23.

Table 9. Number of years on present farm for tenants in Missouri and Southeast Missouri, January 1, 1935

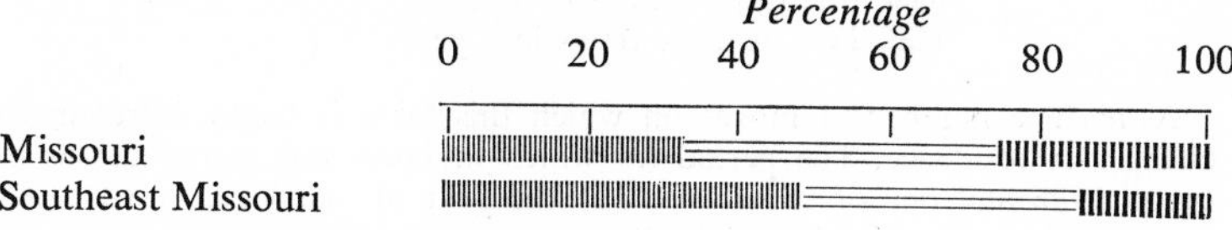

Legend: Percentage of tenants on present farms
Less than one year
1–4 years
5 years and over

Source: United States Census of Agriculture, 1935, *FSA Report*, p. 54.

Table 10. Mobility of 1,091 farm families in Dunklin, New Madrid, and Pemiscot counties, by color and tenure group

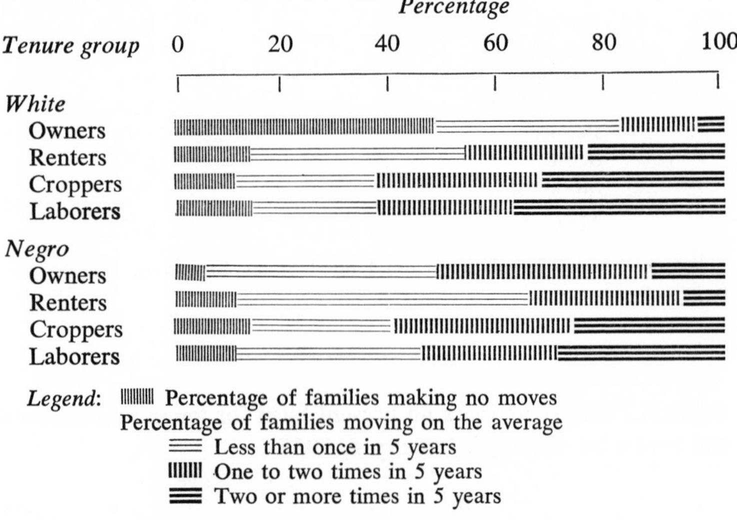

Legend: Percentage of families making no moves
Percentage of families moving on the average
Less than once in 5 years
One to two times in 5 years
Two or more times in 5 years

Note: The number of moves on which this table is based represent the changes in residence. The period for which mobility was recorded was between 1936 and one of two dates: (1) the year of marriage, or (2) 1920, if the head was married before 1920.

Source: Survey of 1,533 households in Dunklin, New Madrid and Pemiscot counties, *FSA Report*, p. 55.

Table 11. Types of tenure among 914 tenants in Dunklin, New Madrid, and Pemiscot counties

	Number	*Percentage*
Renters	313	34.3
Croppers	237	25.9
Laborers	364	39.8
Total	*914*	*100.0*

Source: Survey of 1,533 households in Dunklin, New Madrid, and Pemiscot counties, *FSA Report*, p. 35.

Table 12. Percentage of 1,097 farm families receiving relief in Dunklin, New Madrid, and Pemiscot counties at some time during the year in 1933, 1934, 1935, and 1936, by color and tenure group

Color and tenure group		0 10 20 30
1933		
White	Owners	
	Renters	
	Croppers	
	Laborers	
Negro	All tenure	
1934		
White	Owners	
	Renters	
	Croppers	
	Laborers	
Negro	All tenure	
1935		
White	Owners	
	Renters	
	Croppers	
	Laborers	
Negro	All tenure	
1936		
White	Owners	
	Renters	
	Croppers	
	Laborers	
Negro	All tenure	

Source: Survey of 1,533 households in Dunklin, New Madrid, and Pemiscot counties, *FSA Report*, p. 56.

Resolution of New Madrid planters January 12, 1939*

Whereas there exists at this time in New Madrid County and other cotton-raising counties of southeast Missouri a condition in which a large number of persons have moved from their homes to the rights-of-way of several roadways in these various counties; and

Whereas the metropolitan press and other individuals are responsible for attempting to create the impression that such conditions are a result of evictions ordered by the landowners and landlords of said section of the State of Missouri, or to other causes for the responsibility which the landowners and landlords are all the cause, we, the undersigned representatives of the landowners and landlords of southeast Missouri, do hereby declare that these conditions have not been caused by any responsibility of the landowners and landlords of southeast Missouri: And be it therefore

Resolved, That the landowners and landlords of the southeast Missouri respectfully request that a thorough and complete investigation be made of the conditions now existing in the cotton counties of southeast Missouri, and that a hearing be held at a place which is convenient for the inhabitants of all these counties where it will be possible for the representatives of all the people involved in this matter to be present and be heard; it is further

Resolved, That this body, representing the landowners and landlords of southeast Missouri, respectfully request our United States Senators and Congressmen and the Governor of our State to use all means within their power to bring about a fair and impartial investigation of these matters, in order that the true facts may be known, and in that connection it is respectfully requested that this hearing be conducted by representatives of the Federal Bureau of Investigation, if it is possible for such to be done, in cooperation with a referee assigned for the purpose of hearing these matters by the

* *Cong. Record,* 76th Cong., 1st Sess. (Appendix), Jan. 17, 1939, pp. 143–144.

proper Senate committee, and a thorough report be made to the proper authorities.

It is further resolved that it is our belief that the present conditions exist not because of evictions of any sharecroppers or tenants, but due to the fact that a great percentage of the people who are now complaining have done so at the instigation of certain agitators who claim to be representatives of the United States Government and are telling the people that it is only necessary for them to move out on the highway and the Federal Government will come along and give them 40 acres of ground with the proper tools and teams to cultivate it.

It is further resolved that our information leads us to believe that fully 90 percent of those people who are now camping on the highways are nonresidents of the State of Missouri, or those who have not lived here longer than 5 or 6 months at the most, having come to this section from other States in order to pick cotton for which it is known that southeast Missouri pays a higher price than other parts of the South, and that this excess labor are not the sharecroppers of southeast Missouri.

It is further resolved that it is our information that the great majority of the people now on the said highways are there as a result of their own voluntary act, a great many having moved there from towns, and that there are very few sharecroppers moving.

It is further resolved that this committee requests a thorough investigation of the activities of one Hans H. Baasch, who is the authority in charge of the Resettlement Administration in New Madrid County, at LaForge, Mo., and one of his aides, a colored Baptist preacher by the name of Owen H. Whitfield, because the said Whitfield has been going about southeast Missouri collecting dollars from the poor people of these communities and telling them that if they would move out on the highways the Government would give them 40 acres of ground and the tools to cultivate it, and that the said Hans H. Baasch is reliably reported to have made various communistic remarks leading to this trouble, and that one of said remarks was "it will not be long before all the ground in New Madrid County will be owned by the Government and given to the poor people when divided into 40-acre tracts."

Be it further resolved that this committee representing the landowners and landlords of southeast Missouri requests that this investigation be commenced immediately and that the activities of the persons responsible for the conditions now existing in these counties be reported to the proper authorities in Washington for whatever action is deemed necessary and advisable.

Be it further resolved that copies of this resolution be immediately forwarded to the Governor of Missouri, both the United States Senators of Missouri, the Congressman representing this district, the Dies senatorial committee, the Honorable John Nance Garner, and the Honorable Henry A. Wallace.

I hereby certify that the foregoing is a true and correct copy of the resolution which was unanimously adopted at this meeting the 12th day of January 1939 at the courthouse in New Madrid County, Mo.

J. V. Conran, *Chairman.*

Attest:

O. T. Miles, secretary; Fred M. Copeland; O. H. Acom; Claude Stillman; E. V. Jewett; Roy Dillard; Chas. B. Baker; O. P. Tilghmon; J. V. Conran; W. C. Thompson; S. S. Thompson; O. T. Miles; P. M. Barton; John L. Girvin; S. L. Hunter; T. H. Streeter; A. R. Wrather; A. T. Earls; J. K. Robbins; Paul Crouthers; Jno. P. Jones; O. R. Rhodes; Elon Proffer; H. G. Cathey; Geo. R. Ellis, Jr.; A. F. Stanley.

Resolution of Mississippi County planters January 13, 1939*

Whereas there are now known to be 99 families on Highway 60, Mississippi County; and

Whereas it has been reported in the press that these people have been forced to move by their landlords; and

Whereas the condition of these people has been investigated and the following facts determined: That the people now on the highways fall in the following classes—56 sharecroppers, 1 leaseholder, 32 day laborers, 4 W.P.A. workers, and 6 moved out of town; that 25 percent of these sharecroppers had contracts with landlords and farmers to be retained on the farm in 1939; that 1 had legal notice to vacate and 5 with letters asking them to move; that 87 moved, giving no reason for vacating; that all refused to tell why they moved to the highway and who instructed them to do so; that it was clearly determined that a great majority of the landlords had nothing to do with their moving from the farms and nothing to do with their moving to the highway; and

Whereas the farmers of Mississippi County in joint meeting held at the county courthouse in Charleston on January 12, 1939, determined there are approximately 4,200 tenant farmers and sharecroppers in Mississippi County; and

Whereas the number now on the highways is less than 3 percent of the total tenants and sharecroppers of the county; and

Whereas that is less than the normal moving from farm to farm each year; and

Whereas it is definitely known that numbers of these people had farms rented and crop contracts for 1939 and part of the land prepared for crops: Therefore be it

Resolved, That this movement to the highways of this county is the result of unscrupulous and scheming agitators who have been

* *Cong. Record,* 76th Cong., 1st Sess. (Appendix), Jan. 18, 1939, p. 187.

deceiving the Negro tenants and sharecroppers by making them believe that they were going to be given property and money by the Government and that they will not have to work; and be it also

Resolved, That it would be to the best interests of Mississippi County that Government relief and charitable agencies refrain from encouraging this movement by giving aid and assistance for the reason that landowners and farmers are in a position to take care of them in 1939 by giving them crops and labor; and be it further

Resolved, That it is the opinion of this body assembled that the statements made that the landowners and farmers of Mississippi County are dispossessing their sharecroppers for the purpose of receiving all the Government crop payments are absolutely false and made for the purpose of deceiving the press and public; and be it further

Resolved, That landowners and farmers of this county will welcome any investigation of the facts pertaining to this situation and will cooperate with any properly authorized investigating agency to determine such facts; and be it further

Resolved, That copies of this resolution be forwarded to Hon. Bennett Champ Clark, Hon. Harry S. Truman, Hon. Orville Zimmerman, Hon. J. C. McDowell, Hon. Dan O'Bryan, Hon. Henry A. Wallace, and Gov. Lloyd C. Stark.

Thad Snow's "Confession"*

Outside observers of the recent roadside demonstration have all been impressed by the orderliness of the affair. All have agreed that it was planned by a master mind. It occurs to me that my many friends would be interested to know where, when and by whom the idea was conceived, and what men later were consulted and contributed a part in perfecting the plan.

It was Trotsky's idea in the first place but many others had a part in developing the plot. Like many important historic events, this one started in a casual conversation. I shall tell all about it, although the facts will lessen my own prestige as the sole planning agency.

It all started in Mexico City last summer. I spent a day viewing literally acres of the mural paintings of the great Mexican artist, Diego Rivera. I was so charmed by the powerful technique, the reckless realism and sardonic humor of the paintings that I was overcome by a desire to know the artist himself. Why not just go call on him? I did so, and we became friends almost at once. I told him that some of his murals would fit our cotton country if he would just change his Indians into Negroes. Rivera knew much about our country and asked me endless questions.

"Now," he said, "you must come with me and talk this over with Trotsky." Well, we went together to Trotsky's heavily guarded exile retreat. Strangely enough this great Russian revolutionary knew almost as much about this cotton country as I did. But of course I could give him up-to-the-minute information that he lacked. His questions were incisive and penetrating and his concentration amazing. We talked for two hours. He had me draw him a rough map of Swampeast Missouri for him to study. "Come back to me in the morning," he said, "and I will tell you what to do."

Rivera and I went back next morning. Trotsky had our roadside sit-down strike almost planned out when we arrived. He had writ-

* Snow, *From Missouri,* pp. 262–264.

ten out directions in long-hand, and had located the camp sites on my map. But he would not let me have the papers.

"Wait," he said, "I have promised to do nothing while I am in Mexico that might cause international complications. Let me be sure," he said, "that President Cardenas of Mexico and your Ambassador Daniels approve my action in this matter." So he called them both by phone and in a few minutes they were with us.

The great President of Mexico gave his approval out of hand. Mr. Daniels felt that he should wire Secretary Hull and President Roosevelt and await their reply. It came next morning. Mr. Daniels and I went together to Trotsky's house and showed him the message signed jointly by President Roosevelt and Secretary Hull and authorizing Trotsky to deliver the maps and instructions over to me. He did so.

I then went to Acapulco on the south coast of Mexico with my small daughter, Emily. She kept the plans on her person always, so that if I fell under suspicion and was searched they would not be found. Since we spent much time bathing on the beach, I had an oilskin envelope prepared and she carried the papers in the bosom of her suit while bathing.

The plans were admittedly incomplete, so when we returned to the United States we drove to California to get Upton Sinclair's judgment in regard to the whole matter. He took me to San Quentin prison where we were accorded an hour's conference with Tom Mooney. He added some useful details. Then I had to make a secret trip to Washington because President Roosevelt wanted to see Trotsky's original manuscript and map. He thought of a number of people whose counsel he desired. So he called Al Smith, Norman Thomas and Dorothy Thompson from New York. Tom Girdler and Frank Hague were called in too. These two latter gentlemen thought Hitler and Mussolini ought to be consulted by cable, but that was not done.

Idealists who examined the plan thought that the roadside demonstration might lead to changes in the farm laws, and that the essential kindliness and generosity of the planters might be brought to the surface by the demonstration.

Many others have contributed their part. Whitfield's work and mine have been simplified greatly by all this careful planning by many minds. Then when the demonstration finally came off, the magnificent co-operation of all state and local relief agencies, the churches, charitable organizations, the highway patrol, local enforcement officers, and the citizenry in general, helped to make it the unmitigated success that it was.

I am expected to turn Trotsky's historic script, unfortunately damaged by salt water despite the oiled envelope, over to the John Dewey Commission on February 15. Meantime it may be seen at my home by any planter or other local citizen who is interested and who is sympathetic with the aspirations of the roadside demonstrators.

Bibliographical note

There are three indispensable sources of information on the Southeast Missouri sharecropper demonstration of 1939. Much of the material obtained for this study came from these three sources: (1) The records of the Southern Tenant Farmers Union, deposited in the Southern Historical Collection at the University of North Carolina, Chapel Hill, North Carolina. H. L. Mitchell, the union secretary, was a meticulous record keeper. As a result, from this source, I not only learned of the union's activity in the Bootheel, but I also found here most of the important information relating to the bitter struggle between Whitfield and Mitchell, which occurred at the height of the demonstration and which played a large role in the ultimate destruction of the union. (2) The federal government records in the National Archives in Washington were also a vital source of information. The materials most used were Record Group 96, the Records of the Farmers Home Administration (successor to the Farm Security Administration); Record Group 16, the records of the Secretary of Agriculture; and Record Group 145, the Records of the Agricultural Adjustment Administration. The material used from these sources was mostly memorandums and correspondence of the individuals in the Agriculture Department, especially Secretary Wallace, Will Alexander, C. B. Baldwin, Phil Beck, R. W. Hudgens, and Sam Bledsoe. (3) *The Selected Documents from the Papers of President Franklin D. Roosevelt Concerning Sharecropper Demonstration in Southern Missouri* (Microfilm, Franklin D. Roosevelt Library, Hyde Park, New York) contain a wealth of information on the strike. Those documents most utilized from this source were the on-the-spot reports of government officials at the beginning of the demonstration, the interviews and investigations conducted during the strike, and the reports submitted to Henry Wallace and President Roosevelt afterward.

Other government records relating to the tenancy problem in the Bootheel were found in the Agriculture Department Library in Washington, D.C. By far the most helpful were the numerous studies, reports, and publications of the Farm Security Administration. This information was particularly useful for gaining insight into the difficulties in Southeast Missouri which led to the 1939 roadside exodus.

The author also made extensive use of manuscript sources, both those that have been collected and deposited in libraries and also those in the private possession of friends and relatives of individuals involved in the strike. The following were most helpful: The papers of Fannie Cook (Missouri Historical Society, St. Louis, Missouri); Thad Snow (in the possession of Mrs. Robert Delaney); Owen Whitfield (in the possession of Mrs. Zella Whitfield); and Josephine Johnson (in the possession of Mrs. Grant [Johnson] Cannon).

The author interviewed a number of people who had first-hand knowledge of the demonstration. Those most helpful were: Zella Whitfield, Howard Kester, John Stewart, E. L. Hughes, Jesse Sterling, Mr. and Mrs. Robert Delaney, Cora (Whitfield) Terry, and Sarah Howard. The author also corresponded with H. L. Mitchell, J. R. Butler, Howard Kester, Claude Williams, and Mrs. Grant (Johnson) Cannon.

Newspaper sources were particularly helpful for the story of the croppers during the time they were camped on the roadside. The author examined most papers during the period surrounding the demonstration, especially the closing months of 1938 and the first few months of 1939 and 1940. Of the papers examined, those used most were the St. Louis *Post-Dispatch*, *Southeast Missourian* (Cape Girardeau), Charleston *Enterprise Courier*, Sikeston *Standard*, New York *Daily Worker*, New York *Times*, Memphis *Commercial-Appeal* and Memphis *Press-Scimitar*.

Index